Human Rights in Islamic Societies

This book compares Islamic and Western ideas of human rights in order to ascertain which human rights, if any, can be considered universal. This is a profound topic with a rich history that is highly relevant within global politics and society today.

The arguments in this book are formed by bringing William Talbott's *Which Rights Should Be Universal?* (2005) and Abdulaziz Sachedina's *Islam and the Challenge of Human Rights* (2014) into conversation. By bridging the gap between cultural relativists and moral universalists, this book seeks to offer a new model for the understanding of human rights. It contends that human rights abuses are outcomes of complex systems by design and/or by default. Therefore, it proposes that a rigorous systems-thinking approach will contribute to addressing the challenge of human rights.

Engaging with Islamic and Western, historical and contemporary, and relativist and universalist thought, this book is a fresh take on a perennially important issue. As such, it will be a first-rate resource for any scholars working in religious studies, Islamic studies, Middle East studies, philosophy, sociology, and law and religion.

Ahmed E. Souaiaia is a member of the faculty with joint appointment in International Studies, Religious Studies, History, and at the College of Law at the University of Iowa, USA. He is the author of several books including *Anatomy of Dissent in Islamic Societies: Ibadism, Rebellion and Legitimacy* (2013) and *Contesting Justice: Women, Islam, Law, and Society* (2008). He has published articles in refereed journals and essays in national and international media outlets. He has received a number of other awards including the Presidential Faculty Fellowship, Dean's Scholar Award, and the Provost's Global Forum Award.

Routledge Studies in Islam and Human Rights
Series Editor: Ahmed E. Souaiaia

Routledge Studies in Islam and Human Rights series publishes scholarly monographs that examine the rich and complex intellectual and institutional legacy of Islam relevant to human rights and social (in)justice since the formative period of Islam (seventh century CE). The series aims to integrate knowledge from a variety of disciplines employing new and established methodological and theoretical approaches in human rights research, taking into consideration the consequential legacies of colonialism, imperialism, and globalism on Muslim-majority countries in the modern era as well as the impact of Islam, as an idea and event, on indigenous peoples during the rise and expansion of the Islamic civilization. While acknowledging the fact that the human rights discourse is primarily political, the Series is committed to providing space to critical analysis, advocacy-oriented, and public policy research in an accessible form to students, professors, human rights professionals, and publicly engaged scholars. The series welcomes works dealing specifically with the topic of human rights theories as well as discoveries that connect human rights to social issues, institutions, themes, ideas, and events.

For more information about the Series Editor see - https://ahmed.souaiaia.com

Human Rights in Islamic Societies
Muslims and the Western Conception of Rights
Ahmed E. Souaiaia

For more information and a full list of titles in the series, please visit: https://www.routledge.com/Routledge-Studies-in-Islam-and-HumanRights/book-series/RSIH

Human Rights in Islamic Societies
Muslims and the Western Conception of Rights

Ahmed E. Souaiaia

LONDON AND NEW YORK

First published 2021
by Routledge
2 Park Square, Milton Park, Abingdon, Oxon OX14 4RN

and by Routledge
605 Third Avenue, New York, NY 10158

Routledge is an imprint of the Taylor & Francis Group, an informa business

© 2021 Ahmed E. Souaiaia

The right of Ahmed E. Souaiaia to be identified as author of this work has been asserted by him in accordance with sections 77 and 78 of the Copyright, Designs and Patents Act 1988.

All rights reserved. No part of this book may be reprinted or reproduced or utilized in any form or by any electronic, mechanical, or other means, now known or hereafter invented, including photocopying and recording, or in any information storage or retrieval system, without permission in writing from the publishers.

Trademark notice: Product or corporate names may be trademarks or registered trademarks, and are used only for identification and explanation without intent to infringe.

British Library Cataloguing-in-Publication Data
A catalogue record for this book is available from the British Library

Library of Congress Cataloging-in-Publication Data
A catalog record has been requested for this book

ISBN: 9780367433499 (hbk)
ISBN: 9780367776176 (pbk)
ISBN: 9781003002581 (ebk)

Typeset in Sabon
by KnowledgeWorks Global Ltd.

To Julia.
and then,
To Julia, Fatima, and Mona.

Table of contents

List of tables — ix
Contributor biography: William J. Talbott — x
Preface — xi

1 Introduction: Universalizing the study of the universal human rights through systems thinking — 1

PART I
Human rights as a discourse — 19

2 What we now know: Human rights and post-enlightenment thought — 21

3 Islamic reaction to Western enlightenment — 43

PART II
Human rights in history — 63

4 European Enlightenment, racism, and human rights — 65

5 Islam, supremacy, sectarianism, and human rights — 85

PART III
Globalism, history, and human rights today — 117

6 The case of the 2011 wars in SWANA — 119

7	Actual and instrumentalized human rights	138
8	Conclusions: Human rights, civil society, and the state	162

Appendix   174
Select Bibliography   180
Index   185

List of tables

6.1 State and non-state actors in the Syrian war 126
6.2 Ownership of media outlets used in this study 129
6.3 The various actors' descriptions of their opponents. The use of labels by the warring factions include these tags: Rafida, Nusayri, Persian, Crusader, Apostate, `Ilmani, Regime, Assad Regime, and Daesh 134

Contributor biography

William J. Talbott teaches and has published articles in epistemology, and moral and political philosophy, including the philosophy of human rights, rational choice theory, and the philosophy of law. Bill wrote his dissertation on reliabilist epistemology ("The Reliability of the Cognitive Mechanism," 1990). He is the author of two books in the philosophy of human rights: *Which Rights Should Be Universal?* (2005), the Korean translation of which was named Korean Human Rights Book of the year in 2011, and *Human Rights and Human Well-Being* (2010). He is currently working on a book in epistemology to be titled *Learning From Our Mistakes: Epistemology for the Real World*, in which he proposes a new model of learning that applies universally, even to epistemology itself.

Preface

I suspect that many if not most of the readers of this work are from outside the academic area of inquiry known as Islamic studies. Some will not be familiar with the Arabic, Persian, or Turkish technical words that they may encounter in this book. It is of little benefit, but rather cumbersome, to fully transliterate all the foreign words using diacritics and pronunciation aids. For this reason, I limited the use of diacritics to select words about which I did not want any confusion. In all other instances, Arabic words are presented in simplified rendering without diacritics. A list of such words, with diacritics and or pronunciation aid markings, and voiced (audio clips) is accessed online via author's website.

1 Introduction
Universalizing the study of the universal human rights through systems thinking

The introduction lays out the scope, methodology, and rationale for this work. It establishes the framework within which the topic of human rights is explored, underscoring the interconnectedness of world cultures and world societies in ancient and modern times.

In 1948, 48 out of 58 nation-states endorsed a document containing about 30 statements pertaining to human rights, the Universal Declaration of Human Rights (UDHR). Some observers see this document as a global bill of rights derived from Western Enlightenment thought.[1] Governments, many of them occupying African and Asian countries, adopted ideas in this tradition. It is only natural, then, that countries emerging out of colonialism would be sceptical of the claims made in the UDHR.[2] Nonetheless, in the half-century following the UDHR's signing, it gave rise to more than six binding treaties, which almost all of the world's governments ratified. The energy behind the widespread adoption of these treaties is not solely due to the inspiring words of Enlightenment thinkers,[3] but also, and importantly, on account of a legacy of human rights abuses inside and outside Western countries. Moreover, the occurrence of human rights abuses increases in frequency and severity during violent conflicts: Protests and dissent uprisings, civil wars, and wars among nations.[4] With these facts in mind, when calling for a list of universal rights, the assumption is that human rights should be addressed in the global system and that solutions must be applied across cultures and national borders. Yet more than seventy years after the signing of the historic document, human rights abuses continue to occur in every country. This leads to the conclusion that human rights abuses, not human rights norms, are universal.

Despite setbacks and persistent negative trends on the path to promoting human rights, scholars, rights advocates, and some public servants continue to build capacity in the realms of ideas, events, and institutions to address past human rights violations and deter future perpetrators. Many human rights scholars and advocates believed that the creation of the International Criminal Court (ICC) would change attitudes and establish permanent systems to hold individual human beings, not just States, accountable, by

2 Introduction

charging them with criminal acts including genocide, war crimes, crimes against humanity, and aggression. These four categories of crime capture the most egregious acts of human rights abuse. For new institutions like the ICC, the potential is not limited to punishing perpetrators; they may also define human rights and codify human rights offenses as crimes. For example, while national and international laws have defined and codified genocide and war crimes, crimes against humanity have not yet been codified in dedicated statutes and treaties. Yet, it is the offenses that fall solely under the category of crimes against humanity that are the most egregious and the ones most prevalent. Historically, too, crimes against humanity catalogue atrocities such as slavery, the slave trade, colonialism, mass killings, the crime of apartheid, extermination, deportation, or forcible transfer of populations, imprisonment, persecution, enforced disappearance of persons, persecution, rape and grave forms of sexual violence, sexual slavery, forced prostitution, forced pregnancy, and forced sterilization. Underscoring the State's interest in limiting discourse on rights relevant to crimes that only the State can commit,[5] the drafters of the ICC treaty delayed including the crime of aggression, blaming a lack of consensus on a legal definition of "aggression."

Overall, it should be noted that individuals and governments have committed crimes against humanity during times of both war and peace. For almost all past atrocities, there has been no remediation. Importantly, these crimes continue to occur in every country and across every geographic region. Therefore, when looking at the list of human rights enshrined in the UDHR, one must bear in mind the list of atrocities that have occurred, and continue to take place, to provide context to a clutter of abstract thinking. Similarly, by comparing a list of actual past crimes and atrocities to the list of rights in the UDHR, the drafters' subjective bias and self-interested positions on rights should become evident; the theoretical weakness and veil of ignorance should become transparent.

In this work, I draw on the binaries of theory versus practice and ideas versus events to offer a range of insights into the history and evolution of human rights. In order to develop a new paradigm for framing human rights, I interrogate scholars and researchers who have devoted most of their professional careers to the topic of human rights; I examine the bodies of literature and traditions that inform these scholars' understandings and theories on human rights; I survey the origins and history of Islamic civilization to identify the actors and subjects of human rights abuses; and I present the archetypal cases that combine internal strife and international geopolitics. This introduction will introduce the elements that make each section of the book relevant to the overall theme.

The first section of this book is a critical review of work from two experts representing different disciplinary areas of inquiry, William Talbott and Abdulaziz Sachedina. In addition to their professional backgrounds, these individuals offer insight into the social and cultural environments to which they belong. These experts' perspectives accomplish two important things: They bridge the historical legacy of their sources, and they introduce the theories and ideas of other influential thinkers relevant to human rights.

After examining the views and proposals of each of these scholars, I introduce evidence from their intellectual and cultural legacies. Specifically, I highlight key events and ideas from Western Enlightenment and post-Jahiliyya Islamic traditions and practices to link human rights norms to events and ideas that shaped the way Western and Islamic societies have engaged with the discourse on human rights.

Lastly, I introduce a case involving both Islamic and Western actors, which underscores both the political and global nature of human rights discourse. The presentation and analysis of the 2011 wars in Southwest Asia and North Africa (SWANA) highlights the convergence of regional and global interests; the universality of human rights abuses; the role historical atrocities play in creating new atrocities; the connection of supremacy and racism to human rights abuses; and the culpability of the State in committing and enabling human rights abuses.

Before explaining the theoretical lens I apply throughout this work, and given their frequent citation, I should introduce core concepts and summarize key documents. This will equip readers with a level of familiarity with these ideas and documents, making it easier to visualize this work's full argument and its context.

One of the key documents to this text is the Universal Declaration of Human Rights. This is an official statement signed by representatives of states that are members of the intergovernmental world organization the United Nations. It is often referred to as the Declaration, the UDHR, or the Rights Declaration. A summary of the rights included in the Declaration is provided for convenience. For our purposes, the reader should keep in mind the list of atrocities that have occurred in both Islamic and Western societies, some of which I listed above, to contrast them against the content of the UDHR and other treaties derived there from.

The Universal Declaration of Human Rights is one of the most oft-cited documents in writing about human rights. As the history of the document shows, there has never been strong consensus about all the rights it contains. When it was adopted by the UN, only 58 countries were members of this new post-world-wars intergovernmental organization. Many countries were still under colonization by the same governments pushing for the Declaration's adoption. Nonetheless, the impact and influence of this document is undeniable, notwithstanding the objections and reservations concerning many of the rights contained therein or rights left out. The 1948 Universal Declaration of Human Rights was voted on by the then 58 members of the United Nations; 48 voted in favor, none voted against, eight abstained, and two did not

4 Introduction

vote. The declaration consists of about 30 articles containing over 30 basic human rights claims, abbreviated below:

1 Right to be recognized as a human being, with dignity and rights
2 Right not to be discriminated against
3 Right to life
4 Right to not be enslaved
5 Right to not be tortured
6 Right to use law anywhere
7 Right to equality before the law
8 Right to judicial review
9 Right to not be arrested or exiled arbitrarily
10 Right to presumption of innocence until proven guilty
11 Right to privacy
12 Right to freedom of movement and residence within the borders of each state
13 Right to leave and to return to own country
14 Right to seek and to enjoy in other countries' asylum from persecution
15 Right to a nationality
16 Right to marry and to found a family
17 Right to own property alone and in association with others
18 Right to freedom of thought, conscience, and religion
19 Right to freedom of opinion and expression
20 Right to freedom of peaceful assembly and association
21 Right to take part in the government of own country
22 Right to economic, social and cultural rights indispensable to one's dignity
23 Right to work
24 Right to rest and leisure
25 Right to a standard of living
26 Right to education
27 Right to participate in the cultural life of the community
28 Right to social and international order
29 Responsibility to respect the rights and freedoms of others
30 All of these rights must be respected and protected by law

Since William J. Talbott's work[6] is examined here, it might help the reader to know the nine basic rights that Talbott believes should be universal.

Talbott's List of Basic Rights:

1 Right to physical security
2 Right to physical subsistence (understood as a right to an opportunity to earn subsistence for those who are able to do so)
3 Children's rights to what is necessary for normal physical, cognitive, emotional, and behavioural development, including the development of empathic understanding

4 Right to an education, including a moral education aimed at further development and use of empathic understanding
5 Right to freedom of the press
6 Right to freedom of thought and expression
7 Right to freedom of association
8 Right to a sphere of personal autonomy free from paternalistic interference
9 Political rights, including democratic rights and an independent judiciary to enforce the entire package of rights.[7]

Abdulaziz Sachedina believes that all the rights enshrined in the UDHR should be universal. His stated goal is to convince Muslims that all such rights, irrespective of who drafted them and despite their secular origins, are part and parcel of Islamic tradition and can be naturally discovered through human nature, which he calls *Fitra*, encompassing human reason and consciousness.

The notion of universal human rights is often presumed to be understood, but is rarely defined. Some understand *universal* rights in the sense of the prevalence of a notion of rights across time and cultures. Others consider the normative aspect of *universal*; that is, the forward-looking development and adoption of human rights norms and institutions. In the absence of a specific definition of *universal* rights, both aspects of universality can be considered for the basic idea of human rights norms as they have existed throughout history.[8]

Lastly, human rights cannot be examined and explained without reference to governments.[9] Talbott, for instance, relies on the government to issue and honour legal guarantees to promote and honour his list of basic rights. Similarly, Sachedina wants governmental reform to strengthen citizenship. Most Enlightenment thinkers were interested in projects that yielded a form of government capable of promoting human rights, leading to the idea that only in liberal societies led by liberal governments could human rights norms thrive.[10] Consequently, any work on human rights presumes a specific function for the State and such presumption guides one's understanding of rights.

My critique of the work of other scholars and the framing of my counter-proposals is influenced by an overarching theoretical model: Systems thinking paradigm. In any work of scholarship relevant to social issues with practical implications, the theoretical approach could have significant practical impact on the level of adherence to human rights norms and protection of vulnerable social groups. In the following pages I will introduce and explain the theoretical lens through which I filter, process, produce, and reproduce ideas, promoting a clearer understanding of human rights and new recommendations for the mitigation and remediation of, and restitution for, human rights abuses.

First, I would like to challenge the wide acceptance of a concept often invoked to argue for granting rights: *Equality*. The founding fathers of the

United States of America went as far as qualifying the claim, "all men are created *equal*,"[11] as a self-evident truth. Representatives of member-states of the United Nations, who drafted the Universal Declaration of Human Rights, asserted in the first article of the document that "all human beings are born free and *equal* in dignity and rights."[12] Many of the struggles for civil rights in the United States and in other countries around the world often invoke *equality* as a principle on which governments should grant people rights.[13] However, in order to create a sound foundation for a project intended to be universal, we should ask the questions: In what respect and in how many ways are human beings equal? Should equality be a prerequisite for acquiring basic rights?

Reflecting on these questions and on the theoretical approach I shall employ for this work on human rights and Islamic societies, I recalled an ancient Sufi lesson. In this story, the Knower (*`Arif/Peer*) says to the Disciple (*Murid*): You believe that since you know one, you must know two because one and one make two. However, you neglect that you must also know the "and." This anecdote illustrates the assumption that relationships between seemingly same objects, or *equal* quantities, is simple and automatic: One human being *and* one human being make two human beings. As the Sufi teacher suggests, we must understand the system that relates one to one before making a judgement about the outcome. Positive integers have many functions but, in most cases, these functions involve non-abstract objects. The functions are governed by systems: Equations, for instance, that would produce specific outcomes given specific input within a specific framework. Only in abstractions can we conclude that one + one = two. In most cases, when variables are specified, one and one rarely equal two.

In a social context, one human being is equal to another human being in an abstract sense: As generic persons belonging to the same species. However, humans are hardly generic. Everyone has biological, physiological, mental, cultural, environmental and social traits, circumstances, and markers—variables—that make them fundamentally unique. Understanding these variables is what enables a physician to adequately assess a person's health. No doctor can rely on a chart that simply says: one human ready for check-up. They depend on a chart that contains information about age, sex, gender, race, weight, height, medical history, family medical history, occupation, and other information. An effective physician understands that a person is produced by many systems and that these systems are interconnected. A person's illness cannot be just related to his weight, because their weight is impacted by other systems. A doctor would understand that one man and one man are not equal to two men, and that one woman and one woman are not equal to two women. Indeed, doctors must rely on some abstractions and averages to assess the health of a person. To assess a person's health, a doctor would order a comprehensive metabolic panel laboratory work to evaluate metabolic functions and probe the performance of organ systems. To evaluate cardiac risk, a doctor would compare a person's cholesterol and triglyceride levels to the levels of a "normal" person. To assess organs' health and functioning, a doctor would order tests to measure levels of glucose, sodium, potassium, calcium, chloride, carbon dioxide, blood urea, creatinine, cholesterol, triglyceride, and other substances in the body. All of this probing is designed to assess the status and conditions of all systems. In many cases, one or more systems (such as organs) might be compromised—not producing the desired outcome. However, since the outcome of one system might be necessary for another system to perform its function, the doctor would decide on a solution that could either repair the system or supply the outcome directly (as with medications) in the body so that the rest of the systems can continue to function as normally as possible. Sound medicine starts with the assumption that every human being is unique and that no one person is equal to another in any significant way that would allow for abstract medicine. Good medicine is customized medicine, not generalized based on the principles of similitude. Human rights abuses in society are analogous to disease in human body: They are systemic malfunctions or systemic failures.

Human rights abuses are a chronic harm occurring in every society: Ancient and modern; liberal and conservative; and homogenous and diverse. The widespread occurrence of human rights abuses suggests that humans are more likely to perceive each other as *unequal* than equal. Just like medicine, to assess the cause and likelihood of an illness striking a human being through systems analysis, social scientists should rely on systems thinking to explain and mitigate human rights abuses. In society, systems are as ever-present as they are in medicine, and more complex than in the human body.

Relevant to systems thinking and human interrelationships, a widely shared Islamic tradition (Hadith) also comes to mind. The Prophet Muhammad reportedly struck an analogy between society and the human body, saying that, in terms of their care for each other, members of the faithful community's mercy towards each other and love of one another is like the human body; if one organ complains of an affliction, the rest of body sympathizes, experiencing both fever and sleeplessness.

These Sufi and Hadith idiomatic traditions illustrate two important aspects related to knowledge acquisition and systems connectedness. The first tells us that just because we know components of a system or the connection between systems; it does not necessarily mean that we know the functioning of the system or the nuances of connections between systems. The second suggests that society is, in its own way, a single body. The same way the whole of a human body's system sympathizes with an injury affecting one sub-system, society also reacts to an injured sub-group; or it should.

Neither the principle of equality, nor reasoned and empirical data alone, inform my approach to the topic of human rights. My work is premised on the assumption that human beings are more *unequal* due to chance,

8 *Introduction*

accident, biology, culture, social and economic status, experience, and other factors than they are equal. People are all born into *inequality*. Throughout history, societies and cultures have failed to mitigate inequality, celebrate diversity, and accommodate difference in ways that would honour the dignity and rights of the most vulnerable individuals and social groups. Instead, dominant social groups, through a plurality of systems they have designed, have used difference to exert control, maximize their own benefits, and preserve privilege. Consequently, human rights abuses have become prevalent because dominant social groups often leverage the inherent and acquired inequality among human beings. Facts suggest that because and despite inequality and difference among human beings, human rights should be universalized.

I submit also that human rights discourse is essentially more of a political issue, in the sense that it is more about managing social conflict and human difference, than it is a moral position of innate, reasoned, or empirical origins. As such, the status of human rights is decided by a plurality of systems. Therefore, systems thinking paradigm is most appropriate for understanding human rights in any given society at any given time.

There are many reasons systems thinking bears relevance to human rights. First, the topic of human rights is or has the potential to be present in every academic discipline. Scholars from each discipline rely on the tools and theoretical models most common within their discipline. Therefore, they must subject human rights—the topic of inquiry—to their systems of analysis and exploration. Second, human rights are invoked in every domain of public life; everyone is impacted by them. Inquiring about human rights amounts to inquiring about ourselves, recalling our personal experiences or the experiences of people we know personally, or perceiving our collective history relevant to its promotion of, or failure to promote, human rights norms. The ubiquitous presence of human rights in public life makes it a subject of different social and natural systems. Lastly, our personal stories make our personal biases ever-present. Personal bias, in this context, could be instructive and remedial, not negative or harmful. With all this complexity, I see the systems thinking paradigm as being the most appropriate theoretical lens for investigating human rights. I should start by introducing systems thinking in general terms and, then, explain the framework as I understand it and apply it to the topic of human rights using practical examples and scenarios.

As an approach widely used in most academic disciplines throughout history, systems thinking is based on the idea that the existence of things is not random or purposeless. Rather, things exist within systems and systems are designed to achieve specific things. Therefore, a system consists of components that are deliberately connected to achieve desired outcomes. An outcome could be part of the elemental input for another system.[14] This generic definition of a system calls for three parts: Element, connection, and function. In a system, the various elements work together towards a specific purpose. Once the purpose is achieved within one system, it could become an element of another system, whose function might be enhancing the same purpose (such as a redundancy, parallel output, or scalability) or producing a different outcome (in the case of serial output).

While elements may be system-specific, their connectedness is both intra- and inter-systemic. Systems can be nested within other systems that are working towards interconnected purposes that may not be measurable through the same scale or metrics. Systems are ubiquitous. They are found in nature, in society, in physical and abstract things, in institutions and organizations, and in simple and complex organisms. System interconnectedness makes the identification of a single system subjective, dependent on the nature of the inquiry, but always purposeful when soundly established. In nature, the smallest system is a single unicellular organism, while the largest one is the entire accessible universe. In human society, the complexity of elements makes breaking it down to the simplest single system more challenging—made less challenging only by the level of detail of information about a specific element. Beyond that, a system can be anything one is interested in exploring. A marine biologist might define a lake as a system, while a plant biologist might consider a specific plant, such as an olive tree, a system.

The elements can be simple or complex, involving input, process, and output. Each element can be a subject of inquiry to define or describe its composition, or one can query the entire network between input, process, and output. The main idea behind systems thinking perspectives is that every system, when properly defined, is in relation with other systems. The connection could be obvious and immediate or latent and deferred.

To understand its elements, the system must be properly isolated. That is, one must determine the boundaries of the system within which the system can continue to perform its function without the need for any outside elements for a specific time or under certain conditions. A system can be isolated if its investigated characteristic or event is contained within its borders and not produced by forces from outside the borders. Returning to the topic of human rights and Islamic societies, an example might be human rights (a social phenomenon) in Syria today (a location and time), which cannot be considered an isolated system to study human rights abuses because many of its human rights abuses result from actions by forces from outside Syria. Of course, we can limit the inquiry to human rights abuses in Syrian prisons, which is feasible within Syria as the system's border. However, even then, we would still need due diligence in the selection of elements to ascertain that we are accounting for all internal forces and only internal forces for our analysis to be systemic and accurate.

Because of the potential complexity of elements and the nature and function of connections between systems, the most challenging task in systems thinking analysis is the determination of system boundaries, since what could be an element or component of one system might be mistaken for an output-rendered-component for another system. System-nesting, when poorly understood, could compromise the discovery process and this problem is more acute in disciplines within social sciences and the humanities than in other disciplines. Perhaps these abstract renderings can be made somewhat more concrete by reintroducing systems thinking through examples. Since everything is, at some level, a system, I will start with my work environment, the university, and through the systems thinking perspective I will explain some of the structures of the institution and navigate out of the university system to connect it with the topic of human rights in national and global—that is, universal—systems.

Starting with the general purpose, I could describe a public university, like the University of Iowa, as a system of discovering and sharing knowledge. To achieve this institutional purpose, a university consists of essential elements: Teachers and researchers who create and impart knowledge, and students who learn from and study or train with them. In this setting, the elements are teachers, researchers, and students; the process involves teaching, discovery, or both; and the output objectives are knowledge and skill acquisition and transfer.

As many of us know, however, a university is not simply a place, one physical building housing teachers, researchers, and students. At some level, a university is a microcosm of society. In addition to students and teachers, there are many staff members and volunteers, objects and living things, and events and ideas without which the main purpose of the institution, sharing and discovering knowledge, could not be achieved. Importantly, many of these elements within the university system might have functions and purposes that have no obvious connection to the creation and sharing of knowledge. For example, the groundkeepers' main function is to maintain green spaces and gardens on the campus. While green spaces make the learning environment more pleasant, they are not required for knowledge creation. In fact, even main elements might have purposes different from the general purpose of the university. A faculty member might be interested in earning tenure and securing a stable income. A student might be interested in getting good grades from a "highly-ranked" university to secure a high-paying job. From the university's point of view, an administrator is supposed to balance the budget so the institution can carry out its mission. From the viewpoint of an administrator, their goal might be to advance a particular ideology within educational systems. Given its dependency on human actors and given the different experiences across individuals, the actions each actor takes could vary from the university's stated mission. For example, a student could cheat to earn high grades, a professor could spend less time teaching students and more time publishing books, and an administrator could allocate less money to key resources to save money for something they deem more important. These decisions and actions by different elements could, and often do, conflict with the general purpose of the university. To mitigate the impact of these conflicts, a university might adopt a blueprint for each system to make sure that each system produces the outcomes that it needs to achieve its general purpose.

As it happens, universities do develop manuals of policies and procedures for the entire institution and for each unit, essentially creating sub-systems designed to produce outputs that enable the institution to achieve its mission. Given the critical role universities play in knowledge dissemination and skill development, which have a direct impact on the economic life in society, governments, too, produce public policies—another layer of systems—governing the relationship between universities, society at large, and the government. These internal and external systems are designed to enable institutions to operate and deliver outcomes consistently regardless of the individual actors administering each unit. Importantly, the interconnectivity of systems allows society to create and preserve a socioeconomic order that is stable and predictable. To be sure, the national economic system can be dependent on systems at the university level. Moreover, the various units within a university, as independent systems in terms of function, become autonomous and specialized, insulating the larger system from possible malfunction occurring within one unit. For example, the department of computer sciences might struggle in achieving its purpose, but its struggles will not stop the university from achieving its general goal. The struggling unit, then, could adjust, or the university could remove its output from the list of components, or replace it. If properly applied, systems thinking should be able to help explain how an isolated system governing the operation of a single department within an educational institution can impact economic disparity at the national level.

Relevant to the topic of human rights, the policies and procedures universities create have had direct impact on equity and inclusion in society. Through systems designed and equipped with specialized instruments, including admissions metrics and standardized testing, universities have denied Black people, indigenous people, and women equal access to education and professional training. The denial of education to these social groups has limited their chances for gainful employment, access to resources, an adequate standard of living, and choices for location of residence. Moreover, in affluent societies, dominant social groups' localized practices extend beyond national borders. Because of the dominance of US economic, social, and political systems, conditions created in the United States and other affluent European nation-states often replicate themselves on the global stage. For these reasons, we must address the right to education, healthcare, economic and cultural autonomy, and security in defined systems with clear boundaries.

The prevalence of systems within research and teaching institutions makes it easy to see how systems thinking is relevant to human rights. As it were, systems thinking is appropriate to this study for another important reason: The relevance of human rights to many academic disciplines. In other words, systems thinking is intrinsically interdisciplinary, allowing human rights scholars to work from an augmented body of integrated knowledge. A legal scholar interested in human rights could draw on knowledge of living systems from biology and health sciences, economic systems from economics, social systems from sociology and psychology, technological systems from computational and information sciences and cybernetics, conceptual systems from engineering, ecosystems from ecology and environmental sciences, and institutional systems from political science, law, and religion.

Some systems reflect operational functions and outcomes. Others are made to perpetuate superficial metrics. For example, although there is disparity in resources and assets among educational institutions, university rankings create real and fictional standing, amplifying disparity and reproducing elitism and privilege. The mere name of an institution confers status, entitlement, and superiority. Continuing with the example of the university setting to explain systems, we can take as example the following trajectories of two individuals from different backgrounds.

Mr. Smith,[15] a white man born to an affluent family, earned a degree in business management from a prestigious university. Mr. Smith took over management of the family real estate business. Over the years of his leadership, the business faced financial challenges. Mr. Smith filed for multiple bankruptcy protections and faced hundreds of legal actions. Nonetheless, when he applied for loans to rebuild his business, banks agreed to loan him millions of dollars. Mr. Smith was also able to leverage government resources and assistance to stay in business and build a brand name: When the global financial meltdown struck, the US government was able to print more money and resuscitate the financial sector. Mr. Smith benefited from this governmental intervention as well as from his family, class, and racial privilege. Due to systemic modalities, decisions that impacted Mr. Smith were made not just by formal systems governing public transactions, but also by informal factors—personal bias, cultural norms, and social norms.

Mr. Sulaiman, a Black man born to a poor family on the south side of Chicago, earned a degree in business management from a public university. He started a business remodeling and selling houses. He did well, but he wanted to expand his business to stabilize income for his family and for the people who worked for him. Mr. Sulaiman applied for a loan. As is often the case for Black people, banks denied his applications. Unlike Mr. Smith, and despite his success running a small business, Mr. Sulaiman was not able to overcome the fact that he was Black. The legacy of slavery and racial bigotry, through formal and informal systems, has programmed members of society to associate values and to make judgments based on a person's skin color rather than their professional record.

The disparate fortunes of Mr. Smith and Mr. Sulaiman are not only personal, but represent privilege extending back generations and across borders. Frustrated by the uncertainties of being a Black businessman in America, Mr. Sulaiman decided to relocate his family and business to his ancestral home, Somalia. There, he hoped to borrow money from government-run banks or through private investors. However, the government of Somalia, like that of many African countries, was not able to secure financial assistance from international financial systems. Therefore, there was not enough money in government-run banks. The government could not even support its own bureaucracy to run the country, let alone provide loans to private businesses. Somalia became a failed state. The only money coming in was from wealthy individuals and governments of oil-rich countries like Saudi Arabia, Qatar, and the United Arab Emirates. However, money from both came with conditions: Political and cultural realignment and patronage, through which a specific brand of Islam was imported with the money. Some business owners took the money; Somalia became a breeding ground for extremism, intolerance, and exclusion. Somalia fell deeper into instability, violence, and fragmentation. Mr. Sulaiman soon realized that his chances of achieving his business goals in Somalia, while upholding his values, were no better than his chances of success in the United States, albeit for different reasons.

These scenarios, which represent real cases, illustrate the interconnectedness of systems not only within national borders, but on a global scale. One could argue that what happens in Africa is due to the actions of Africans. Yet slavery, colonialism, and sanctions tell a different story: What happens in Africa is only partly due to the actions of Africans. What happens in Africa is also decided by a global order built on systems and institutions designed, created, and maintained by dominant social groups in dominant societies run by dominant governments. One might explain an event in small neighbourhood in Mogadishu, Somalia through explaining the workings of a university system in a small town in Iowa; or by a belief system preached in a mosque in small town in Saudi Arabia, or both. The same applies to a human rights case: Mass killings against members of a clan in Somalia might be explainable by the workings of systems in DC and Riyadh, and the systems in DC and Riyadh might be designed by racism, supremacy, and sectarianism originating in the seventeenth and seventh centuries, respectively. Systems thinking analysis enables us to identify the origins, evolution, and functions of ideas, events, and institutions in some of the most complex environments.

Systems thinking is both specific and holistic. When a border of a system is properly identified, the system's outcome will be specific. However, since the output of a system is rarely an end-goal for itself—rather, it is component that another system is using for another purpose—systems thinking contributes to the understanding of the whole. As such and when appropriate feedback loops are in place, the knowledge relevant to one system can amend, enhance, or reaffirm knowledge in other systems. Critical components, because they are necessary to deliver main institutional outcomes, might require duplicated functions in a system—intentional redundancy— to enhance overall systemic performance. Other systems may end up performing the inverse of the desired outcome. Even though understanding such a system can be irrelevant to the larger system, it has a value in that it explains the system, though through an alternative perspective. This complication can be resolved through awareness of the researcher's epistemological position, inherent in the multidisciplinary nature of systems thinking paradigm.

To the subject of human rights, systems thinking is an essential paradigm because most human rights problems were not deliberately created. I like to think that no one person or social group decided to intentionally create poverty, degrade the environment, deprive people of food, deny people work, cause illness, unleash pandemics, widen inequity, torture people, pay women less than men, or launch wars. However, individuals and social groups deliberately created systems to augment wealth, increase productivity, enhance efficiency, reduce the cost of labor, exploit natural resources, and hoard resources and means. These intentionally created systems have had direct or indirect effects on poverty, crime, hunger, the environment, and a litany of other abuses, making it arguable that these negative outcomes are ultimately systemic. These and other problems in the area of human rights persist because they are system problems; to that end, they can be resolved through systems thinking.

When I apply systems thinking to the subject of human rights, it yields a system in the form of an equation in a state of dynamic equilibrium, consisting of civil society institutions on one side and the State on the other side. The isolation of the system in such a way identifies the State as the principal culprit of human rights abuses and that the State's abuses can be addressed internally—within systems—and through actions of civil society institutions.

With the same forcefulness with which I identify the State—an entity with overwhelming power—as the sole abuser or potential abuser of human rights, I also identify racism, or its derivatives, other systems of supremacy, as the sole motivating force behind the most egregious human rights abuses in history. This work is informed by these two assertions, for which I will present ample evidence and argue throughout.

While I identify the State as the only entity responsible for human rights abuses, it must be noted that the State (along with its agencies and the systems controlling them) is the creation of society. In a popular democracy, society is abstracted by the will of the majority and the preferences of the dominant social groups. In non-popular democracies, society is abstracted by the institutional powers that produce the governing entity—clan dominance, constitutional terms, military force, and other forms through which power takes shape. In all cases, the governing power is beholden to the wishes of an interest group. In such a setting, human rights abuses occur through formal and informal channels. The State commits its abuses through formal actions: Public policies, allocation of resources, and access to services. Society, through social norms and cultural practices, acts in an injurious manner, violating the rights of some social groups informally: Racism, bias, discrimination, exclusion, and other methods of intolerance. These actions, while they amount to human rights abuse, are still crimes of the State, for it is the State that did not act to prevent them. Moreover, the State's formal abuse of human rights is simply reflective of an informal societal inclination to abuse the human rights of marginalized social groups. For instance, if we grant the proposition that racism is the motivating force behind most human rights abuses, it becomes clear why only the actions of the dominant social group that both empowers the State and is enabled by the State would qualify as acts of racism. A disempowered social group, even if they hold racialized views, cannot be considered racist for *racism exists when racialized views are enabled by power.*

Moving from the general to the specific, systems thinking allows us to analyze and understand how the various systems within society impact human rights norms. Systems thinking allows us to contextualize human rights abuses within Western societies, during and after the Enlightenment era, because during this era Western society developed and employed ideological, normative, and institutional systems that produced prosperity while causing abuses. An economic system designed to maximize wealth necessarily produces extreme poverty. An ethical system that positivizes riches and problematizes[16] poverty necessarily stigmatizes the poor. Racism, before it became a potent instrument of social control in the hands of dominant social groups, not only problematized Blackness, but connected it to ethical value systems. Such ethical value systems instilled the supremacy impulse in the dominant social group and were used to strip the oppressed social groups of feelings of self-worth. In the end, one cannot justify hoarding resources without glorifying greed. Consequently, some members of oppressed social groups, and some people of colonized nations, came to believe that only through oppressor-produced systems could a person of color or a people of exploited nations prove their self-worth. Some have come to believe that they must use the tools of racism to defeat racism; in reality, what they need is the development of new systems that would positivize poverty and problematize extreme wealth.

Similar to post-Enlightenment Western societies, Islamic societies have prioritized their goals and set up systems to achieve those goals. During the rise of Islamic civilization, the dominant social groups were not white, they were brown. The dominant ideology was not liberty, it was Sunnism. Islamic society produced a worldview rooted in ethnic supremacy and sectarian purity. The dominant social groups designed efficient and deliberate systems to positivize these ideals, which led to committing genocide against those who challenged their worldview and to establishing a political order that denied non-Arabs any path to political leadership. It is no surprise, then, that the violent conflicts in twenty-first century Islamic societies are unresolved conflicts and ideas from the seventh and eighth centuries.

16 *Introduction*

Subjecting ethical and social ideas and institutions, or individual cultures and societies, to systems thinking analysis reveals the forces that predetermine outcomes (social and institutional determinants). This is not to say that human rights cannot be understood outside limited systems, such as within a specific culture or society. By understanding human rights abuses in isolated systems, by developing a catalogue of common elements and the connectedness of systems that produce human rights abuses, we should be able to explain their persistence globally. Indeed, the most important fact that guides this work is the fact that human rights abuses *are* universal. The universality of abuse, if properly contextualized, could lead to developing universal safeguards and harm reduction measures that could universalize human rights norms.

By examining Enlightenment thought's legacy and the evolution of that tradition in Western society, we should be able to explain slavery and the dehumanizing of treatment of specific social groups. However, slavery is not unique to Western societies. Islamic civilization was built, in part, on the backs of enslaved human beings and exploited social groups. Specific cultural and societal practices governed slavery in Islamic societies just as specific factors initiated and dictated slavery in Western societies. The same can be said about all human rights abuses throughout modern Western civilization and its predecessor, Islamic civilization. How could two different systems produce the same social scourges? In the next four sections, I will layout evidence from both Western Enlightenment and Islamic thought and practices to highlight the motivating forces, persistent conditions, and deliberate systems that universalized human rights abuses, and I will suggest a revised framework for discourse on human rights.

Notes

1. Zehra F. KabasakalArat, "Forging a Global Culture of Human Rights: Origins and Prospects of the International Bill of Rights," Human *Rights Quarterly* 28, no. 2 (2006): 416–37.
2. See, generally: Bonny Ibhawoh, *Imperialism and Human Rights: Colonial Discourses of Rights and Liberties in African History* (Albany: SUNY Press, 2008).
3. Tu Wei-Ming, "Beyond the Enlightenment Mentality," *The Bucknell Review* 37, no. 2 (1993): 19.
4. Tim Delaney, *Darkened Enlightenment: The Deterioration of Democracy, Human Rights, and Rational Thought in the Twenty-First Century* (New York: Routledge, 2020).
5. See, generally: William A. Schabas, *An Introduction to the International Criminal Court* (Cambridge, UK: Cambridge University Press, 2011) and Kamari M. Clarke, Abel S. Knottnerus, and Eefje de Volder, *Africa and the ICC* (New York: Cambridge University Press, 2016).
6. William J. Talbott, *Which Human Rights Should Be Universal?* (New York: Oxford University Press, 2007).
7. Talbott, *Which Rights*, 178–179.

Introduction 17

8. Micheline Ishay, *The History of Human Rights: From Ancient Times to the Globalization Era* (Berkeley: University of California Press, 2008).
9. See, generally: Andrew Clapham, *Human Rights Obligations of Non-State Actors* (New York: OUP Oxford, 2006); Cohen, Stanley, "Human Rights and Crimes of The State: The Culture of Denial," *Australian & New Zealand Journal of Criminology*26, no. 2 (1993): 97–115; Catherine A. MacKinnon, "Rape, Genocide, and Women's Human Rights," *Harvard Women's Law Journal* 17 (1994): 5; Claudia Card, "Rape as a Weapon of War," *Hypatia*11, no. 6 (Fall 1996) 5–18; Margaretha Wewerinke-Singh, *State Responsibility, Climate Change and Human Rights Under International Law* (Oxford, UK: Hart Publishing, 2019); K. Mills, D. Karp, David Jason Karp, and Kurt Mills, *Human Rights Protection in Global Politics: Responsibilities of States and Non-State Actors* (Basingstoke: Palgrave Macmillan, 2015); and David Jason Karp, *Responsibility for Human Rights: Transnational Corporations in Imperfect States* (Cambridge: Cambridge University Press, 2014).
10. Nannerl O. Keohane, *Philosophy and the State in France: The Renaissance to the Enlightenment* (New Jersey: Princeton University Press, 2017), 13 and 370; William A. Galston, *Liberal Purposes: Goods, Virtues, and Diversity in the Liberal State* (Cambridge: Cambridge University Press, 1991), 91–93, 153, and 264; and, generally, Nicholas P. Higgins, *Enlightenment Legacies: Colonial Reform, Independence, and the Invisible Indian of the Liberal State* (Austin: University of Texas Press, 2009).
11. Emphasis on *equal* mine.
12. Emphasis on *equal* mine.
13. Mike Cole, *Education, Equality and Human Rights: Issues of Gender, "Race," Sexuality, Disability and Social Class* (London: Routledge, 2017); Andreas Føllesdal, Johan Karlsson Schaffer, Geir Ulfstein, *The Legitimacy of International Human Rights Regimes: Legal, Political and Philosophical Perspectives* (Cambridge: Cambridge University Press, 2013); Michael Goodhart, *Democracy as Human Rights: Freedom and Equality in the Age of Globalization* (New York: Routledge, 2005); Allen Buchanan, "Equality and Human Rights." *Politics, Philosophy & Economics* 4, no. 1 (2005) 69–90; Wouter Vandenhole, *Non-discrimination and Equality in the View of the UN Human Rights Treaty Bodies* (Oxford: Intersentia, 2005); Rezvan Ostadalidehaghi and Daniel Béland, "Women without Guardians' in Iran: Gender, Cultural Assumptions, and Social Policy," *Journal of International and Comparative Social Policy* 29, no.1 (2013): 48–63.
14. I prefer not to use the term "sub-system" because that risks hierarchizing systems. Systems, as I understand them, are functionally independent but connected through their outputs. However, in some contexts, using the term "sub-system" might better help illustrate a point.
15. While these stories reflect real-life individuals and circumstances, the names and identifying details of both men have been changed.
16. The word "problematize" is often used to mean different things; I am using it here in the context of coloring something, in this case poverty, as a problem. The same logic applies to my use of the word "positivize," assigning a positive ethical value to something, in my example being wealthy.

Part I
Human rights as a discourse

Very few subjects stir emotion as does human rights. This is even more so when the argument asserts that the very topic of discussion, human rights, must not only be recognized, but universalized. The chief challenge against universalizing human rights norms is the argument that any attempt to make rights norms universal will result in legitimizing moral imperialism and executing cultural genocide.

In the first two decades of this century, the authors of two monographs—one on the universality of human rights and the other on the resonance of human rights within an established religion—contend that at least some human rights claims should overcome political and cultural challenges and be normalized across humanity. One author grounds his argument in moral philosophy, consistent with a long line of liberal political thought. The other grounds his analysis in moral reasoning framed in Islamic classical thought and practices.

In his monograph, *Which Rights Should Be Universal?* Philosopher William J. Talbott asserts that some rights should be universal, and that this position is not necessarily one of moral imperialism. Responding to a widely held view that religion in general, and Islam in particular, is incompatible with human rights, scholar of religious studies Abdulaziz Sachedina indirectly supports the idea of universal human rights while asserting that Islam, as he interprets it, is compatible with human rights norms. He further contends in his monograph *Islam and the Challenge of Human Rights* that any theory of universal rights necessarily emerges out of specific cultural contexts.

I foreground my own work with these ostensibly unrelated yet thought-provoking works to bridge the gap between cultural relativists and moral Universalists in relation to human rights and to increase the scope of human rights discourse beyond the limits of a single academic discipline and a single society. I accomplish this by integrating settled knowledge from relevant disciplines to probe both the discovery-rooted argument and the malleability of religious traditions, while focusing on the source and nature of conditions that compel a forceful engagement with the idea of human rights and its derivatives. First, I will introduce, discuss, and critique the ideas that comprise Talbott's writing on universal rights.[1]

2 What we now know
Human rights and post-enlightenment thought

By way of engaging with the writings of two scholars, a moral philosopher who draws on the legacy of Western Enlightenment thinkers and a comparative religion historian who draws on classical Islamic texts, ethics and law, this chapter lays out the case for the struggle of modern thinkers to define human rights and to appreciate the function of academic disciplines, societal norms, and institutional authorities as systems of power that inform and/or limit our understanding and reproduction of the discourse on human rights.

Before even reading the full text, the title of Talbott's work—*Which Rights Should Be Universal?*—is significant. Considering his background as a Western philosopher, we can fairly deduce that the title announces his presumptive position that not all human rights claims enshrined in the Universal Declaration of Human Rights should be universal. Moreover, it would be a mistake to think that Talbott's position is decidedly a moral proposition, existing only within the confines of epistemology. His monograph comfortably engages with historians, sociologists, political scientists, political economists, psychologists, and ethicists. Though he notably omitted the many contributions of law and jurisprudence scholars, Talbott engages whom he calls "moral philosophers," scholars of religious studies or religious persons who "develop and exercise their own moral judgment."[2] He references Islam and Muslims to contextualize his argument apropos to cultural relativism, imperialism, and individual and group autonomy.

Human rights abuses are as pervasive now as they have been in every civilization throughout human history. Talbott ascribes the drive behind developing basic human rights norms to the pervasiveness of patriarchy, religious intolerance, and absolute monarchy. Talbott observes that "the idea of rights develops as a response to the oppression of one group by another."[3] Considering the development of human rights in American and Western European societies, Talbott contends that human rights values are a reaction to these societies' human rights abuses, including government taxation of property-owning males without representation, the enslavement and subsequent segregation and marginalization of Black people, the colonization and exploitation of indigenous peoples in Africa, the Americas, and Asia, and the subjugation of women. Talbott argues that in each of these cases,

> The oppressors have attempted to justify their oppression *paternalistically*, by claiming that members of the same oppressed group were not good judges of what was good for them and that the oppressors were really acting for the good of those they oppressed.[4]

As will be made clear by the end of this work, I assert that the context, justification, and motive for human rights abuses are critical for developing human rights norms and safeguards. For this reason, I will briefly respond to this justification of human rights abuses.

First, Talbott generalizes that men in patriarchal societies subjugated women.[5] To be able to develop sound public policy to address the historical subjugation of women, it is imperative that attribution of responsibly is based on facts. The subjugation of women was not and could not have been done by men, especially if we are noting women's grievances in the same stream of thought when noting the grievances of people who were enslaved. Enslaved men did not and could not have subjugated women, let alone white women, for they lacked the freedom, and, importantly, institutional power to do so. It was governmental structures and agencies which subjugated women in all societies. Members of the elite, a majority of whom were men belonging to the dominant social group, authorize government abuse. However, this elite class has included white women (as in the case of US society). This is crucial information because it is based on the facts which public policies, intended to address historical injustices, are built. If the facts are skewed, so will be the policies. And if the policies are skewed, then they will fail to mitigate, remediate, and make whole the harm and damage specific social groups experienced, suffered, and sustained.

Second, there is no reason why the "justification" of human rights abusers, such as those who enslaved Black people out of ostensibly paternalistic intentions, would be of any significance to a project aiming to develop a list of basic universal rights. The justification is *post hoc*. It could have been proposed only belatedly: After having travelled to distant lands, kidnapped people away from their homelands, and using their bodies and energies to augment the wealth and power of white men. Likewise, it would not make sense for white Europeans, living in Europe without any Black people around, to decide to go to another continent and provide the people there with the "care" white people thought Black people deserved. Meanwhile, when enslaved and abused Black people, already living among whites, objected to the way they were treated and claimed their dignity, the slaveholders justified their actions "paternalistically," claiming that Black people "were not good judges of what was good for them," and that slaveholders "were really acting for the good of"[6] the Black people.

Moreover, it defies reason to believe that slaveholders were thinking and telling the people they were lynching that being lynched was in their interest. It is absurd to believe that those being lynched could see such reasoning as sound. The act of enslaving other human beings and the actions taken thereafter to keep them in bondage in perpetuity were intended to break down their humanity, including their capacity to reason, feel, think, and act autonomously. Enslaving others, and building the narratives and institutions to preserve slavery, was deliberate and systemic beyond any paternalistic impulse and intent.

Slavery is a crime; a crime of the State, to be exact. Governments allowed intercontinental trade in human beings. Governments also allowed some of its citizens, the dominant social group to whom the State is beholden, to own human beings as property and exploit them to augment wealth. A government capable of prohibiting the sale of liquor should be able to proscribe the sale and exploitation of human beings. Since slavery, as is the case with other egregious human rights offenses, is a crime, one should be interested in the motive, not the justification, of the crime. Paternalism could not have been both.

Faced with mounting criticism and opposition to the treatment of enslaved people and the institution of slavery in general, those profiting from slavery grounded their argument for keeping slaves in normative terms. Their actions, some argued, were good because they provided care for people who would otherwise have none. Such a posturing justification is patently false: Slaveholders did not enslave Black people out of a motive to care for them. Since Talbott is arguing for set universal rights, his repeating a false claim attempts to absolve those who used it to escape responsibility. By giving credence to false justifications, Talbott perpetuates a myth that there was an ethical basis for slavery. The veneer of paternalism masks slavery's cruel, degrading, and abusive nature.

Talbot could have objected to referencing paternalism as justification for some human rights abuses in passing, since it is true that some have indeed tried this justification. However, using it as a diagnostic tool in a project aimed at universalizing basic human rights lays a weak foundation for such a towering project. Talbott might have included it to augment his claim that illiberal societies make decisions "on the basis of paternalistic judgments" when he emphatically declares that "no illiberal government can be relied upon to adequately promote the good of the groups it treats paternalistically."[7] Though it might be pure optimism, Talbott appears to suggest that a package of basic universal rights is achievable only in liberal societies that produce liberal governments. Such optimism is so overwhelming that it incites the fervours of imperialism and hegemony. It raises the other critical question: If the realization of universal rights can only be achieved in the context of liberal societies led by liberal governments, should liberal societies engage in a global mission to eradicate all illiberal societies and replace them with liberal ones? Moreover, given that the discovery of human rights often happens in environments abusive to human rights, how would the eradication of hostile environments to human rights impact the discovery process after illiberal societies are eradicated? Talbott may avoid being a moral imperialist only to risk becoming a social imperialist.

Talbott's emphasis on paternalism as the impediment to moral progress of developing universal human rights might be convenient for formulating an abstract argument. However, it is not useful when actually developing a package of basic human rights that can inform public policy addressing historical instances of abuse and many other grievances yet to be fully discussed and remediated. Enslaving human beings belonging to a specific racial or ethnic group is more than paternalism. It is about leveraging a power differential to exploit, dehumanize, and impose physiological and mental shackles that endure beyond the removal of physical chains. In the context of Western societies, supremacy and racism is the common thread present across all major human rights abuses. Adopting systems thinking as a framework is more useful to understanding human rights abuses than accepting false justifications. I will address this common thread and the theoretical approach in more detail later on in this work.

Returning to Talbott's account of human rights norms, Talbott posits that discovering basic human rights is the result of a historical "bottom-up process" of "moral development" and "social transformation." That human beings, he argues, "should have certain legally protected basic rights is a partly moral, partly empirical discovery based on thousands of years of accumulated experience of human existence."[8] He does not consider whether any rights are universal; instead he considers whether "in light of what we now know about human beings, any rights *should* be universal." He finds that we "now have sufficient understanding of the nature of human beings and of the moral constraints on how they should be treated to realize that governments everywhere ought to guarantee certain basic rights to everyone within their borders."[9] These basic rights materialize from social pressure centres and modalities including competing discourses, contestation of values and ideas, and grassroots social movements emerging to challenge established moral and political elites. Now, Talbott declares, and after "thousands of years of human moral development," we discover that "certain basic rights should be universal."[10] These statements are significant because the implications, at first glance, are dramatically transformative.

Reading through the first chapter of Talbott's book and thinking through the statements above, my first reaction was to pause and reflect on time and place. What is special about now? And, though implicitly if not explicitly present, what is special about here? Talbott is suggesting that here, at the centre of gravity of the Western civilization, at the start of the twenty-first century, finally, we have the moral development to agree that some basic rights should be universal and that any government aspiring to be recognized as legitimate must guarantee these rights. Embedded in this stream of thought is the idea that moral development is linear, accumulative, and progressive.

The second issue, though not as explicitly argued, is related to place, or the kind of society with Talbott's required moral judgement. Because Talbott references other, non-Western, communities and other societies primarily to introduce a negative "for-instance,"[11] it is reasonable to assume that the place or the society Talbott has in mind is a Western society with roots in Enlightenment. These are the hallmarks of moral imperialism and cultural supremacy. Since imperialist and supremacist are grossly inaccurate descriptors of Talbott's personal character, it may be worth looking for an alternative interpretation and the impact of systems on his thinking. Additionally, the reader must contextualize this part of the argument with Talbott's explanation of why holding such position does not make him *ipso facto* a moral imperialist.

Talbott may not be using the concept of "now" in the way I interpreted above, since he also holds that the development of human rights is a *fallible* historical process. In other words, human moral development is not linear. At one moment, there might be some progress. At another, there is only regress. In a third instance, there is progress and regress with varying degrees of success, cancelling portions, or all, of each other. The actions of any given generation of human beings determine whether there is progress or not. Now, at this moment, Talbott finds that based on what he knows now, governments should guarantee nine basic rights and these rights should be considered universal. However, with the same certainty he proposes those rights; he also submits that anyone can recognize injustice and any culture can transform itself from a culture that violates human rights to one that respects human rights. This position is predicated on epistemic modesty, which leads one to acknowledge one's fallibility on reasoned judgment and empirical evidence. Whether the force of epistemic modesty is enough to overcome the inertia of a moment defined by supremacy is another question.

According to Talbott, the discovery of rights occurs despite some top-down social forces, like religious or political elite, who "admonish their adherents to follow the directives of the relevant moral authority unquestioningly, and not to exercise their own moral judgment."[12] However, he adds, religious traditions may also "produce at least some people with the capacity for independent moral judgment."[13] Without saying so explicitly, Talbott connects the moral philosophers who are *not* members of the elite—those who rule and impose their values from the top—to those who develop human rights norms from the ground up. Through historical examples, reasoned arguments, and some assumptions, Talbott introduces his readers to nine basic rights that he believes a government should guarantee to secure its legitimacy.

It is a mistake to assume that the list of nine basic rights is Talbott's main contribution to the discussion of human rights. Such an assumption diminishes his entire body of work, which consists of two volumes and a number of presentations and essays. Indeed, producing such a list is neither significant nor original. Every semester, in an undergraduate course on human rights, I assign students a small group task to collectively develop and produce a list of universal rights. What is deeply instructive in this activity, and the reason I keep assigning it, is not the various lists that groups of students produce, but the discussions and negotiations they engage in to build a list that all, or most, members of each group support. When each small group presents its list, the greater class discussion is equally instructive. Talbott's list is not much different from any one of the lists my students produce. What is significant about Talbott's work is the processes and the conditions that he used to produce the list of basic rights.

To generate the package of rights that should be universal, Talbott examines historical records from the last 300 years of human experiments and experiences in mainly Western societies, measures them against ideas and theories proposed by other political and philosophical thinkers from the same era and the same societies, and amends them in light of what we (as moral philosophers, per Talbott's definition) now know about human moral development. This process is not simple and for that reason, readers must allocate considerable efforts unpacking Talbott's arguments and distinguishing them from the thinkers he cites. A reader cannot fully appreciate Talbott's position on human rights without considering it in its particular and general contexts.

I share Talbott's wariness of society's elite minority who impose their values from the top down. I believe Talbott identified the proper agents of oppression and sources of oppression. I am sceptical, however, that members of the elite in and by themselves—neither directly in charge of the government nor influencing those in charge of the government—are the real threat to human rights. I am also perplexed by Talbott's distrust of illiberal governments and his confidence in liberal ones when he emphatically declares that "no illiberal government can be relied upon to adequately promote the good of the groups it treats paternalistically." When taken in conjunction with the fact that Talbott's project takes *society* as the platform for normalizing the rights he deems universal—not individuals—this statement become problematic in its meaning and implications.

Some of the obvious questions in reaction to the above declarative statement are these: Can all liberal governments reliably and adequately promote the good of the groups they treat paternalistically? Do liberal governments treat all groups non-paternalistically? If universalizing human rights is dependent on creating liberal societies that are run by liberal governments, should liberal societies, interested in universalizing human rights, engage in liberalizing all illiberal societies and installing in them liberal governments?

How does proselytizing for liberal societies differentiate from missionizing for a particular religion?

These questions are critical. If Talbott conceives of liberal societies run by liberal governments that do not treat any social group paternalistically, he would need to solve the process of creating such a government, because at present there exists no such system. In most liberal societies, governments emerge out of competition: That is, elections. During the time leading up to the elections, people with different ideas and different policies propose them and ask the people to vote for the person with the proposals they prefer. In the end, one side wins and one side loses. The winner implements their ideas and proposals to the objection of the losers. The winner has the authority to paternalistically impose their will and the will of their supporters on those who lost the vote. Even in a democratic liberal society, a government must implement policies that some reject, and, in many cases, which go against the wills of those who lost the election. The point here is this: All governments, liberal or not, treat one group or another paternalistically because no government can promote the good and interests of all who are under its rule at the same time. A clan-based illiberal government will promote the interest of its clan and treat all others paternalistically. A popular democracy-produced government will represent the interests of the majority, the influential, and powerful, and treat others paternalistically. There will never be a government that promotes the good of all and treats no group paternalistically; historical data supports this conclusion. There has never been a government that did not treat one social group or another paternalistically. Therefore, a reasonable policy related to human rights must be built on verifiable evidence, not on aspirational theory. Based on historical records, human rights are most at risk when a dominant social group with an anti-human rights agenda aligns itself with, or gains full control over, the governing institutions. This difference might be minor at this stage, but its significance will become evident when proposing an alternative scheme for safeguarding human rights. For now, I will continue with a general critique of Talbott's ideas and proposal, with a focus on his theoretical approach.

*****

Talbott may have misidentified his audience. Although he initially defines his readers as moral philosophers, individuals who "have developed and exercise" their own moral judgment, many of his arguments are written in a way that is only accessible to academic readers. On its own, writing about human rights is likely to intrigue readers from outside philosophy, not just the sub-tract of moral philosophy. Moreover, the authors and scholars he cites and the examples he invokes are decidedly from outside moral philosophy. These factors open Talbott up for criticism beyond the actual scope of this specific work. Presuming that this work is useful outside a narrow window, I will uncover insight within the monograph that is enriching, complex, and necessary to understanding human rights in theory and practice.

To emphasize the diligence needed when reading Talbott's book, I highlight his position on the role of reason and emotion in human moral development. Talbott considers the distinction between reason and emotion a false dichotomy. Instead of believing that a judgment must be based on either reason or on sentiment, he suggests that emotions themselves can be a result of reasoning, leading to judgments on what is right or wrong as well as what is true or false. Additionally, he believes that people progress towards recognizing basic human rights through inevitable moral development. Returning to the case of American natives, Talbott asserts that even "if the Spanish colonists could not see anything wrong with their treatment of the American natives," there is still "an objective moral standpoint from which it can be seen to be wrong, and the American natives themselves would easily be able to see that it was wrong."[14] Failure to see objective, universal moral truths, according to Talbott, can be the result of psychological experience or evolutionary processes.

To better understand Talbott's answer to the question of which human rights should be universal, a reader should understand Talbott's monograph as a non-prescriptive endeavour, for Talbott sees discovering human rights as a fallible historical process. Such development is different from empirical knowledge in that it is dependent on the social forces, and the degree and direction, with which people are engaged. It is a bottom-up process and, as such, the outcome does not result from the special epistemological insight of anyone, and certainly not Talbott's. He professes an "epistemic modesty"[15] that ensures that even his proposed list of basic rights might be revised; but for now, based on what he knows at this point in time, he believes that the list is a prerequisite for any government to claim moral legitimacy.

In addition to the general context a reader needs, critical readers need to be mindful of a somewhat stylistic fact as well: Talbott seems to think through his ideas as he writes them. This habit is engaging to read, but it sometimes appears as inconsistency or hesitancy. For instance, at the start of the book, Talbott suggests that "governments everywhere ought to guarantee certain basic rights to everyone within their borders."[16] By the end of the book, however, he stresses that a government must adopt his package of basic rights—rights of citizens who meet certain conditions, not of everyone within a national border—to be recognized as legitimate. I will address the list of basic rights separately. Before that, let's start with a general analysis and critique.

The same way Talbott faulted other thinkers for relying on false dichotomies, he errs in connecting knowledge to acts. It is unclear what exactly he means when contending that, on the one hand, the Spanish colonists could have accessed the objective moral truth that it was wrong to treat the American natives the way they treated them, yet they treated them so; and on the other hand, it is irrelevant that American natives knew that the way that the Spanish colonists treated them was wrong. The more important question is whether the Spanish colonists knew then that their treatment of the American natives was wrong and, if so, how they justified treating others wrongly. Considering Talbott's pondering the accessibility of an objective moral truth to the Spanish colonists and American natives in the context of his discussion of a "Universal Moral Standpoint,"[17] a reader can assume that Talbott's answer is that the Spanish colonists lacked proper judgment attached to their actions. Had they lived in another time (say, the twenty-first century) or in another place (say, in the Northwest United States), they would have known, and they would not have treated the American natives the same way they treated them three centuries ago. That is a problematic position for several reasons—even if we assume that moral development is not a linear function.

First, we have no evidence that supports the proposition that knowledge and understanding lead to acting in conformity with the knowledge. There is enough evidence suggesting that most peoples' actions, especially when carrying out "official" instructions, are independent from their knowledge and understanding of the judgment attached to such actions.[18]

Second, the Spanish colonists' treatment of American natives is not a time-dependent or context-dependent event impossible to replicate in another time and circumstance. Indeed, many other European colonists inflicted the same treatment on indigenous peoples in Africa and Asia in the twentieth and twenty-first centuries. Liberal democracies inflict or abet similar wrongs around the world today, and it does not seem that their knowledge of moral truths has altered their abusive treatment or course of actions.

These objections lay the groundwork for my alternative framing of human rights norms and the conditions under which human rights norms are abused: There is an undeniable connection between the psychological impulse of racism or supremacy and the propensity to engage in human rights abuses; knowledge alone is incapable of severing the connection between racism and human rights abuse. With that said, I will now consider specific themes in Talbott's rights project.

While developing his list of nine basic rights that should be universal, Talbott often invokes principles of justice and fairness. However, since fairness and justice cannot be applied as absolute norms, Talbott adopts frames of reference such as equality and affinity to calibrate the measure of such principles. It is not fairness if men and women in patriarchal societies are subject to "unequal division of benefits and burdens of social cooperation between them… Even girls raised in rigid patriarchal families can recognize that they are not treated fairly."[19] The assumptions here are many.

First, on the matter that men and women are equal, we must ask, in what way are men and women equal? It is not explicit whether this is in reference to legal equality—that is, guaranteed legal rights that ensure equal treatment across the diverse spectrum of humanity—or inherent equality—that is, alike in attributes and experiences. As I previously demonstrated, men and women are not equal in the sense of inherent sameness or equivalence, the same way no two men and no two women are equal. Each human being is unique physically, mentally, and temperamentally, and these predetermined identifiers are often transmitted to make each individual unique socially as well. When we insist on ignoring difference and diversity, we leave no room to combat those who will inevitably use it as leverage for supremacy. The problem is not inequality in the sense of diverse standings; rather, it is with the judgments and practices societies attach to difference and how they use difference to create inequality, establish caste systems, and deny certain social groups access to education and some vocations.

Second, Talbott seems to subscribe to the idea that social affinity is a basis for equal access. In other words, a man and a woman, members of the same family, clan, or nation should be able to share the benefits and burdens equally. We know that now, and throughout history, sex, gender, skin color, and age are variables and such variables have often, if not always, been used to construct hierarchies that supersede the bond that connects a parent to a child, a woman to her clan, or a citizen to their government.

Third, Talbott appears to suggest that *similar* circumstances, conditions, activities, or events should result in equal distribution of benefits and burdens. Yet similarity is not the same as sameness, and people have always used that distinction to custom-make privilege, deny it, or both. Therefore, it is reasonable to challenge Talbott's presumption that "girls raised in rigid patriarchal families can recognize that they are not treated fairly."[20] Classical Islamic law, as understood by the majority of established Sunni religious scholars, does not allow a woman—regardless of her nearness to the deceased—to inherit a share equal to or above that of a man, regardless of his distance from the deceased. In most cases, according to classical Sunni law, a woman would inherit half what a man would inherit. Talbott, or a Muslim moral philosopher as Talbot would define them, might argue that these are rules based on archaic *understanding*,[21] and that they must be changed based on what we now know. In fact, many Tunisians made that same argument after the 2011 uprising. However, when Tunisian women were surveyed to gauge their support for a proposed law to make men and women equal in inheritance, a majority of women opposed it.[22] Notably, Talbott only said that girls in rigidly patriarchal circumstances "could recognize" fairness, not that they would invariably support action based on fairness. This example underscores the weakness of his reasoning, as he has yet to demonstrate linkage between knowledge and action to uphold human rights norms. It is one thing to know and understand what is fair and unfair, but it is another thing to act on that knowledge.

Notwithstanding his failure to prove knowledge's connection to acts, Talbott's prescription for moral development is successful in its argument that the bottom-up structure of inductivist models does not result in the discovery of absolute principles (e.g., killing another human being is always wrong). Rather, it results in the discovery of the conditions under which a principle may or may not apply (e.g., It is wrong to kill another person unless that other person is failing or has failed to respect another person's right to life).

Before human rights became embedded in civil and governmental institutions to the extent that the majority of governments around the world ratified numerous binding treaties, human rights was merely a moral aspiration enshrined in a relatively short document called the Universal Declaration of Human Rights. Before that, and centuries before 1948 when the document was signed, many Western countries made similar declarations in the forms of bills of rights and constitutions. Human rights discussions and debates have found a natural home in philosophy, specifically in the branch of philosophy called ethics or moral philosophy. Some thinkers have concluded that the idea of human rights is essentially a moral one.[23] I started this work by introducing the thinking of a passionate moral philosopher whose academic career has tapered into advocating for a set of universal basic human rights. That is not an easy position, especially for someone from the Western world, because the most compelling challenge to the idea of universal human rights is the destructive imperialist attitude inherent to that position. That was the criticism levelled against those who promoted the Universal Declaration of Human Rights and, inevitably, it is a path to undermining Talbott's suggestion of a list of universal basic rights—even if his list is considerably shorter than the Universal Declaration of Human Rights and its derivatives. Talbott's defence is anchored in two things: Epistemic modesty and moral discovery derived through bottom-up reasoning.

While Talbott's epistemic modesty is an effective response to the charge of moral imperialism, the bottom-up discovery of moral truths needs more development. A bottom-up project, I presume, would imply large participation in the discovery processes. However, the example of Bartolomé de las Casas, which Talbott uses repeatedly, weakens his contention that moral discovery is collective. Las Casas's moral discovery was not bottom-up; it was a top-down discovery given his position among the colonists and within the Church. In many cultures and civilizations, a lone voice, a single charismatic activist, or a determined minority social group is usually what has initiated real social change.

Talbott proposes a package of rights that are discovered bottom-up. But such a discovery is not entirely rooted in moral development. The discovery is also longitudinal, reasoned, and empirical, derived from a body of accumulated human social experience going back thousands of years (Talbott's account only covers hundreds). Because the discovery of basic human rights took thousands of years, Talbott suggests that members of prehistorical human communities cannot have been expected to respect each other's rights.[24] Based on the necessary empirical discovery of rights, it is unclear whether Talbott is minimizing humans' innate moral sensibilities or making it entirely dependent on social experience. Moreover, this point of view makes moral discovery—be it social- or moral-based—a decidedly linear process, privileging the "now" of this moment and perhaps "nows" of the future, but not the past. Talbott would object to the interpretation that his moral discovery claim is linearly produced. He would argue that a moral development that enables humans to discover basic rights is a factor of fallible historical processes. In theory, that may be true. In reality, however, given the dearth of examples from historical records, it would require more evidence to support.

If Talbott's claim is true that only the most recent discoveries are likely to be sound, a claim which cannot be found in his work, such a position would rob other civilizations of ever getting credit for discovering and respecting each other's basic rights. Such a position steers its holders away from culture- and race-cantered imperialism but devalues ancestral accomplishments, diminishes the discoveries of our predecessors, and robs ancient civilizations. In this case, epistemic modesty might empower us to acknowledge that we do not know the conditions under which our ancestors labored while inventing social institutions and scientific tools, without which none of today's achievements and discoveries would have been possible.

Talbott does not specify whether the order of his list of basic rights is important. That is significant because while some may agree with Talbott that education should be a basic right, others may consider education, depending on the curricula, to work against bottom-up reasoning given the potential for education to indoctrinate, domesticate, and propagandize.

In terms of framing Talbott's scope, approach, and theoretical position, and in addition to what I have already stated about his works' value as one with which scholars from a plurality of disciplines must engage, I would situate this specific work by Talbott—a moral philosopher—in the genre of political philosophy in the tradition of John Locke and Immanuel Kant. With that in mind, Talbott, in my view, would consider liberal democracies legitimate governments, regardless of whether they subscribe to his package of basic rights; because, I suspect, he would argue that even liberal democracies are works-in-progress. These basic rights, then, are an alternative path to legitimacy for governments not recognized as legitimate, or for liberal democracies progressing towards more functional legitimacy. Talbott posits that a government, such as an autocratic government, becomes legitimate if and only if it guarantees nine basic rights to its citizens with cognitive, behavioural, and emotional functioning. This appears to be the main conclusion and purpose of the book. However, there are some omissions and failures to clarify worth noting.

First, Talbott does not provide an adequate definition of what he means by "guarantee." We are left to speculate whether such guarantees are explicit laws in statutes and constitutions. If the answer is in legal guarantees, it is relevant whether historical records can show that the government has never violated these basic rights so that we can rely on this path in the future.

Deductively, I believe that Talbott conceives of legal guarantees.[25] If this is correct, and legal guarantees are all that he requires, the package of basic rights becomes weaker, regardless of how he discovered it. All the basic rights on Talbott's list appear in legal documents, in constitutions, or both from some of the most autocratically run countries, but that has not stopped these governments from violating the rights listed. Additionally, while I am aware that Talbott is drawing on the legacy and experiences of the Western world from the last three centuries, his confidence in liberal societies and governments could undercut the universality of basic rights.

Talbott insists that the guaranteed rights are for citizens with functional cognition, behaviour, and emotion. However, he offers no details about the meaning, procedure, authority, and standards that determine being functional. What does it mean for a person to be functional? Who will make this determination? What procedure and what standard will they use to assess the functional standing of a citizen?

Many communities throughout history have deemed certain social groups dysfunctional, lacking, or suffering from compromised cognitive, behavioural, or emotional abilities.[26] In the United States, high courts ruled that "three generations of imbeciles are enough"[27] and approved government-forced sterilization programs that impaired hundreds of thousands of persons with disabilities. Governments in many Muslim-majority countries, invoking classical interpretation of Islamic law, barred women from serving as judges, citing women's inability to use reason. Enslaving specific racial or ethnic groups, across all known human civilizations, almost always came with the justifying claim that such social group was fit only for certain tasks and that it was the responsibility of the "able" people to provide them with food and shelter while employing them in the specific tasks of which they are capable. A colleague once pointed out to me that, depending on what standard one uses, up to 70% of Americans could qualify as mentally ill. Would this exclude them from Talbott's list of basic human rights?

It is curious why Talbott limits his proposed list of universal rights to people with what he calls "normal" cognitive, emotional, and volitional capacities. He might have limited the list of rights for logical consistency or some other compelling but unstated reasons. However, the power differentials between social groups can only further empower the State to discriminate against the most vulnerable social groups and individuals in society. Talbott's framing of human rights—and his limits on who is deserving of those rights—creates a path for the State to commit and justify human

34 *Human rights as a discourse*

rights abuses. This is the antithesis of what any project for universal human rights should focus on, which is limiting the paths through which the State can justify and excuse its abuse of rights. Moreover, while some of the basic rights Talbott lists are applicable to "normal" people, other rights expressly apply to individuals whom he would not classify as "normal." Specifically, the first four rights on the list are all necessary for minors and others with limited functioning: The right to physical security, right to physical subsistence, the rights of a child to development, and the right to an education. So, either these rights are out of place on this list, or the limit is not applicable in all cases; hence, this qualification is not only unnecessary but potentially harmful. Talbott objects to John Rawls's desire for, and faith in, illiberal societies. He rejects Rawls's argument that liberal societies should not interfere with or encroach upon decent illiberal societies.[28] Rather, Talbott is deeply sceptical of the pass Rawls would give to an imagined Islamic society where "dissent has led to important reforms in the rights and role of women."[29] He imagines that Rawls's exemption might prevent liberal societies from "offering support to groups advocating rights for women."[30] Talbott does not discuss the Responsibility to Protect (R2P) theory and principle[31] directly, but based on his objection to Rawls and on numerous other statements, he is most likely not an advocate for it. However, it is also fair to conclude that Talbott advocates soft intervention in non-liberal societies to bring about change, creating these societies in the images of the liberal ones. While Talbott would object to the use of the military or hard economic and financial sanctions to bring about change, he would not object to making aid, loans, and exchanges among civil society institutions contingent on adopting or implementing the values of the donor liberal society. This aspect of globalizing human rights, and its reference within this context, is critical.

Before addressing liberal societies' interventions in non-liberal societies, and whether Talbott's soft intervention differs meaningfully from military intervention under the R2P principle, I should address a methodological concern.

Talbott invokes in his work some Islamic practices, Muslim women, and idealized Islamic societies. I gather that he would also accept conditioning economic or political exchange with illiberal societies, with the requirement that the illiberal society adopt liberal causes. For instance, a Western liberal government could extend economic aid to a Muslim-majority country if the latter's government adopted a new policy or law granting Muslim women a right that the liberal society considers universal. I presume Talbott will accept this transaction; however, it compromises his reasoning and the approach he adopted to develop his package of basic rights in at least two ways.

One, Talbott's project is built on critical conditions whereby human rights norms are developed bottom-up and in a space that allows everyone to participate in the discovery process. In fact, that is Talbott's strongest defence against the charge of moral imperialism. He does not claim that he, or any other authority, has some special moral insight. Instead, what we have is a market of ideas and contestations, accumulated over thousands of years by reasoned individuals in social settings. Yet based on Talbott's cited works, he did not appear to have engaged Muslim "moral philosophers," nor did he examine their historical record of experiences and insights. He therefore assumes that their insight and their experiences conform to his. Talbott might reasonably respond that he had neither space nor interest to extend his discussion to works from outside the ones he used. However, since the main thesis of his work is determining which human rights should be universal, and since he invokes Muslims' ideas and practices, he has already engaged them imaginatively. Talbott could have chosen not to imagine idealized or non-idealized Islamic societies and focus on actual cases from the societies he chose to work with (Western societies of the last 300 years); he could have relied on the hope that other scholars would take on a similar project to his but focusing only on Islamic societies. This could have resolved his work's framing problem.

The case against military intervention under the principle of R2P has been made. The United States' invasion of Iraq in 2003 was a compelling argument against it, and a tangible example of the possibility for abuse under the R2P principle. Many human rights advocates continue to push for soft intervention. Based on the examples in his work, Talbott appears to be an advocate for soft intervention as well: He rejects military intervention outside the UNSC, and he is against economic sanctions. There is a strong body of evidence that harsh economic sanctions inflict profound harm on vulnerable people in sanctioned countries, and any reasonable observer can see the disproportionate effect sanctions have on people relative to their sanction-bearing government. It is therefore appropriate to outline the harmful impact that even seemingly innocuous interventions can have on other countries.

The US government has determined that economic and financial aid is one of the most effective tools in furthering US interests. In one of these decades-long aid projects, the US government has shipped tons of used clothes to poor countries. One such country is the North African republic Tunisia. The Tunisian government receives these donated clothes and distributes them (sometimes selling them) to merchants. The merchants then sell the used clothes to thousands of low-income citizens as *ruba fika*. At first glance, this is a perfect arrangement: The US government helps the Tunisian government provide a source of income to otherwise unemployed people, while providing quality used clothes at a fraction of the cost of new clothes. In return, the U.S. has a reliable ally and the Tunisian government takes credit for creating employment opportunities for hundreds of people, while providing others with clothes. To understand the actual impact and real economic and political costs of this arrangement, one must examine it in the proper context.

Economically, dumping free, high quality used clothes kills any local business engaged in making and selling clothes for the same class of consumers. So while hundreds of merchants may be gainfully employed reselling these recycled clothes, local manufacturers, distributers, and even these sellers are priced out of business; no business can compete with "free." Reselling American used clothes has no added economic value; thus there is no real local economy.

The harsh economic cost of this free aid is matched only by its cultural cost. To illustrate the cultural cost of such a soft intervention, consider this image: A young man wearing a t-shirt with the words *Fuck Authority* written across the back, standing in line performing mandatory religious prayer in a mosque. In the eyes of Talbott, this young man would qualify as a moral philosopher, for it takes tremendous courage to not only challenge authority, but do it using obscene words in a house of worship. The reality tells a different story. From the outside looking in, based on the way they dress, Tunisians seem to be very westernized, modern, and progressive. From the inside, Tunisian indigenous culture, clothing styles, economy, and way of life has been erased and replaced by something that they do not fully understand. This example is not an argument against aiding communities in need; it is a warning to pay extreme care, to provide support without committing cultural genocide or economic wipe out.

Reaching into the lively sociological discussion on human rights, Talbott touches on another framework for explaining human rights: The equilibrium model. Although his discussion of the equilibrium model[s] as proposed and applied by John Stuart Mill, Rawls, and Jürgan Habermas is cursory, I highlight them because I will rely on a variation of the equilibrium construct to frame my understanding of human rights. Suffice it to say at this point that Talbott, like Rawls, conceives of an equilibrium that is "intrasubjective," one which contrasts with Habermas's "intersubjective, or social" equilibrium.[32] Because Talbott believes that moral development is essentially epistemic, by agency; but social because of its accretive nature, historically; and the discursive environment, procedurally; his conception of moral principles includes human rights norms.

When Jean-Jacques Rousseau, Mill, or Rawls (who died just over a year after September 11, 2001) wanted to construct an illiberal society, they imagined an idealized Islamic society with little social dissent and an aversion to reason. Now, in the twenty-first century, and with the United States (and many of its Western allies) still fighting its longest war in a Muslim-majority country, and when Muslim-Americans are an increasingly growing segment of America's citizenry, and during the age of globalization and globalism, inventing an imagined Islamic society instead of engaging with Islamic thinkers (modern, classical, or both) seems unjustified, especially given Talbott's insistence on human moral development and bottom-up discovery. If Talbott's discovery of basic human rights and moral principles is contingent on a free and open exchange of ideas among individuals committed to reasonable discourse, then, for his claim of universality to be compelling, this discovery should be contingent on the exchange and contestation of such ideas with people outside of Western societies. He did not have to invoke imagined social relations and structures of an Islamic community; but, choosing to, he might have made time and space to engage with the subject—one with which much of our dealings are intertwined—on an informed level.

At this juncture, and without going into details, it is relevant to point out that the examination of 300 years of Western history is a sliver of the lifetime of Islamic civilization, whose thinkers, like Talbott, struggled with questions about the place of reason-, emotion-, and authority-driven moral and legal judgments. For the first 300 years of Islamic civilization, thinkers who believed in the supremacy of reason, called Reasonists (*Ahl al-ra'y*), dominated public discourse to the extent that Muslim governments adopted their thinking as a form of public orthodoxy, which led to the first Islamic inquisition or *mihna*, a curious case of rationalist fanaticism. In other times, Islamic governments aligned themselves with top-down moral authority that showed disdain to reason and dissent; that, too, collapsed under the weight of its own extremism. In modern times, these extremes, and all the shades in between them, exist in some Muslim-majority area or another.

I will conclude this section by discussing Talbott's main theoretical flaw, which relates to his choice of framework. Talbott set himself the challenging task of identifying and defending a set of rights that should be universal. By the end of the book, he produces a list of nine rights. It is not the list that is original. Rather, his originality lies in his process of discovering these rights, which others could apply because it employs techniques and capacities common to other "moral philosophers." However, to buy in to this argument, we have to accept that other things are common as well: Reason; meaning, function, and structure of society; nature and function of government; inertia of history; processes, concepts, and events. All of these must be shareable and replicable to universalize human rights. Answering the question *which human rights should be universal* presumes a shared understanding of all these concepts, ideas, institutions, and events. That presumption is the flaw that limits the chances of seeing these basic rights universalized. Granted, Talbott might not be interested in seeing everyone everywhere adopt his list of rights. He might be interested instead in seeing his process adopted to develop other packages of rights. However, if that were the case, it would defeat the purpose of universalizing human rights: It is not "universal" if each society, at any given time, has a different set package of basic rights. Does that mean that there is no path for developing a list of universal human rights? I would argue that there is. But we have to adjust the framework for identifying such rights and setting up appropriate goals.

Moral philosophers, because of the nature of their discipline, struggle with topics that are primarily social rather than normative. They face the hazard of abstraction present in social sciences, a hazard which is manageable in philosophy and other disciplines of the humanities. Abstraction becomes even more problematic when applied to the topic of human rights. For example, appealing to reason, fairness, and equality, to generalize rights beyond a specific set of circumstances, can be presumptive and tenuous. Talbott would argue that a woman in Tunisia should be able to recognize that she should have the right to her father's legacy equal to that of her brother. We now know that most Tunisian women either do not make that recognition or they do and do not wish to change the law. He also might want to see a woman teaching moral philosophy at the University of Washington, where he works, getting paid as much money as he is paid. Yet most women in American universities make less than their male peers. Why? Is it because men and women in Tunisia and the U.S. do not believe in fairness and equality?

The idea that two people doing the same job should receive equal pay is an abstraction. A man and a woman are equal only in the abstract sense: As two human beings. In society, human beings do not perceive themselves and are not perceived by one another in abstract terms. They are what they tangibly are to each other: Mother, father, daughter, son, aunt, uncle, friend, neighbour, student, teacher, client, boss, citizen, ruler, and so on. In addition to this network of relationships, society assigns other layers of identifiers and descriptors and each comes with an attached value system, like beauty, ugliness, strength, weakness, intelligence, foolishness, and, of course, male and female. Most, if not all, individuals see themselves and others around them through these systems of networks, values, relationships, functions, and power. As these systems apply to human beings, therefore both fairness and equality are rendered real and tangible through a plurality of systems that produce specific outcomes. To determine if a man and a woman are equal, or if a man and another man are equal, one would need to determine through which systems they are being compared.

Equality that would necessitate fair pay or fair inheritance can only be realized through a plurality of systems that contribute to an ultimate outcome. The biological system that resulted in the birth of the male and female, the upbringing system that reared each to become a man and a woman, the educational system that taught the man and the woman, the assessment systems that tested the man and the woman, the standardized testing system that granted (or did not grant) the man and the woman access to educational institutions, the value system that rewarded the achievements of the man and the woman, and every major and minor event that had an impact on the man and the woman, contribute components, which a system of assigning inheritance rights or paying for labor must process. Many of these events may even appear arbitrary, but their effect is deliberate because they are part of a network of systems that are designed to produce specific outcomes. The place a person is born, the neighbourhood they live in, the name of the school, the quality of the school, the resources at the school, status of the college that conferred their degree, the social associations, the professional and connections, the attire they wear, their height, their weight, how society perceives and judges the height and weight of a person, and many other small and large events that imprint something on the person is processed through systems. These systems are connected to other systems, in different locations, geographies, and times, designed to produce specific outcomes. Even when one of the connected systems malfunctions or is modified, the network of systems continues to operate towards a final goal, which those in power set. Systems are in place to make the biological and social worlds work in some predictable way.

In a social context, and in an interconnected world, systems outcomes become universal when the impulses inherent in the individuals and social groups that designed these systems are similar. For this reason, many human rights abuses are universal, but safeguards against them are not. The propensity to abuse human rights, and the historical disinclination to promote them, speak to conditions created through systems, not from abstract ideas and concepts. The fact that human rights abuses are already universal suggests that something universal about human beings is the motivating force behind human rights abuses. Talbott engages with the justification of those who abuse human rights: Paternalism. If paternalism has any value, it is only as a weak excuse, a way to explain away atrocities such as slavery, genocide, mass killings, colonialism, and exploitation. In regard to the true reasons for these horrors, I find racism and supremacy as the singular forces that motivate a social group, which the State then enables or carries out, to abuse the human rights of vulnerable social groups. That Talbott managed to write an entire monograph on the subject of human rights, without a single reference to racism, is evidence that social and moral systems work as designed: To make an entire academic discipline overlook inconvenient truths.[33]

None of the objections I raise in this work about Talbott's ideas are objections to Talbott. Rather, they are objections to the discipline, philosophy—political philosophy to be exact. Western philosophy, given its track record, is unprepared to address topics with social justice implications, such as the topic of human rights. It is the least diverse discipline in the humanities, and more work is needed within the discipline before it can become a platform for proposals to address the rights of vulnerable social groups. Philosophy is not just an academic discipline; it is a system designed to produce and reproduce specific outcomes, including the philosophers themselves. To underscore this point, I propose this analogy: If a city's fleet of buses used for public transportation runs on diesel engines that burn too much fuel and produce too much pollution, hiring drivers who

40 *Human rights as a discourse*

are zealous environmentalists will not solve the problem. Similarly, a philosopher who might be a committed human rights advocate, who is committed to the Enlightenment legacy or was produced by the systems rooted in Enlightenment tradition, cannot produce a human rights discourse free from the limitations of that system.

For these reasons, and to further test the theory of universal human rights norms, we must go beyond three hundred years of Western European history and beyond the legacy of Western moral philosophers. I submit that systems thinking would enable us to explore the origins, functions, and history of social, institutional, and conceptual systems and how they work in real life, across culture, and throughout history. We must look at other human civilizations with systems divergent from European Enlightenment ones and those that mirrored them. For that, I think it is apt to interrogate another expert, a "moral philosopher" representing the Muslim, Islamic, and modern intellectuals. Islamic thought and institutions have not been appropriately represented in Western scholarship despite its span of over one thousand years and its role as a critical bridge that allowed the modern Western world to access, adopt, and appropriate Greek philosophical and political legacies. Additionally, some of the systems which powered Islamic civilization were radically different from the determining[34] Enlightenment systems, including the religious system and its place in the functions and institutions of the State. It is timely, because since 2011, Muslims living in Southwest Asia and North Africa have been going through transformative events that not only have changed the dynamics between the ruler and the ruled, but which have exposed Western powers' direct and indirect involvement in shaping the discourse on human rights in Islamic societies and beyond.

Notes

1. I wish to disclose that I know personally Prof. Talbott. I admire his passion and his courage to speak out about consequential topics related to social justice, inequality, and human rights. I see the areas of disagreement as a result of systems' influence rather than personal positions. Given our persistent differences, which I consider to be more instructive than obstructive, I suggested that he write a short essay to include with this work. He graciously agreed.
2. Talbott, *Which Rights*, 4.
3. Ibid, 10.
4. Ibid, 11; emphasis of *paternalistically* is mine.
5. Ibid.
6. Ibid.
7. Ibid.
8. Ibid, 3.
9. Ibid.
10. Ibid, 4.
11. I sometimes use the phrase "for-instance," thus written, in reference to what I also describe as "essentialism" which denotes the tendency to reduce other cultures or other peoples to simple traits, events, and ideas, often negative or unimaginative, to explain an idea. For example, if one were to explain

women's subjectivity to a Western audience, one would invoke Muslim women, reinforcing the perception that all Muslim women are subjugated, or that subjugation is more common in Islamic societies, and/or that Western women are not subjugated; hence we use as for-instance, or for-example, from a catalogue of stereotypes.
12. Talbott, *Which Rights*, 4.
13. Ibid.
14. Ibid, 170.
15. Ibid, 15.
16. Ibid, 3.
17. Ibid, 76.
18. Timothy K. Earle, *How Chiefs Come to Power: The Political Economy in Prehistory* (LA: Stanford University Press, 1997), Ira Chaleff, *Intelligent Disobedience: Doing Right When What You're Told to Do Is Wrong* (Berrett-Koehler Publishers, 2015), Dennis Wrong, *Power: Its Forms, Bases and Uses* (New York: Routledge, 2017), Robert W. Cox and Michael G. Schechter, *The Political Economy of a Plural World: Critical Reflections on Power, Morals and Civilization* (London: Psychology Press, 2002).
19. Talbott, *Which Rights*, 171.
20. Ibid.
21. Recall that the discipline that determines these legal rules in Islam is aptly called, *fiqh*, "understanding," not law or dogma.
22. Ahmed Souaiaia, "Hope Springs Eternal: Reforming Inheritance Law in Islamic Societies,"*Hawwa*17 –> I couldn't find the volume/issue number for this (2019): 1–18.
23. The discussion of morality, law, politics, and human rights is lively and ongoing; see, generally: B.S. Turner, "Alasdair MacIntyre on Morality, Community and Natural Law," *Journal of Classical Sociology* 13, no.2 (2013): 239–253; Bassam Tibi, "Islamic Law/Shari'a, Human Rights, Universal Morality and International Relations," *Human Rights Quraterly* 16 (1994): 277–299; John O'Manique, *The Origins of Justice: The Evolution of Morality, Human Rights, and Law* (Philadelphia: University of Pennsylvania Press, 2003); Ryan Thoreson, "The Limits of Moral Limitations: Reconceptualising Morals in Human Rights Law," *Harvard International Law Journal*59 no. 1(2018): 197; Michael J. Perry, "The Morality of Human Rights," *San Diego Law Review* 50 no. 4 (2013): 775; and Michael J. Perry, "Human Rights as Morality, Human Rights as Law, "*Boletim d Faculdade da Direito da Universidad de Coimbra*84 (2008): 369.
24. Talbott, *Which Rights*, 3.
25. Talbott says that his proposition is that "human beings should have certain *legally* protected basic rights..." Ibid. Italics mine.
26. I will provide examples from the writings of key Enlightenment thinkers who held that certain ethnic and racial groups lacked the emotional, intellectual, and other abilities to make them equal to while men.
27. Thus, writes Justice Oliver Wendell Holmes, Jr. in Buck v. Bell, a 1927 Supreme Court case upholding a Virginia law that authorized the state to surgically sterilize certain "mental defectives" without consent.
28. It should be noted that Talbott's characterization of Rawls's discussion of decent peoples is not accurate. Rawls does not identify countries like Oman and Kuwait as decent peoples; he would measure them against his list of "core human rights." Societies that violate those core human rights, according to Rawls, overstep the limits of toleration, and may be subject to economic sanctions and/or military intervention. Talbott has a different list of basic rights and he does not support economic sanctions and military intervention.

29. Talbott, *Which Rights*, 18.
30. Ibid, 12.
31. Responding to the atrocities of the 1990's (Bosnia, Rwanda, and Kosovo), the United Nations started a discussion to address the worst forms of violence and persecution. During the 2005 World Summit Outcome Document (A/RES/60/1) Heads of State and Government affirmed their responsibility to protect their own populations from genocide, war crimes, ethnic cleansing and crimes against humanity and accepted a collective responsibility to encourage and help each other uphold this commitment. Some human rights advocates want one sovereign state to intervene militarily in another country under the principle. Given that such action can be used as excuse by powerful countries to coerce or invade weaker countries, the resistance to R2P was strong. Some human rights advocates promote soft intervention as an alternative to violent intervention.
32. Talbott, Which *Rights*, 29.
33. I should emphasize that Talbott's avoidance of the use of the word "racism" is a systemic problem, not personal negligence or a deliberate omission. John Rawls, who wrote a book on justice and inequity, did not reference slavery; and many other influential political philosophers of the twentieth and twenty-first centuries wrote on the ideals of liberal societies and their legitimate governments, yet they all avoided addressing how these states' practices have contradicted their stated ideals.
34. Systems whose function and output are necessary but not sufficient to achieve the overall purpose.

3 Islamic reaction to Western enlightenment

How have Islamic intellectuals and Muslim scholars handled the question regarding the compatibility of human rights with Islamic thought and institutions is captured in the summary of the work of Abdulaziz Sachedina on human rights, with a focus on his monograph, *Islam and the Challenge of Human Rights*. Discussion of this work brings in insight of other scholars with whom Sachedina engaged, responded to, and critiqued. This chapter introduces Sachedina, his book *Islam and the Challenge of Human Rights*, and adds context to position Sachedina's views within broader Islamic thought. Additionally, this chapter reveals some of the key areas of similarity and difference between the two scholars in regard to human rights discourse. Talbott and Sachedina both place the impetus for discovering and protecting human rights on instances of egregious rights abuses, such as the religious wars in Europe. However, unlike Talbott, Sachedina views religious ideas as a necessary component of moral reason, and he aims to show how Islamic thought has already offered a foundation for human rights norms. Furthermore, although Sachedina's basis of thought is, like Talbott's, rooted in his Enlightenment training, he critiques its limited ability to apply across diverse religions and forms of government.

Generally speaking, and when discussing human rights in particular, Islamic thinkers and traditional Muslim scholars tend to react to and reproduce ideas and institutions, not invent new ones. There is a simple reason for this: Modern civilization is not theirs. They are part of it, and Muslims may have bequeathed the building its blocks. However, Islamic cultures, ideas, and institutions that produced and sustained Islamic civilization for hundreds of years are no longer the dominant systems. That role has fallen to Western European societies. Muslims' dominant role in the preceding civilization, and the traumatizing impact of colonialism on most Muslim-majority counties, has caused Islamic thinkers and Muslim scholars' reactions to range widely: From nostalgic attachment to the once-dominant culture, resulting in rejecting anything modern as being un-Islamic; to full adoption of a Western worldview, resulting in fractured individual identity and conflicted national characteristics. Within this range of reactions to the emerging Western civilization there are those who hold on to both classical

Islamic thought and modern ideas and institutions with equal passion. This particular group of thinkers expands the breadth and depth of the conversation to involve not only contemporary communities from diverse cultures and geographies, but also communities, ideas, events, and institutions from hundreds of years past. The second thinker whose work we are going to review, Abdulaziz Sachedina, belongs to this group.

The author of *Islam and the Challenge of Human Rights*, Sachedina is both a compelling subject and an informed interlocutor. First, he is a practicing Shia Muslim and a provocatively independent thinker.[1] He contends that Islam, like any culture, is open to development and change; he rejects the idea of Islam as incompatible with modernity in general, and human rights norms in particular. Second, given his personal background, Sachedina is the unlikely kind of moral philosopher with whom Talbott is already in indirect conversation; in *Islam and the Challenge of Human Rights*,[2] Sachedina engages in the kind of bottom-up work Talbott describes. Uniquely, however, he is comfortable applying the linguistic, logical, and religious tools and instruments of reasoning and argumentation of classical Islamic scholars of *kalam* and *fiqh*, theology and law/jurisprudence, to make his case for human rights. Third, the space of academic inquiry which Sachedina inhabits is one which Talbott has not visited to the extent that he would be able to engage with its diverse scholars and plurality of approaches. Since the topic and cause of human rights find homes in so many disciplines and public spaces, framing my own work alongside the work of a moral philosopher and a historian of religion from radically different backgrounds will situate the topic in its natural context, the integrated knowledge research framework.

It must be noted at this juncture that the source Sachedina often cites for rejecting human rights norms in Islamic societies, *fiqh*, literally means human understanding, knowing, and acquainting with law derived from Islamic sources. That happens to be the precise definition of epistemology, the Greek concept referring to knowledge and understanding, which is Talbott's area of expertise and one of the filters through which he processed his research. Together, with Talbott's ideas and critique of other theories on human rights and governance, Sachedina's personal experiences and theories provide the needed coverage of the full range of ideas which Muslim scholars and Islamic thinkers face related to human rights. Sachedina, in many ways, represents more than a moral philosopher.

First, Sachedina adheres to an established religion. A Shia Muslim with education and training in both secular Western institutions as well as in religious seminary, this dual belonging has tested his commitment to both worlds. Traditional Shia Muslim scholars questioned his faith following his dissertation, in which he theorized on doctrinal concepts dealing with the imamate, or Shia religious leadership. Western readers of his work raised questions about his scholarly objectivity, a frequent critique levelled against Muslim academics.

This plurality of ideas and experiences from, by, and around Sachedina and his work make him a good representative of the moral philosopher Talbott envisions. Talbott argues that moral philosophers can belong to a religion that restricts moral judgment to a specific moral authority. Most Catholics do not take their cues from the Pope on a range of issues like divorce and family planning; Sachedina belongs to a school of Islamic thought similar to Catholicism. Unlike Sunni Muslims, who do not believe in an infallible religious authority, *Imami* Shia Muslims follow, or *Taqlid*, the teachings of a living religious authority, *Marja`*. This means that Sachedina is a moral philosopher who is not a moral authority, but who is expected to defer to one. Knowing the fundamental differences between Sunnism and Shiism make the selection of an intellectual conversant from Shia Islam inclusive to the extent that whatever conclusions we draw about the Shia moral philosophers we can extend to their Sunni counterparts, for reasons that will be made clear in the next chapters.

In a sense, Sachedina is already unknowingly in conversation with Talbott. Explaining the purpose and approach of his work, Sachedina argues for a "foundational capacity in Islamic tradition to sit in dialogue with the secular human rights theorists to make a case for inclusive notions of human entitlements."[3] I am confident that he would consider Talbott a "secular human rights theorist" and it is likely Talbott would accept that description. Elaborating on what he means by a "foundational capacity" of Islam, Sachedina qualifies it as a "foundational theory of human rights based on some of the pluralistic features of Islam and its culture," features which are "totally ignored by Muslim traditionalist and fundamentalist discourse."[4] Sachedina's foundational theory of human rights stands in opposition to what he calls the "secular theory of moral development" on human rights. He objects to the secular theory because it

> Favors exclusively reason-based morality founded upon human experience in the context of everyday life situations. In contrast, moral development, as it emerges in the Islamic creation narrative, takes revealed guidance as well as naturally endowed intuitive reason as two interrelated sources of moral knowledge that humanity needs in order to avoid moral perdition.[5]

Though stated as a generality, Sachedina's critique of moral development theory applies directly to Talbott, given that Talbott used almost the same language to describe the basis of his discovery: Society-based, experience-rooted moral development that is not imposed from the top-down. As it happens, Talbott invoked examples from Islam and Islamic societies, in part when he was responding to Rawls's discussion of decent society. Sachedina, too, engages Rawls, for he sees in him a representative of secular human rights theorists. In this context, however, Rawls supports Sachedina's basic contention that Western thinkers have their own

46 *Human rights as a discourse*

circumstances that have allowed them, or forced them, to decouple human rights from the religious discourse.

> In *Political Liberalism* (1993), John Rawls identifies the origins of liberalism in the aftermath of the wars of religion and maintains that one of the significant achievements of liberalism is advancing religious tolerance by privatizing religion and clearing the public domain of religious interference.[6]

Sachedina's reference to Rawls serves at least two purposes. First, it reminds readers of the specific circumstances from which the discussion of human rights was born: Wars of religion. If religion was part of the problem, Sachedina reasons, religion cannot be part of the solution. Therefore, it was only natural that religion was excluded as a vehicle for advancing human rights norms in favor of secularism. However, secularism did not just supersede religion in the discussion of human rights; it reduced religion's role and exiled it from public domain.

Second, the absence of religion made room for public reason, regardless of whether religion took part of such reason. Sachedina thinks that political circumstances and the role Islam has played in public life create a different context for debating human rights in Islamic societies. Specifically, Sachedina argues that Islam depends on public reason to formulate right and wrong. Sachedina adopts the word *Fitra*, which he translates in some instances as intuitive reason, to contend that every human being, regardless of religion, is endowed by nature with intuitive reason, which guides moral development.

> Islamic religious thought is based on the human ability to know right from wrong. Through God's special endowment for all of humanity, each and every person on earth is endowed with a nature (*fitra*), the receptacle for intuitive reason, that guides humanity to its spiritual and moral well-being. On this notion of divine endowment, moral cognition is innate to human nature and gives human beings the capability to discern moral law.[7]

Those who argue for both universal rights and religion-excluding secularism create a conundrum. To make something universal, something applicable and supported by all, significant social groups must be included. Excluding them deceases the level of universality. It is reasonable to argue that faith-based reason is incompatible with the kind of public reason that supports and sustains human rights norms and therefore, religion should be excluded. Such reasoning seems to apply to Islam. Muslim thinkers are often said to be too limited by their religious commitments to accept the idea of universal human rights. That view rings true when applied to Muslim political leaders: When called upon to sign international treaties enshrining human rights norms, most leaders of Muslim-majority countries invoke cultural and religious reasons for resisting ratification unless the treaty is gutted with exceptions and reservations. What is also true is that leaders of Muslim-majority countries use religion domestically to preserve and extend their rule, not to honour religious dogma. Independent thinkers are not driven by the same political calculus.

> The moment one admits cultural relativism in the application of universal moral values, one is face to face with the flouting of all those concerns that we have about the violation of human rights of individuals and, more particularly, the most vulnerable in the autocratic and totalitarian political systems that crowd the political landscape of the Muslim world (not to mention in other regions of the world).[8]

Scholars are the product of their choices: Their employment, the books they read, and the society in which they live. Personal bias is inevitable, but in academia most people insist that they have no personal bias. They believe their training and knowledge lifts them above and beyond the social and cultural filters that stream the world before their eyes. Yet even the language they speak connects them to the society they live in, subtly instilling in them the values and norms of the dominant culture to the extent that makes it impossible to distinguish between various influences in a multicultural person until they are directly challenged. A Muslim-American, like Sachedina, thinks that they can be fully Muslim and fully American or Western. They are often surprised to find that they speak a foreign language when they encounter interlocutors who are only Muslim, raised in Muslim-majority country:

> The subtlety of this ethnocentric facet of the language that I had assumed to be inclusive and had used so confidently to argue about the moral comprehensiveness characteristic of Islamic revelation shook my confidence in the universality of any idiom that claimed cross-cultural applicability, regardless of whether that idiom was secular or religious… If what I have observed about the problematic of translation of secular political-cultural idiom into an Islamic one were impossible to overcome through cross-cultural communication, then the entire project of demonstrating that Islam was compatible with democracy, or that Islam legitimized the Universal Declaration of Human Rights as a valid source of directives to protect human agency and human dignity, would have to be abandoned as impracticable.[9]

Sachedina concludes that a project to advance human rights norms based on cultural or value translations would be futile. He insists that epistemological and ontological discussions about the foundations of human rights are controversial and divisive. Instead, he recommends that both secular and religious thinkers emphasize the "moral and metaphysical foundations of human rights norms" to overcome Muslims' fear that human rights discourse is "a ploy to dominate Muslim societies by undermining their religiously based culture and value system."[10] Sachedina identifies the absence of interest in natural rights and natural law in classical Muslim theology or philosophy, signalled by the absence of discussion thereof, as the reason for difficulty in rooting human rights norms in Islamic thought and practice. His goal, then, is to develop an ethical foundation that could serve as "a springboard for international conventions about common moral standards for the entire human race, the very secular foundation of the Declaration." He is confident in this approach because he is confident that "even the staunchest opponents of the Universal Declaration of Human Rights, who regard the document as being morally imperialistic and culturally ethnocentric, concede the fact that human beings have rights that accrue to them as humans."[11] Sachedina does not want to interpret Islamic tradition based on what we now know to accommodate modern human rights norms. Instead, he believes that he is merely providing a context for Islamic texts, a context that has been missing because Muslims neglected the ethical and theological dimension of Islamic texts in favor of juridical and legal enterprises. Sachedina's confidence in this approach stems from his conviction that the challenging circumstances in Western societies were the reason Western societies adopted human rights.

> The language that was constructed at the height of European colonialism over the ruins of the world wars and atrocities committed by humans against humans (under various pretexts of racial or religious claims of superiority of one people over another) could not have evolved without some kind of soul-searching into the depth of moral and spiritual heritage of the colonizers (the power wielders and political brokers of the 1940s).[12]

Though neither Talbott nor Sachedina elaborated enough on this, both of them claim that the cruelty of the world wars and other atrocities forced European societies to consider a path unlikely to reproduce the same events, and that path led to them committing to human rights norms. In other words, the discovery of human rights was not a moment of enlightenment or an informed discovery occurring during times of peace and prosperity. Rather, adopting human rights norms was a response to unjust conduct, abuses of power, war crimes, and other acts that dehumanized disempowered social groups at the hands of those in power.

> The ultimate support for the Declaration cannot simply come from its pragmatic purpose of protecting human agency; rather, it can come from the reasons as to why that personhood deserves to be protected from unjust conduct of those in power.[13]

Instead of looking for experiences and events in Islamic societies similar to what happened in Europeans societies and which inspired them to embrace human rights norms, Sachedina defaults to the hypothesis that connects Enlightenment, Christianity, and abstract thought as the forces that produced human rights norms. He draws on normative works by Western intellectuals to connect abstract thinking to human rights.

> Johannes Morsink's valuable study of the history of the drafting of the Declaration, by affirming the ways in which metaphysical and philosophical issues connected with Christian experience of the Enlightenment provided the drafters a language that could claim universal application, affords the opportunity to engage Islamic universalism.[14]

The reason Sachedina gravitates towards this hypothesis, in my view, is because it resonates with his project. In a sense, what he is engaged in throughout this work is an enlightened rereading of religious texts to discover threads of public reason that connect human rights to Islamic tradition. The same way Morsink examines the language of the Declaration to confirm "a connection between the universal Declaration and Enlightenment ways of thinking about morality that is universal and at the same time secular," Sachedina proposes to do the same with Islamic tradition after having established that "this secularism is not totally non-religious in the sense that nature and reason, 'the two secular components of the triad—were still kept in close proximity to the God from which they flowed.'"[15] Furthermore, Sachedina qualifies the Enlightenment view of humanity as deriving "from natural rights philosophies, which located human equality and inalienable rights in human beings simply by virtue of their own humanity and not because of some extraneous reason."[16] The secularization of the language of the Declaration was useful for the pursuit of universal morality to support human rights across traditions, but not across religions. This is Sachedina's first criticism of the framing of human rights through secular discourse.

Sachedina's second criticism concerns the Declaration's linking human rights norms to a specific form of government. He argues that the language of the Declaration empowers individuals to protect themselves against injustices in liberal democratic societies. However, this language is limiting; it would not apply to abuses within societies that lack a democratic system for redress. Sachedina argues that people in Darfur, for instance, cannot protect themselves with "this kind of empowerment when they have had no experience of seeing their agency or their rational capacity as important instruments to assert their human rights and defend themselves."[17]

Unlike Talbott, who developed his own list of basic rights that should be universal, Sachedina does not believe that the UDHR "can be dismissed outright as merely a product of Western secular philosophy with deep roots in Enlightenment thought." Furthermore, Sachedina thinks that the often-levelled critique of "Eurocentric bias" as the document's flaw is not valid because "liberal views about human individuality, dignity, and agency are compatible with Islamic revelation as developed in Muslim philosophical theology and juridical methodology to understand human personhood."[18] Sachedina rejects these charges against the UDHR because, in part, he has already identified that it was the violent wars and cruel events which forced Western societies to commit to the UDHR, whereby the "the true purpose of the international document" is the "protection of human beings from abuse, oppression, and cruelty."[19] Like most other advocates for the adoption of the UDHR, Sachedina does not explicitly name the agent or agents of abuse, oppression, and cruelty; that, in my view, makes his entire endeavour fruitless. Human rights abuses do not happen unless there is a full equation that accounts for the subjects of abuse as well as the agents or perpetrators. I would argue that leaving out the agents of abuse makes social groups suspicious and defensive, and that that is the main reason behind Muslims' resistance to endorsing the Declaration. Sachedina would disagree.

Sachedina believes that Muslim thinkers and political leaders were left out from the conversation when drafting the UDHR was underway because Western leaders spearheading these efforts presumed that "just as the philosophy of the Enlightenment in its conflict with Christianity sealed the fate of religion in the public square," Islam, too was not compatible with the demands of "modernity and that has also dealt the same blow to Islamic political theology and its ability to deal with universal morality grounded in the autonomous individual's ability to reason and to negotiate his or her spiritual destiny."[20]

> It is not surprising that Max Stackhouse, a Christian theologian, who had probably very cursory knowledge of Islamic tradition, regarded Islam as a religious tradition that simply does not maintain the free agency of human beings for freedom of action and association to develop democratic governance in Muslim societies... As a matter of fact, in his study of human rights in three cultures he indicates that Islam, in comparison to Western Christianity, is ill suited to a democratic concept of society.[21]

Responding to the comparison of Islam to Christianity, Sachedina points out another element that contributes to human rights abuses: "Official" readings of religious texts that work against pluralism, when pluralism is critical for developing a culture that respects human rights norms. In that respect, Sachedina points out that Islam, unlike Christianity, does not have "a religious institution like a church" that decides from the top-down on public morality and orthodoxy. He contends that there existed an "antiauthoritarian theological stance adopted by a number of classical jurist-theologians,"[22] who opposed government-sanctioned orthodoxy.

Focusing on Muslim thinkers and religious scholars, Sachedina identifies three major trends within Islamic societies in relation to their stances on human rights: Traditional Muslim scholars, secular Islamic thinkers, and secular Islamic thinkers who apply classical Islamic tools and sources to reject the Declaration. Despite their differences in terms of background and expertise, they all have failed to appreciate the ethical dimension of Islamic tradition, which, according to Sachedina, provides a path to reconciling Islam with human rights norms as stated in the UDHR.

Sachedina's comparison of Christianity and Islam relevant to their reliance on reason is a reaction to Western thinkers and Christian religious authorities who have argued that Islam does not value reason because reason has never been part of the culture, processes, and tools to developing public morality. He appears to be responding to a common charge against Islam and Muslims, made formal, through curious citation work, by Pope Benedict XVI in an address given in the Aula Magna of the University of Regensburg in Germany. In this address, the Pope indirectly and creatively suggests that Islam is a religion spread through violence and that it is not bound by rationality.[23] Sachedina's work reveals challenges emerging from two tracks. The first, highlighted above, is historical colonialism. He contends that Western thinkers, religious leaders, and governments are the forces making Muslims suspicious of any idea or institution proposed by the West. Christian bias, Enlightenment thinkers' baseless assumptions, and political, military, and economic interventions in Muslim majority countries have given Muslims ample reason to reject any grand project coming from the West even if it could be beneficial to ordinary Muslims. The second challenge Sachedina says is internal: Muslims' uninspired appreciation for their own ethical and moral heritage. Especially when contrasted against Talbott's proposal, Sachedina faults Muslims for favoring law and jurisprudence over an ethical and theological grounding of moral development. Recalling that Talbott believes that human rights can be advanced through legal guarantees, Sachedina, in balance, favors an epistemic grounding of rights rooted in morality (and secondarily in jurisprudence), not an epistemic grounding rooted in social experience and secular public reason only.

> [W]hat leads to further contempt for the Declaration is the epistemological denial that morality or jurisprudence has serious metaphysical or epistemic grounds to serve as a foundation for human rights. If the secular intent of the Declaration is defined by circumstance and history rather than any metaphysical notions such as human nature and the inherence of rights, what is so universal about the Declaration's intellectual and moral appeal that it can reach out to other cultures in a global context today?[24]

Sachedina recognizes that changing Muslims' attitudes towards human rights norms is a challenge not only because of the reasons mentioned above, but, importantly, because there are institutional and methodologic currents either hostile to human rights norms or unfit to engage in a discourse on human rights. To address these internal challenges, Sachedina invents new categories and interpretations, and criticizes dominant institutions and approaches. Such an approach also involves new language, a very risky endeavour as it can be interpreted as convenient, opportunistic, or simply false. For instance, to make his favored ethical approach relevant, Sachedina presents the disciplines of theology, *kalam*, and jurisprudence, *usul al-fiqh*, in a parallel arrangement. That representation is true only in some Islamic schools of thought and practices (*mathahib*). The facts overwhelmingly point to a serial, not parallel, arrangement of Islamic disciplines. In other words, Muslims thinkers and scholars first adopted theology to adapt religious beliefs and practices to the real world. Theologians harmed the reputation of the discipline when they applied it to more hypotheticals and less relevant topics such as lived experiences. Theology was supplanted by the more practical disciplines of law and jurisprudence by the end of the first Islamic century. By the third Islamic century, Muslim scholars and thinkers became familiar with other cultures and communities and that allowed them to assimilate their intellectual legacies, including Greek philosophy, Indian literature, Persian sciences, African arts, and Byzantine and Roman politics and economics. A serial arrangement of ideas and disciplines would place inconvenient filters before original texts, limiting access and claim to authenticity. Consequently, Sachedina would prefer to present theology and jurisprudence as two disciplines that co-exist in the same time at any period, including now.

> Moreover, political theology (*al-kalam al-siyasi*) in Islam correlates reason and revelation in such a way that political jurisprudence (*al-fiqh al-siyasi*) undertakes to translate personal faith into social action through judicial decisions that envision and endeavour to motivate the faithful to establish just institutions in society so that they objectively reflect God's will for humanity.[25]

Sachedina makes it clear that it "is the ethical dimension of Islamic legal methodology," not the proscriptive one (law), "that holds the potential for an inclusive universal language that can engage the universal morality of the Declaration."[26] Where Talbott prefers universalizing basic human rights through legal guarantees, Sachedina insists that human rights can be universalized through a system of ethics, one that distinguishes between right and wrong innately. The contrast is stark: While the moral philosopher sees the solution for challenges to human rights through legal regimes and political action, the religious scholar and "moral philosopher" rejects the privileging of reason, public or otherwise, as the only "source of moral deliberation," as is the case with the "secular model of human rights."[27]

Sachedina views Talbott's approach as inorganic since it does not appeal to human nature, which, he argues, includes reason, "the divine endowment of humanity through the very *fitra*, creation of human nature, the receptacle for intuitive reason."[28] Reflecting on the Shia doctrine of mind or intelligence, `aql, Sachedina claims that in Islam,

> human ability to know right from wrong is part of the divine endowment... Moral cognition, in this notion of creation, is innate to human nature and because of it human beings are capable of discerning moral law. There is no discussion about natural law or natural rights in Muslim theology.[29]

Sachedina contends that the portrayal of Islam as anti-rationalism is systemic in the West because "a number of Western scholars of Islamic legal tradition" were informed by the writings of "mainly Sunni jurists" who "have erroneously excluded any organic relationship between theological and legal doctrines."[30] He contends that the majority of Muslims, including Shia, "have not severed their epistemic correlation."[31] He correctly points out that the field of Islamic studies as an area of inquiry in Western higher educational institutions, historically dominated by Orientalists, has been mainly limited to the so-called orthodox Islamic tradition, which was filtered through "Sunni-Ash`ari thinkers, who denied human reason any ability to understand the rightness or wrongness of an act independent of God's revelation." In contrast, Sachedina contends that "Sunni-Mu`tazilite and Shi`ite theologians, who form a minority theology in Islam"[32] have always stressed reason, free will, and justice as foundational to Islam.

Related to the ethical and legal Islamic discourses and whether they are able to accommodate the language and substance of the UDHR, Sachedina thinks that the problem is with the schools of thought, not with the discipline, text, or tradition. Specifically, he identifies Sunnism as a track within Islamic thought that made it impossible to embrace human rights norms. For Sunni traditional scholars, Sachedina argues, an action "is not good because it is construed so by the essential nature of a human being, but because God so wills." In other words, Sunni scholars have rejected reason as un-Islamic.[33] Sachedina implies that for Islamic tradition to be made compatible with the Declaration, Islamic thinkers must discard most Sunni thought in favor of "the Mu`tazilite and Shi`ite deontological-teleological models that shape human action."[34] He contends that the Mu`tazilite and Shi`ite theology was abandoned in favor of a divine command ethics, and that the Ash`arite doctrines that emphasize the will of God as the source of morality—and that law is an expression of God's will—do not just establish barriers to human rights, but also provide justification for authoritarian Muslim rulers as manifestations of God's authority and power.[35]

At this juncture, I should discuss some of Sachedina's claims, because they are critical in understanding Islamic legal and ethical tradition and I shall return to them in more detail in the next chapters. Sachedina appears to bend the arc of history in a way that allows him to organically connect his interpretation of Islamic tradition to its primary sources. While that might be an acceptable methodologically, it lacks a basis in fact. His presentation of Sunnism, Mu`tazilism, Shiism, and Ash`arism is oversimplified to a level that rends it impossible to accept. For example, while Shiism has been a minority sect in Islamic societies throughout its history as it is now, Mu`tazilism is no longer a sect or school of thought in Sunni Islamic societies and therefore cannot become a minority or a majority. While it is true that some Shia scholars have been influenced by Mu`tazilism, Sunni Muslims have shunned Mu`tazilism since the end of the inquisition (*Mihna*), on account of the caliph's enforcement of reason-based doctrines from Mu`tazilite thinkers. Since then, Sunni scholars adopted Ash`arite doctrines as the only form of orthodoxy, while Imami Shia have continued to hold their own doctrines, some of which may resonate with Mu`tazilism. This clarification is an appropriate segue to analyzing Sachedina's discussion of political ideas and institutions.

When I qualified one of Sachedina's statements defining human rights as representative of only half the equation of human rights, it was not based on a partial assessment of his work. It applies to his entire work, because despite the fact that governments are central to any scheme dealing with human rights, Sachedina's discussion of State functions relevant to this matter is marginal. This critique applies to Talbott as well, despite the fact that he wants the government to guarantee his package of basic rights and Sachedina believes that a "commitment to human rights is necessarily tied to a legitimate political system that recognizes its limits and that empowers its citizens to seek remedies for the violation of their human rights."[36] Moreover, Sachedina asserts that the assumption behind the "idea that since in Islam religion and politics are inseparable, the traditional paradigm of Islamic political society" is incompatible with modern human rights and therefore false.[37] He correctly points out that many Muslim religious scholars have been more interested in preserving institutions and public order than in protecting vulnerable social groups from governmental abuse.

> The de facto differentiation between the religious and the political was never accepted as fully legitimate. Muslim political thinkers from Mawardi (d. 1058) through Ghazali (d. 1111) to Ibn Taymiya (d. 1328) increasingly tended to legitimate any political regime that would guarantee a modicum of protection to Muslim institutions by requiring people to obey them. Political authority remained suspect not only to rural activists, who from time to time engaged in armed insurrection to replace a ruler with a more acceptable candidate, but also to urban ulema, who viewed political authority as a necessary evil to avoid political turmoil.[38]

Islamic reaction to Western enlightenment 55

The role and function of the `Ulama in granting legitimacy to political leaders, argues Sachedina, suggests that the coupling of the legal/juridical and political authorities was mere theory.[39] Moreover, Sachedina contends that the function of the government in Islam is to administer justice according to Sharia, which is deeply secular due to the distinction of its branches (human-God versus Human-Human subdivisions).[40] Nonetheless, it is clear that Sachedina's project for promoting human rights in Islamic societies is discursively ethical, lacking any functional connection to legal or political action plan.

> My overall objective to uncover the foundational sources for human rights norms in Islam, then, depends upon unfolding the universal content of some key Islamic concepts so that it can stimulate and engage the secular advocates of human rights in a meaningful conversation to appreciate an inherent secularity that exists in the Qur'anic concepts of human dignity and moral worth of all human beings without any extraneous conditions.[41]

Ultimately, Sachedina envisions an articulation of "natural law as a human rights foundation in Islam"[42] by engaging the Islamic tradition in order to

> respond convincingly to the violations of human rights that plague contemporary Muslim societies in three important areas: (1) Intolerance and even institutionalized violence against different sects and religious minorities; (2) rampant disregard for the rights of women; and (3) lack of any democratic constitutional and conceptual development of the notion of citizenship. By simply declaring the superiority of human rights guaranteed in the Islamic tradition without accounting for their exclusiveness in the Shari`a over the current legal protections offered by an inclusive human rights regime, Muslim religious scholars are failing to challenge autocratic regimes in the Muslim world to accept their moral and religious responsibility in protecting the human rights of the people they rule.[43]

Having presented a detailed, specific survey of Sachedina's key ideas, I now provide a general critique of his work. The same way Talbott establishes in the title of the book his position on the rights spelled out in the Universal Declaration of Human Rights—that not all of those rights are universal—Sachedina, too, announces in the title of his book that Islam has a problem with human rights. That position places the author in a precarious defensive position made even more difficult by his unqualified "unflinching support for the Universal Declaration of Human Rights."[44] Sachedina, as he summarizes at the end of his book,[45] is committed to two things: The UDHR and the Quran as lived by Muhammad. He is determined to reproduce a religious tradition, through new narratives, purged of any conflict with the letter and spirit of the UDHR. That is a real challenge indeed. I will leave it to other readers, however, to determine if his endeavour was successful. Instead, I will comment on the substantive, political, and theoretical implications of his position.

First, Sachedina overstates the function of ethics and morality in shaping social behaviour and political life. I say this as person who believes that morality and ethics is a testing ground, a space used to ready society for hard social change. Sachedina believes that ethical discourse can be so transformative that it can solve problems once and for all. The difference between the ethical and legal discourses is significant; it is the distinction that renders the UDHR a mere declaration, not a binding treaty or law.[46]

Second, Sachedina's proposal for promoting an ethical discourse on human rights that is organically tied to the primary sources of Islam is outdated by Muslims' standards. If one takes his proposed discourse to mean the discipline that was all-inclusive, *kalam*, which included ethics, then historical records show that *kalam* was a precursor to Islamic law and jurisprudence; *kalam* faded out because it lacked the power to force compliance in society and because early Muslim scholars found it too abstract and impractical. To pin hopes for changing Muslims' attitudes related to human rights through an expired discourse puts one on a course to regress, not progress.

Some would understand ethical discourse as intertwined with jurisprudential discourse. Scholars of Islamic law and jurisprudence have distinguished five Rules (*Ahkam*) along ethical and legal categories. The legal rules covering proscription and obligation (*haram, wajib*) are concerned with law, whereas the rules covering desirability and undesirability (*mustahab, makruh*) are concerned with ethics. Rules of law, when broken, are remediable. Rules of ethics, when followed, are enhancements. In other words, while law breaking results in punishment, ethical action results in a positive reward only. If Sachedina's proposal is one that emphasizes ethics and morality, which appeals to the innate reason as he suggests, such a proposal is unlikely to achieve its goal. For instance, the Quran and other primary sources of Islamic authority have already established that slavery is immoral and unethical. The Quran orders Muslims to free slaves to atone for one's inability to undertake some obligations, such as fasting, or to atone for breaking an oath. However, Muslim scholars did not proscribe slavery and Muslims continued to enslave people until it was abolished by the world community. This demonstrates that ethical judgments did not nudge Muslim scholars to upgrade an ethical norm to a legal rule. In fact, some Muslim literalists (*Zahiris*) have thought—and some continue to think—that since the Quran did not prohibit slavery, slavery must be legal and cannot be abolished. Those who benefited and profited from the exploitation of other human beings found it convenient to leave slavery in the moral domain of the public discourse, or to abolish it gradually, which could last indefinitely.

Third, Sachedina's project amounts to a purging project through reclaiming and narrating. Such projects rarely succeed, and when they do succeed, they do so by splitting communities, not uniting them behind the cause of human rights. It is possible that at the end of this reform endeavour, Sachedina's reasoning will convince a fraction of Muslims, but others will persist. What then?

Sachedina seems to concede ground to those, like the European Union and—most recently—French President Emmanuel Macron—who contend that Muslims must purge their tradition of any textual reference or practice that is incompatible with human rights norms. These authorities have not asked the same of Jewish scholars or Jewish authorities, nor have they expected these authorities to purge their traditions of anti-human rights teachings and practices despite the fact that most Western societies consider themselves to be rooted in Judaic-Christian tradition. One could argue that Judaism and Christianity in the West operate in secular societies and therefore there is no expectation of involving them in the discourse on human rights one way or another. In response, I would point out that out of 57 Muslim-majority countries, only two nation-states can be classified as non-secular. The rest are modelled on Western societies and Islam is as much of an influence in public as are Christianity and Judaism. Even these two countries, where classical Islamic thought and law plays a greater role than in other Muslim-majority countries, the political institutions (including the form of government) are not based on the same classical theories of sovereignty and power. Iran is based on Imami Shiism, a sect that has never been in power before, which is one of the reasons they call their state a republic. The other, Saudi Arabia, is modelled on the Umayyad dynasty, but the government is a hybrid combining tribalism, clannism, and institutional governance. The modern Western nation-state is as much alive in Muslim-majority countries as it is in non-Muslim majority countries.

Moreover, Islam should have the space and guarantees to exist in the public sphere as any other religion in any other modern society. In Western societies, governments are secular, but societies hardly are. Political life and the public sphere in Western countries are full of examples that show the extent to which Christianity shapes public life. If nearly 50% of adult Americans would deny women the right to abortion, which is clearly motivated by religious dogma despite the claim that it is motivated by a desire to protect life, why can't 50% of adults in Muslim-majority countries vote based on their faith as well as public policy and yet find ways to protect human rights as Western societies do? The answer again is in the framing of the question: It is not Islam that stands against women's rights, for it has and it will continue to stand against them the same way Christianity does. The resistance to protecting women's rights is political and comes from the State, in both Western and Muslim-majority countries. If, as I contend, the State is the only violator or potential violator of human rights, then it stands to reason that the State—not culture or religion—has the greatest interest in claiming that certain rights are not universal or applicable for religious or cultural reasons so that it is not found guilty of violating human rights. If any follower of any religion were to be told that the State should not have the power to do certain bad things to people or not do certain required positive things for people as part of its main function, they would agree. But if they feel that they need to make their religion responsible for those accommodations, of course they will oppose. That is why it is important that the full equation of human rights is explicit: Human rights abuses are violations of basic rights of certain social groups by the State. The question becomes which of those rights should be universal, not whether there should be universal rights at all. The question of which human rights should be universal is not particular to Islam and Islamic societies, as evidenced in Talbott's book. The more important question becomes: Why should Muslims purge their religion to conform to a declaration that advocates religious freedom?

While Talbott seems to imply that the rights mentioned in the UDHR are not tenably universal, Sachedina appears to make the same mistake as many Muslim thinkers who take the UDHR is an all-or-nothing deal. The reality is that many Western governments, including the United States, do not accept or adhere to all of the UDHR's terms. Some Muslim thinkers, including Sachedina, think that the UDHR is all-or-nothing because the West has leveraged the concept of human rights for political purposes. A powerful Western nation-state with a national interest in a particular region can identify any right in the Declaration and accuse a government opposed to its plan of violating human rights. Such a government would be pressured to strike the deal that the Western country wants or face economic pressure, military pressure, or both.

The reverse is not true. For instance, leaders of the European Union have established that the death penalty is a form of cruel and unusual punishment and therefore consider it a human rights violation.[47] Consequently, any country wishing to join the EU must abolish the death penalty. European states have allocated resources to nudge other countries, most of them in Africa, to abolish the death penalty. However, the US government continues to execute prisoners, primarily members of disempowered social groups, and yet European states do not interfere in US affairs related to this matter. American and European governments, on the other hand, would not hesitate to use human rights norms as a pretext to interfere in the affairs of developing countries. This is another reason why scholars of human rights must have a clear position relevant to the principle of R2P.

There is a very important similarity between Talbott and Sachedina in regards to the basis they use to universalize human rights. Talbott thinks that liberal governments guaranteeing his list of basic rights is the shortest way to establishing a liberal society that adheres to human rights norms. Sachedina believes that secularism excludes religious communities and therefore will continue to fail to universalize human rights. Only a foundational conception of human rights, he argues, can universalize human rights. Yet three hundred years of a secular experiment in liberal societies did not bring an end to human rights abuses. In fact, many of the most egregious human rights abuses occurred in this time period. The same applies to a foundational concept of human rights based on Islamic morality: In 1000 years, Islamic civilization did not realize a universal version of human rights. The problem with both models is that they put too much faith in governments when the problem has always been with governments, and with governments adopting some particular orthodoxy and imposing it internally and externally, leading as it always has to human rights abuses. Muslim governments embraced reason-driven theology and made it public orthodoxy, which resulted in an inquisition and human rights abuses. In liberal societies, governments aligned themselves with liberal thinkers and imposed a kind of liberal public reason from the top-down, which did not prevent abuses of power at home and genocidal interventions abroad. The problem, then, is not determining whether secular or non-secular models are best; the problem is that when a given value system is born in society and that value system is made part of the mission of the government, the road to abuse opens wide.

Salafism is not a threat to human rights on its own, but it has been a deadly threat when empowered by the State and the institutions of the State, the same way Mu'tazilism became a threat when the government embraced it as the only form of public reason. Looking at liberal societies, and all the wars they have been involved in, their interventions in other societies imposed political- and religion-forced conversions. When it comes to human rights abuses, there is a common thread that runs throughout history: A government representing the interests and values of the dominant social group that sustains it becomes a vehicle for exporting and imposing those values and interests, and it often does so through violence and coercion—the ideal circumstances in which human rights abuses are most likely to occur.

We have seen how Talbott and Sachedina recognize the fact that the discovery of human rights norms was driven by the desire to avoid reliving the cruelty of wars and violence. That recognition, however, is secondary to how each author built a discrete narrative for his project. Talbott would like to see governments of liberal societies guaranteeing a package of basic rights, and in return, such governments would be recognized as legitimate. Sachedina, too, is interested in creating a new narrative that would present an Islamic ethical discourse as open, if not conforming, to universal human rights. Neither addresses the main concern for human rights: Liberal or not, Islamic or not, all governments have committed human rights abuses. In the light of that fact, what remedial action does either narrative propose, and what recommendations are there to discourage governments from abusing human rights; what actions should counter the abuses when—not if— they happen? To these questions, neither Talbott nor Sachedina provides

60 *Human rights as a discourse*

answers in their respective works. The two projects seem to achieve goals that are unhelpful in the fight against human rights abuses: Embellishing governments and religious traditions, respectively, making it harder to fight human rights abuses when they occur in a supposedly enlightened liberal society or a re-imagined Islamic tradition.

All scholars on human rights point out the fact that human rights are often violated. Yet most scholars on human rights do not say explicitly who is the actual or potential violator of human rights. Such an omission relativizes human rights because when a perpetrator is not named, many individuals, social groups, cultures, religions, associations, and any other social entity perceive the accusation of a human rights abuse as directed toward them. In this particular context, Muslims feel defensive because they think that it is their religion, irrespective of the sect or school of thought, that is abusive to human rights. The question that scholars rarely ask is: Why aren't Christian and Jewish communities defensive about their traditions' unconformity to human rights norms, since many of the teachings of those two Semitic religions are also anti-human rights or interpreted as such? Respect for human rights would be less controversial if the full equation on human rights abuses were explicit: The frequency and preponderance of human rights abuses *and* the identity of the primary violator of human rights. The incompleteness of the human rights equation creates a problem that is insurmountable for many communities around the world.

Relevant to human rights in Islamic societies, Sachedina concludes that there are three areas of concern: (1) Intolerance and institutionalized violence against different sects and religious minorities, (2) rampant disregard for the rights of women, and (3) lack of democratic constitutional and conceptual development of the notion of citizenship. Given his stated commitment to the totality of the UDHR, this list of concerns is disappointing. It might be a result of Sachedina's fundamental understanding of the meaning and function of human rights. I would use this context to transition into stating the real challenges that face Muslims as they adapt to conditions and circumstances that makes human rights central to any configuration of society today.

First, Sachedina dedicates a full chapter to the topic of women's rights. The chapter does not provide anything original or concrete to remediate the historical injustices Muslim women have suffered. I think that Sachedina dedicated the chapter to women's rights for the same reason he wrote the book: Defensiveness against charges that Islam is anti-human rights. In other words, Sachedina accepts the often-cited charge that women have it worse in Islam and as Muslims, just as we saw with the references Talbott invokes. I do not consider injustice against women to be Islam-specific. Discrimination and exploitation of women is universal, but it manifests itself in different ways in different societies.

Second, Sachedina is right in identifying sectarian strife in Islamic societies. Indeed, in the past and today, Muslims have a supremacy problem, rooted in sectarianism and as grave as the West's supremacy problem rooted

Islamic reaction to Western enlightenment 61

in race. Three of the first so-called civil wars in Islamic societies during the formative and post-formative eras were sectarian wars, produced sectarian fissures, or both. The current wars in Syria, Yemen, and Iraq, though ignited and sustained by regional and world powers, are driven by sectarian hate and bigotry, as I will later discuss.

There is one possible reason behind Sachedina's "unwavering commitment" to all of the rights declared in the UDHR while glossing over the most egregious human rights abuses specific to Islamic civilization. He, like Talbott, is a product of educational and professional systems rooted in the Enlightenment legacy. I am, too. We are subjects and objects of the dominant global system. In the next two chapters, I introduce historical evidence from the legacy of Western and Islamic thought and institutions, to better contextualize ideas regarding human rights in modern societies.

Notes

1. After writing his dissertation, which was a study of the Shia Imamate, Shia scholars took exception with his characterization of the religious doctrine. Sachedina, a practicing Shia Muslim, needed to sit down with a council religious leader to explain his position.
2. Abdulaziz Sachedina, *Islam and the Challenge of Human Rights* (New York: Oxford University Press, 2009).
3. Ibid, 39.
4. Ibid, 40.
5. Ibid, 47.
6. Ibid, 51.
7. Ibid, 52.
8. Ibid, 5.
9. Ibid, 4–5.
10. Ibid, 5.
11. Ibid, 6.
12. Ibid, 7.
13. Ibid, 8.
14. Ibid, 9.
15. Ibid.
16. Ibid, 9–10.
17. Ibid, 15.
18. Ibid, 16.
19. Ibid, 17.
20. Ibid, 27.
21. Ibid, 28.
22. Ibid.
23. Pope Benedict XVI, "Faith, Reason and the University Memories and Reflections" (address), September 12, 2006, University of Regensburg, Germany, "Libreria Editrice Vaticana," document, https://familyofsites.bishopsconference.org.uk/wp-content/uploads/sites/8/2019/07/BXVI-2006-Regensburg-address.pdf, p. 2:
    Show me just what Mohammed brought that was new, and there you will find things only evil and inhuman, such as his command to spread by the sword the faith he preached... The editor, Theodore Khoury, observes:

For the emperor, as a Byzantine shaped by Greek philosophy, this statement is self-evident. But for Muslim teaching, God is absolutely transcendent. His will is not bound up with any of our categories, even that of rationality.
24. Sachedina,*Human Rights*, 34.
25. Ibid, 25.
26. Ibid, 41.
27. Ibid, 58.
28. Ibid.
29. Ibid, 38.
30. Ibid, 42.
31. Ibid.
32. Ibid, 59–60.
33. Ibid, 86.
34. Ibid, 79.
35. Ibid, 86–90.
36. Ibid, 54.
37. Ibid, 44.
38. Ibid, 143.
39. Ibid, 207.
40. Ibid, 77–8.
41. Ibid, 57.
42. Ibid, 92.
43. Ibid, 101.
44. Ibid, 208.
45. Ibid.
46. The treaties that were inspired/derived from the UDHR include the International Convention on the Elimination of All Forms of Racial Discrimination (ICERD; 1965), the International Covenant on Civil and Political Rights (ICCPR; 1966), the International Covenant on Economic, Social and Cultural Rights (ICESCR; 1966), the Convention on the Elimination of All Forms of Discrimination against Women (CEDAW; 1979), the Convention against Torture and Other Cruel, Inhuman or Degrading Treatment or Punishment (CAT; 1984), the Convention on the Rights of the Child (CRC; 1989), and the International Convention on Protection of the Rights of All Migrant Workers and Members of Their Families (ICMRW; 1990).
47. European Convention on Human Rights, Protocol No. 6, Article, 1: "The death penalty shall be abolished. No one shall be condemned to such penalty or executed."

Part II
Human rights in history

I started with a detailed review of Talbott's work to frame the Western conception of human rights in the history of Western Enlightenment thought and institutions, and the legacy of human rights abuses that accompanied it. My treatment of Sachedina's work is intended to produce the mirror image of that framing in the context of the history of Islamic civilization. My approach presumes that every civilization has its unique point of reference that points to their break with old world views. In European societies, thinkers and scholars, including religious authorities, point to the Enlightenment as the moment that marked their new beginning. Muslims, too, represented by the dominant Arab culture that produced the leadership of the new era, have their own turning point; curiously, they use the term *Jahiliyya* (ignorance; unawareness) to denote it. For them, there was the time of ignorance, and then came Islam. For this reason, many Muslim thinkers who argue for Islamic reform in any area of social life tend to invoke the formative period of Islam, since it provides the clearest contrast between what was during the *Jahiliyya*, and what came after it. In other words, for many Muslim thinkers, the Enlightenment started much earlier than the eighteenth century. This expansion of the scope of the timeframe will help place our human rights discourse in broader religious, cultural, and societal context than the limited Enlightenment timeframe, and make the argument for universality of human rights values more meaningful, for it becomes unbound by time and culture.

4 European Enlightenment, racism, and human rights

Some philosophers, more so than scholars from other disciplines, credit thinkers of Western Enlightenment with progress on human rights. William Talbott is a philosopher in that tradition. His first work, which I examined in the first chapter, touches on the common thread among moral and political philosophers of the Enlightenment. My selection of his work is deliberate. It is appropriate to scrutinize his work in order to assess the progress scholars connected to this intellectual tradition have made and whether they have addressed some of the serious shortcomings of Enlightenment thought, especially relating to human rights and racism. Expanding that examination, this section assesses whether the attitudes and substance of political and economic Enlightenment philosophers have evolved in a measure that would redeem their explicit and implicit moralizing which justified, encouraged, and executed human rights abuses within Western societies, and more importantly, in indigenous communities in Africa, Asia, and the Americas.[1]

Close examination of the works by early Enlightenment thinkers reveal a troubling and persistent essentialization of other cultures and communities. In this context, I use the word "essentialization" to mean a couple of things. First, I use "essentialism" to refer to some Enlightenment scholars' tendency to think of other cultures or communities as having natural, innate characteristics that are inherent and persistent beyond change.[2] I also use "essentialism" to describe some Enlightenment scholars' invocation of negative examples (of events, ideas, or practices) from a culture that they associate with self-evident representation of the desired negativity. It might help descriptively to refer to this aspect of essentialism as *for instancism*, since it is often signalled by saying, *for instance*. To be specific, if a philosopher wants to invoke an example of a common human rights abuse case, they would say, "Women are subjugated by men in Islamic societies and under Islamic rule." Such an assertion is common without citing supportive evidence because, in the scholar's mind, it is a self-evident fact that needs no supporting. This practice was rampant among early Enlightenment scholars and, I would submit, among scholars of any society suffering from the supremacy impulse. Thinkers from the early and middle periods including Hume, Kant, Locke, Voltaire, Marx, Engels, Weber, and Durkheim, and even some of the most recent political philosophers such as Rawls (who died in this century) all essentialized indigenous people and, specifically, Islam and Muslims. Some used the offensive epithets *Mohammedanism/Mohametanism* and *Mohammedans* instead of Islam and Muslims.[3] In all cases, the reference was not drawn from rigorous research and verifiable facts, but from stereotype and baseless generalizations.

Western political philosophers of the 21st century have not totally abandoned the essentialism Enlightenment thinkers instrumentalized, despite an abundance of information and the ease with which one can engage with representatives of these once distant, imagined communities. Talbott essentialized Islam and Muslims when he could have engaged with a scholar specializing in Islamic and African political philosophy, read works by Muslim classical political philosophers—from al-Farabi in the east to Ibn Rush in the West—or simply lived up to epistemic modesty and declined to essentialize communities and cultures about which he is not fully informed. In order to provide more context for the importance and relevance of essentialism and racist views to the question of human rights, I will present samples of essentializing non-Western communities and ideas.

It must be noted that, in the view of many European Enlightenment scholars, their intellectual projects were relevant and applicable to all human beings; they presented information as if everyone was emerging out of theocratic or autocratic monarchical rule, and ushering in the era of rationality, liberty, and civil and individual rights. The Enlightenment era was the age of reason.[4] But it was during this age of reason that some of the most egregious human rights abuses took place, including crimes of genocide and colonialism, the kidnapping and transfer of human beings from Africa for the purpose of enslavement, and the exploitation and abuse of human and natural resources of indigenous peoples. Enlightenment scholars had the option of speaking out against these events and conditions, or justifying them. Some justified them through racist theories.

The 18th century philosopher, economist, and historian David Hume suspected "the Negroes to be naturally inferior to the Whites." He based this belief on his presumption that "there scarcely ever was a civilized nation of that complexion, nor even any individual, eminent either in action or in speculation. No ingenious manufacture among them, no arts, no sciences."[5]

On Muslims, Hume's judgement on the language of Islam, Muhammad, and the Quran is clear: If Arabic had words analogous to English ones referring to equity, justice, temperance, meekness, and charity, those words do not hold the same meaning to Muslims who speak them. Words' meanings are connected to the person speaking them and since Muhammad is a pretend prophet, his words must be imaginary moralizing. Muhammad, according to Hume, "bestows praise on such instances of treachery, inhumanity, cruelty, and revenge." Therefore, there is no place for Muhammad and his followers in civilized societies.

It is reasonable to suspect that Hume's negative views about Islam and Muslims are consistent with his skepticism about religion in general. After all, Hume explains God as an idea originating from our own minds. However, Hume also made the argument for the existence of "genuine theism" consisting of belief in only one god, an invisible one, and a creator of everything. Hume conceives of religion as having origins not in reason or philosophical argument, but in human fear and lack of understanding. Hume's view of God and religion mirrors the common belief in Jesus Christ as presented in Christianity—the incarnation of God. In the end, Hume cannot be pinned down to a specific position on religion, for he asserts that "genuine theism" points to a God that is sublime and magnificent, but it is religion, in the generic sense, that disfigures and corrupts the idea of god. Like Thomas Hobbes, who wished to build a secular, scientific account of morality and public life, Hume wished to build a system of secular ethics shaped by both emotion and reason. Such a system of ethics, however, did not extend to understanding Islam and Muslims.

> The admirers and followers of the Alcoran insist on the excellent moral precepts interspersed throughout that wild and absurd performance. But it is to be supposed, that the Arabic words, which correspond to the English, equity, justice, temperance, meekness, charity, were such as, from the constant use of that tongue, must always be taken in a good sense; and it would have argued the greatest ignorance, not of morals, but of language, to have mentioned them with any epithets, besides those of applause and approbation. But would we know, whether the pretended prophet had really attained a just sentiment of morals? Let us attend to his narration; and we shall soon find, that he bestows praise on such instances of treachery, inhumanity, cruelty, revenge, bigotry, as are utterly incompatible with civilized society. No steady rule of right seems there to be attended to; and every action is blamed or praised, so far only as it is beneficial or hurtful to the true believers.[6]

Hume establishes the standard for who is compatible with civilized society, and that standard excludes those who praise—not necessarily undertake—cruel, inhumane, and bigoted actions. In principle, this seems a reasonable position. Substantively, Hume has no basis in fact to conclude that those he derogatorily calls "Mohomet" and "Mahometans" were all committed to treachery, inhumanity, cruelty, revenge, and bigotry more than any other social leader and their followers in his own society. Hume authorizes the essentialism invoked by his fellow Enlightenment thinkers, especially those who confess admiration to his ideas and judgments. His characterization of Roman Catholicism—something he would be more familiar with than

Islam, and a proselytizing, missionary religion built on the idea of converting all of the people it encounters—suggests that Hume's generalizations are assumption-based, not rooted in the nature of things ignoring the overriding principles of ideas.

> It is essential to the Roman Catholic religion to inspire a violent hatred of every other worship and to represent all Pagans, Mahometans, and heretics as the objects of divine wrath and vengeance. Such sentiments, though they are in reality very blameable, are considered as virtues by the zealots of that communion and are represented in their tragedies and epic poems as a kind of divine heroism.[7]

Hume understands human difference in what he calls "moral causes," and defines moral principles and individual characters in terms of "all circumstances, which are fitted to work on the mind as motives or reasons, and which render a particular set of manners habitual to us."[8] Keeping this in mind, it is clear that "'Mahomatans' temperament," in the mind of Hume, is shaped by the circumstances that made them treacherous, inhumane, cruel, and vengeful.

Hume's influence on later moral and political philosophers is clear from work that has emerged from and continues to emerge from the disciplines of moral and political philosophy. Essentialism, however, neither originated nor ended with Hume. Equally influential Enlightenment thinkers produced stereotypical narratives about non-European societies and non-white social groups. Perhaps there is no Enlightenment thinker more consequential and influential on the discourse of morality and rights than Immanuel Kant. Kant not only wrote seminal works that have informed all his successors but also invented systems of creating and sharing knowledge. From a systems-thinking perspective, Kant's legacy is powerful evidence in support of inherited systemic advantages and disadvantages. Kant founded new academic disciplines in German universities, "anthropology" and "physical geography," to amplify his own work and systematize these disciplines in ways that ensured their permanence and influence.[9] The content of Kant's new courses was integrated into work on ethics and metaphysics, and it was in these areas of inquiry that Kant's theories on race, biology, and knowledge lead some to conclude that he "produced the most profound raciological thought of the eighteenth century."[10] For instance, Kant held that some differences between humans are innate ones, and this view contributed to and even encouraged the establishment of racial biology. He claimed that not all races could reach the same level of being "civilized."[11]

> The Blacks of Africa have no sense naturally which exceeds the childish. Mr. Hume requests that anyone cite a single example when a Black has shown talent, and observes: That among the hundreds of thousands

of Blacks who were kidnapped from their lands, although many have been set free, not a single one has been found who has exhibited greatness in art or science or in any other notable area, although among the Whites there are those who constantly rise from the lowest rabble and achieve notice in the world through their notable gifts. So evident is the difference between the two races, that it seems as great in the abilities of the mind as in their color.[12]

Kant, citing a fellow Enlightenment authority, appeals to reason to make the point that reason cannot save certain people because of their biology. The challenge Hume issues proves Black people's mental weakness. Among the hundreds of thousands of Black people enslaved by Europeans, Hume exclaims, show just one who would meet the white standard of greatness.[13] Kant seems to agree with Hume's expectation for individuals who were kidnapped from another continent, subjected to methodical control, systemic abuse, crippling illiteracy, paralyzing fear, and consuming terror to become scientists and artists in an environment designed to exclude them and deny that they have abilities and capacities. Hume finds that even the most uncivilized whites are more eminent than the best of non-whites because they have no record of ingenuity.[14] Hume's reasoning for his generalizations, which Kant cites as well, is stunning in its implications. Hume's ignorance is evident: If he does not know of a Black artist, scientist, or genius, then no Black artist, scientist, or genius had existed or could exist. It is the burden of non-white peoples to prove to white people that they are "civilized."

Absent any evidence produced by non-white peoples, some Enlightenment thinkers are satisfied with the physical markers that allow them to judge other peoples' aptitudes. They viewed blackness as evidence of Black people's limits and disabilities. Being white and being Black are not mere physical markers to Kant; being Black expresses not only a deficiency in the mind, but a deficiency in outlook: Black people's disabilities of the mind match their skin color. Blackness, therefore, is not about being stupid; it is also about being not beautiful. Kant cites an anecdote from Father Labat to prove his point:

> Of course, Father Labat reports that a Negro carpenter, whom he reproached for haughty treatment toward his wives, answered: "You whites are indeed fools, for first you make great concessions to your wives, and afterward you complain when they drive you mad." And it might be that there were something in this which perhaps deserved to be considered; but in short, this fellow was quite black from head to foot, a clear proof that what he said was stupid.[15]

Kant signals his racism and his sexism in the same breath. The hearsay story provides another function: It promotes the idea that Black people are or can be arrogant, superiority-prone, and disdainful actors amongst themselves and in the treatment of their wives. Furthermore, it is the role of the religious authority, Father Labat, to intervene on behalf of the wives. The Black carpenter responds by accusing white folks of being detrimentally accommodating to their wives. Kant finds this response almost worthy of consideration, if it did not come from a Black person who must be stupid, as evidenced by his skin color. The entire report could be believable if Kant did not reveal his belief that "blacks are very vain but in the Negro's way, and so talkative that they must be driven apart from each other with thrashings."[16] If Blacks risked being flogged for carrying on conversations among each other, then it is unlikely that a Black carpenter derided Father Labat, an authority of some sort, about the way white folks treat their wives.

Kant did not simply think that Black people occupied a lower position than white people; he held that all peoples other than white people occupied graded lower positions, to the extent that "the Native Americans have less talent, but Negroes occupy even a lower position,"[17] and other races and ethnicities occupied space on the evolutionary scale.

> If we cast a fleeting glance over the other parts of the world, we find the Arab the noblest man in the Orient, yet of a feeling that degenerates very much into the adventurous. He is hospitable, generous, and truthful; yet his narrative and history and on the whole his feeling are always interwoven with some wonderful thing. His inflamed imagination presents things to him in unnatural and distorted images, and even the propagation of his religion was a great adventure. If the Arabs are, so to speak, the Spaniards of the Orient, similarly the Persians are the French of Asia. They are good poets, courteous and of fairly fine taste. They are not such strict followers of Islam, and they permit to their pleasure-prone disposition a tolerably mild interpretation of the Koran.[18]

Turning his attention to people of the Orient, Kant considers religion, religious texts, and culture in a way inconsistent with how white people of Europe interacted with Christianity and the Bible. Kant's reasoning suggests that Arabs were shaped by their character and sense of adventure, and that they produced a religious text, the Koran, which matched their temperament. Kant submits that Arabs relied on their adventurous nature to propagate Islam through the sword. Ignoring Kant's lack of self-awareness relevant to the Crusaders, he nonetheless suggests that Persians, for being non-Arabs, had a different relationship with the Quran and Islam. Because of who they were as a race or ethnic group, Persians reproduced the message of the Quran; the Quran did not shape Persians. After placing the peoples of the Old World on the evolutionary scale, Kant turns to the indigenous peoples of North America:

> Among all savages there is no nation that displays so sublime a mental character as those of North America. They have a strong feeling for honor, and as in quest of it they seek wild adventures hundreds of miles abroad, they are still extremely careful to avert the least injury to it when their equally harsh enemy, upon capturing them, seeks by cruel pain to extort cowardly groans from them. The Canadian savage, moreover, is truthful and honest.[19]

The indigenous peoples of North America were a plurality of nations, cultures, and languages; they were as diverse as the environment in which they lived. Yet Kant, based on some special insight, reduced them to a group of people with limited emotional, temperamental, and reasoning abilities. Even that which was an otherwise praiseworthy characteristic when applied to white people is a burdensome infliction when encountered among the indigenous peoples of North America: They were prisoners of their own commitment to honor and honesty.

Notwithstanding his racial categorizations, and relevant to the topic of this work, Kant considers the idea of human rights a political matter, not a moral one as seen by other thinkers. Echoing Talbott's call for a government to provide legal guarantees in return for recognition of legitimacy, Kant conditions the promotion of natural rights, such as liberty, equality, and autonomy of citizens, on the existence of "a legitimate government." In this thinking, granting and protecting rights are essentially contingent on the State's functions. Moreover, according to Kant, society's function is dependent on the State's success in granting fundamental rights, laws, and entitlements. What appears to be a circular argument is ostensibly resolved by Kant's assertion that principles of liberty, equality, and autonomy are not granted by the State, but are required for people of the State to create and legitimize it. However, once the State is established, Kant argues, individuals must obey coercive and unjust laws and amend them by appealing to the sovereign using the freedom of the press. This model is incapable of delivering justice for those who lack freedom, or for those whom the State sees and treats as incapable of using reason since the overarching doctrine Kant holds is that only rational nature possesses intrinsic worth. For these reasons, Kant's view on race and biology are critically important.[20]

Like Kant and Hume, Georg Wilhelm Friedrich Hegel, too, held that race is more than a superficial difference signalled by the color of the skin. Hegel saw humans dialectically, with white people and Black people as opposites.[21] He proposed that to understand race relations, Western thinkers must forget all the ways in which they see things: They, Europeans, must think of neither a spiritual god nor a moral law; they must suspend every respect and every morality of what they call emotions.[22]

> The Blacks must be understood as an infantile nation which has not transcended its disinterested or uninterested ingenuousness. They are

sold and permit themselves to be sold without thought whether this is right or not. Their religion has something child-like about it. The higher sensation which they feel, they do not preserve. It passes quickly through their head. They transfer this higher sensation to the first best stone. They make this into their fetish and cast this fetish aside if it does not help them. Good natured and harmless when in a passive state, they commit the most horrible bestialities in a state of sudden frenzy. One cannot deny their possibility for education. Not only have they accepted Christianity with great thankfulness and have spoken with compassion about this after achieving freedom following a long period of slavery of the mind but they have formed in Haiti a state based on Christian principles. But they have not shown an inner drive for culture. The most horrible despotism dominates their homeland. They never achieve the sense of human personality—their spirit sleeps, remains sunk in itself, makes no advances and thus parallels the compact, undifferentiated mass of the African continent.[23]

Hegel turns slavery into an imperative that other people made, not Europeans. As such, he sees slavery as the only thing that connects Black Africa to Europe and that connection can be used to save Black people from themselves, or more appropriately, from their own nature. Hegel thinks North Africa was different because it made contact with northern civilizations—Phoenician, Greek, and other Asiatic or European civilizations. He presents slavery and colonialism as endeavours to uplift Black people. Hegel would oppose the abolition of slavery in favor of its gradual dismantling to give Black people the chance to educate themselves:

The only essential connection that has existed and continued between Blacks and the Europeans is that of slavery. In this the Blacks see nothing unbecoming them, and the English who have done most for abolishing the slave-trade and slavery, are treated by the Blacks themselves as enemies. For it is a point of first importance with the Kings to sell their captured enemies, or even their own subjects; and viewed in the light of such facts, we may conclude slavery to have been the occasion of the increase of human feeling among the Blacks. The doctrine which we deduce from this condition of slavery among the Blacks, and which constitutes the only side of the question that has an interest for our enquiry, is that which we deduce from the IDEA: Viz, that of the "Natural condition" itself is one of absolute and thorough injustice—contravention of the Right and Just. Every intermediate grade between this and the realization of a rational State retains—as might be expected—elements and aspects of injustice; therefore, we find slavery even in the Greek and Roman States, as we do serfdom down to the latest times. But thus, existing in a State, slavery is itself a phase of advance from the merely isolated sensual existence—a phase of education—a mode of becoming participant in a higher morality and the culture connected with it. Slavery is in and for itself injustice, for the essence of humanity is Freedom; but for this man must be matured. The gradual abolition of slavery is therefore wiser and more equitable than its sudden removal.[24]

Enslaving people is abrupt and cruel. In Hegel's time, it involved travelling to a distant continent, kidnapping free people from their homeland, transporting them in degrading conditions, forcing them to perform tasks, and employing all instruments to make sure that they are not free to leave. White people who profited from the slave trade used law, torture, lynching, threats, degrading treatment, and all other physical and mental tools to break down any sense of dignity and self-worth and to ascertain full control of enslaved individuals. However, now that some Enlightenment thinkers have discovered that "slavery is in and for itself injustice," emancipation of these enslaved people must happen gradually because slavery is the "only essential connection that has existed and continued between Blacks and the Europeans." Slavery, in a perverted way, becomes an opportunity for Black people to learn from Europeans; a Black person's chance for "becoming participant in a higher morality and the culture connected with it."[25]

In order to justify the continued promotion of racist Enlightenment thinkers, some philosophers today propose this argument: Those were men of their time and it is not fair to hold them to the standard of our time. It has been suggested that these thinkers, when given the opportunity, changed their views.[26] Such an argument seems reasonable, but the facts do not support it.

First, there were other thinkers and philosophers from the same era who recognized the many inconsistencies of ideas and practices within society's principles of fairness and justice. Even then, there were some who held the view that some norms are universal, and who did not wish to justify what was done in the name of the crown, liberal society, or the church. But society and the systems in place opted to promote the ideas and teachings of those who justified colonialism and genocide.

Second, there are thinkers and philosophers who live in the 21st century and who hold views from the seventeenth and eighteenth centuries. Given the discoveries of the last 200 years, and using the same argument, it is fair to say that these men and women are not of their time. Time does not make truth; people find truth and produce narratives based upon it. There should not be one scale for thinkers of the past and another scale for thinkers of today; doing so relativizes facts and absolves people of responsibility for principles and values thought to be universal. The universality of a norm is easier to prove if its universality is unbound by time, culture, and geography. In other words, if one were to argue that torture is universally blameworthy, one must show that some people held that view thousands of years ago, and that some people from all cultures and regions subscribed to

74 *Human rights in history*

it as well. The multidirectional universality is not a requirement for arguing for a universal rule, but it is a bellwether for it.

Among Enlightenment thinkers, Jean-Jacques Rousseau stands out. Not because he did not contribute to the body of theories that promoted racist ideas, but because his views are so nuanced that one must work hard to connect any racist tendencies with his views on the difference between peoples. I find his assertion about the corrupting power of colonial intrusions in distant lands striking. It could be interpreted to advocate for indigenous autonomy, a position rarely appreciated, even by thinkers of the 21st century, in a time when greed-driven globalism is on full display. Highlighting his bias towards liberal societies, Rousseau can be the least overt contributor to racism through theories on the difference between peoples. Nonetheless, he is believed to argue that:

> For all their defects Europeans were a stage closer to creating legitimate societies than other peoples and consequently that they should conquer the New World societies to prepare them to establish such societies… The social contract in *The Social Contract* is an account of the foundation of a legitimate society, and it does not posit a war of all against all. It requires only that people have "reached the point where obstacles to their self-preservation in the state of nature prevail by their resistance over the forces each individual can use to maintain himself in that state."[27]

Bernard R. Boxill interprets Rousseau's project for civil society and legitimate government to involve colonialism:

> On this account, the European conquest of the New World was one of the greatest catastrophes in human history. Besides the needless death of millions, the conquest and destruction of these societies and the introduction of European social institutions drove the possibility of ever establishing legitimate societies further and further out of reach. When the whole world joined Europe in its greed, pride, hypocrisy, deceitfulness, and cunning, humanity would probably descend into a maelstrom of corruption, war, and death.[28]

I disagree with Boxill. Considering Rousseau's works together, he appears to favor non-intervention or expansion beyond national borders. Granted, Rousseau's disdain toward colonialism is not motivated by care for indigenous peoples. Rather, he sees colonial adventures as a threat to national unity and a strain on national resources. It is, in the end, motivated by self-interest. Rousseau's view of colonialism is not motivated by his desire to universalize human rights norms. It was motivated by his grand project aimed at creating a model society within national borders. Such a project hinges on creating a model citizen since, in Rousseau's view, virtue is embedded in citizens. The glue that cements individuals together is patriotism, which is contingent on liberty, a virtue that must be instilled in citizens through public education. Patriotism cannot be expanded to people in other parts of the word. Therefore, human rights, which are supposed to apply to human beings, not just citizens, are not part of Rousseau's grand project of building a liberal society, a government responsive to public good, and patriots willing to die for the common interest. Taken together, his ideals cannot be a foundation for basic universal rights because they are decidedly nationalistic. Patriotism does build virtuous citizens, but not virtuous human beings, because patriotism is taught as an instrument of the State. Rousseau argues that "patriotism is the most efficacious," because "every man is virtuous when his particular will is in all things comfortable to the general will."[29] However, Rousseau contends that patriotism cannot be built on universalized sentiments.

> It appears that the feeling of humanity evaporates and grows feeble in embracing all mankind, and that we cannot be affected by the calamities of Tartary or Japan, in the same manner as we are by those European nations. It is necessary in some degree to confine and limit our interest and compassion in order to make it active… It is proper that our humanity should confine itself to our fellow citizens, and should receive a new force because we are in the habit of seeing them and by reason on the common interest which unites them.[30]

Rousseau's paradigm cannot produce a universal human rights program that honors the rights of human beings, not just citizens, since committing to ideals that further the interests of non-citizens dilutes patriotism, which he sees as the engine of modern society. With this view in mind, one can see that his opposition to colonialism is a self-interested position, not a concern for the harm European colonialism has inflicted on indigenous communities.

Despite Rousseau's passionate argument for putting the government on the side of the poor citizens, and even in the context of a nation-state, Rousseau's model cannot advance the rights of vulnerable social groups. This is because all the elements that build and sustain the modern state are reflective of the interests of the dominant social group, and there is no mechanism that safeguards marginalized groups' rights. Rousseau's model is built on good morals, respect of the laws, patriotism, and the influence of the general will.[31] All these elements presuppose a homogenous society with similar interests fractured only by economic inequality, which he recommends the wise government deals with for the good of the collective. But this paradigm does not account for a diverse society fractured by sexism, ethnicism, racism, and other persistent forces of discrimination that break society into smaller and radically different groups with very few common values and interests.

76 *Human rights in history*

Rousseau's virtuous society is built on an establishment of public law and public funds. Public funds come from taxation of private property, which in his eyes is the most sacred right of a citizen. The same way public law is borne out of citizens' competing interests, public funds come from money (*ararium*) or land (public *demesne*). Rousseau thinks that public *demesne* is the most important means of providing for the needs of the State. However, he correctly predicts that the State will never be satisfied with a constant amount of taxes, for "no State can subsist unless its revenues constantly increase." This is where Rousseau's republic is firmly set on rails that lead nowhere near universal human rights: A State founded on a system that requires increased revenues, and where revenues are tethered to land, is destined to colonize countries and usurp their land to increase its coffers. Colonialism, therefore, was inevitable, and human rights abuses were certain.

Living and writing during the century in which the French revolution took place, but before such a radical, transformative event that lasted nearly a decade, Rousseau must have been an aspirational figure. However, with the benefit of hindsight, we now know that more of his fears and less of his aspiration were realized. The revolution was mostly in name; colonialism and occupation of African countries occurred faster than the realization of equality in France; and no educational system was able to create moral citizens and responsive heads of State. Fewer than three decades following the revolution, France began its expansion into Africa and, later, into other continents. Rousseau thought that such expansion, though it may increase "public funds" in the short term, would, in the long run, weigh heavily on the bureaucracy of the State. He did not envision the resistance by indigenous communities and the human toll it would take on them. Related to this development, but which Rousseau did not predict, was how French society transformed after absorbing many people from formerly colonized countries. The sense of patriotism that Rousseau envisioned to be the motivating force that would drive "freemen" to fight for the republic has become harder to define and instil in a more diverse society. Even when the adopted peoples were willing to completely and totally assimilate and buy in into the narrative that unites citizens, a large segment of French society rejected them. This development exposed the short-sightedness of a national project that assigns virtue to citizens only, not to all humans irrespective of their background. France, like many other European colonial countries that absorbed people from former colonies, is yet to find a solution to the inconsistencies and contradictions within their human rights discourse.

Rousseau's prediction, more relevant to the dangers to the republic than to its promise, came true. France's expansion in Africa, specifically the occupation of Algeria, my ancestral homeland, turned out to be more damaging to the French republic than beneficial. The intervention was economically costly, but socially and ideologically transformative. Before the liberation of Algeria in 1962, Algerians authored their own revolution, for which they paid 1.5 million lives. France is yet to remedy the war crimes it committed there, and it has failed to integrate (rather than forcefully assimilate) millions of Algerian and African collaborators who have since made France their home.

Rousseau commits to the idea of a country of citizens who are taught to be virtuous and obey the law and the people who administer the law. Rousseau, like Talbott, has faith in law and administrators of law. As someone whose experience and profession biases me in favor of the victims of human rights abuses—and while I share their view that laws are necessary and the rule of law is the ultimate social equalizing tool—I do not share their faith in the State and agents of the State when it comes to protecting human rights, for it is only the State which violates human rights. Human rights norms can be universalized when the State is identified as the actual or potential abuser of human rights and when institutions and public policies, based on this understanding, are put in place.

The theories of many Enlightenment thinkers demonstrate a conception of the Enlightenment as a linear progression. They also hold that some people were not civilized and could not be civilized without intervention, even if such intervention involved abhorrent practices such as slavery and colonialism. Because of this position, they view things that happened in their time such as colonialism, genocide, and slavery as a by-product of this progress and, therefore, acceptable as prerequisites for progress. Those who followed Kant and Hegel, like Hannah Arendt, Jean-Paul Sartre, Martin Heidegger, and Bruce Gilli, have held similar views.

It is a mistake, I would argue, for political and economic philosophers of today to either ignore or gloss over Enlightenment thinkers' contribution to the legacy of racism and the spread of human rights abuses. Racism has deep roots in Western thought and culture. Because of the persistence of racism, and its connection to human rights abuses, we cannot excuse the racist legacy of the Enlightenment by arguing that early Western thinkers were the products of a time when racism was legally and morally acceptable. The flawed nature of such an argument is clear in the few Enlightenment thinkers who categorically rejected racism during the same historical period.

For many Enlightenment thinkers, invoking human rights norms was more important abroad than at home. A civilized society with a liberal government has relatively little fear of human rights abuse. Enlightenment thinkers envisioned human rights abuses as occurring outside of European society and thought that it was Europeans' burden to stop it. That was the logical point of view that allowed many Enlightenment scholars to reconcile their theoretical commitment to rights with their governments' colonization and exploitation of indigenous communities outside Europe: That colonialism, like slavery, was a blessing in disguise for non-white people. If enslaving people from another continent and bringing them to Europe and the Americas was a "civilizing" mission for Black people amongst white people, then colonialism was a civilizing project for non-white people in their homelands. However, since the act of cultural assimilation does not take the black color off Black people, Western Christianity was the indispensable tool to "civilize" African peoples. Many influential Enlightenment scholars believed in the liberating power of Christianity, but some did not.

Arthur Schopenhauer, for instance, takes issue with Hegel's basic premise that it is Christianity which marks the distinction between civilized man and the barbarian (at the close of the 19th century, Friedrich Nietzsche echoes this debate). Schopenhauer inverts the common position of some Enlightenment thinkers who held that progress is pegged to the lapse of time. Schopenhauer holds that religious communities of the past may have held humane interpretations of their faiths and practiced a tolerant version of rituals and conduct.

> In comparison with the Christian centuries that followed, the ancients were unquestionably less cruel than the Middle Ages with their exquisite tortures and numberless burnings at the stake. Moreover, the ancients were very tolerant, had a particularly high regard for justice, frequently sacrificed themselves for their country, and showed every kind of magnanimity and generosity, and such a genuine humanity that even to this day an acquaintance with their thoughts and actions is called the study of the humanities. The fruits of Christianity were religious wars, religious massacres, crusades, inquisitions. Together with other courts for heretics, extermination of the original natives of America, and the introduction of African slaves in their place. Among the ancients nothing analogous to, or in any way like them is to be found; for the slaves of the ancients, the familia, the vernae, were a contented race, faithfully devoted to their master, and as different from the unfortunate Negro slaves of the sugar plantations, who are an indictment against mankind, as are their two colors. The tolerance of pederasty which was certainly reprehensible and with which we mainly reproach the morals of the ancients, is a trifle when compared with the Christian atrocities I have just named. Even among the moderns, this vice has not become anything like so, rare as would appear on the surface. All things considered, can you maintain that mankind has actually become morally better through Christianity?[32]

While Schopenhauer does not believe that followers of the same religion do not necessarily become more humane in their treatment of followers of other religions, he nonetheless held that all religions have objectionable practices. Slavery in the modern Western world is a unique institution, unique in its lack of humaneness, because of its roots in the Judeo-Christian system. Indeed, Schopenhauer sees classical slavery as a different quality than the contemporary institution:

The believers of every religion regard themselves as justified in committing every crime against those of all the others and have, therefore, treated them with the greatest wickedness and cruelty; thus the Mohammedans against the Christians and Hindus, the Christians against the Hindus, Mohammedans, American natives, Negroes, Jews, heretics, and others. Perhaps I go too far when I say all religions, for in the interest of truth I must add that the fanatical cruelties arising from this principle are really known to us only from the followers of the monotheistic religions, thus Judaism and its two branches, Christianity and Islam.[33]

The European colonial powers were not civilizing indigenous peoples; they were competing with other imperial societies and imperial religions. In Africa, for instance, they were not dealing with African religions and African peoples; rather, they encountered there an imperial religion, Islam. Africans, including those affiliated with the European projects, experienced both Islamic and Christian expansion in their continent and recorded the encounter:

> In Central Africa, the religion of Arabia shows its pristine vitality and expansive power, carrying on its operations by indigenous agents and simple methods; while Christianity attempts to confront it by an expensive missionary system and exotic agencies—by various sects and a complicated ecclesiasticism. The experience of each day, especially when we contrast the results of the two systems, convinces the careful and earnest student of the question that an effective missionary among the Natives of interior Africa, whether Pagan or Mohammedan, must begin with "Silver and gold have I none" and continue with, "Stand up; I myself also am a man." And it is becoming more and more apparent that an enterprise which requires so much and such continuous foreign aid and oversight—such an apparatus of alien training and directing agencies—is ill-adapted to compete with that energetic and cosmopolitan system from Arabia, whose agents are indigenous and stand on their own legs, pursuing methods, which, if under the inspiration of the Koran.[34]

David Hume is correct on one account: People's moral development relevant to human rights norms is the product of their circumstances. Abuse of human rights and supremacy views are universal; respect for human rights and for each other is not. If we factor out citizens' rights, there has never been a nation-State in any liberal society that has observed, respected, and upheld universal human rights. Supremacy is the norm; civility is the aspiration.

Since the start of the Enlightenment age, governments of some of the most "Enlightened" and developed countries of Europe have committed some of the cruellest acts and developed some of the most inhumane tools of killing and destruction. The only constant among these cruel acts and instruments is a racist impulse, used to dismiss any claim to dignity and humanity by those exploited, murdered, incarcerated, or killed en masse. More than 500 years have passed and the world is yet to see a fair resolution to genocide against indigenous communities, usurpation of indigenous peoples' land, enslavement of Black people, colonialism, the Holocaust, use of weapons of mass destruction, systemic racism in public policies and institutions, illegal wars, and inhumane economic sanctions. Every one of these crimes and abuses stems from supremacy and racism, the seeds of which can be found in the ideas of most of influential thinkers of Enlightenment and their disciples, who have inherited their legacy and their privileges.

Borrowing Talbott's phrase, what we now know, based on facts, events, and laws and policies, and what is also qualifiable, is that some liberal governments of liberal societies had and will continue to commit human rights violations despite having laws that prohibit them from doing so. They have ignored these laws, repealed them, or interpreted them in ways that have allowed them to infringe on the human rights of disempowered communities at home and abroad. In some cases, they created new laws, new categories, loopholes, and networks to allow them to commit violations. What should not be forgotten is that some of the obscenest human rights crimes, like the Holocaust, were not totally illegal.

It is not expected that all moral philosophers of Enlightenment thought abandon their connection to and reliance on some of their ancestral Enlightenment thinkers who racialized human worth and human aptitude. Indeed, even some thinkers who are descendants of the social groups excluded and demeaned by such thought contend that it is possible to instrumentalize the Enlightenment legacy to reclaim Black people's dignity if the discourse is first de-racialized.

> [T]he key principles and ideals of Kant's ethico-political thought are, once de-racialized, very attractive: The respect for the rights of individual persons, the ideal of the *Rechtsstaat* (admittedly somewhat modified from Kant's own version), and the vision of a global cosmopolitan order of equals.[35]

This approach to thought that once served to systemize racism and supremacy misdiagnoses the consequential impact and the functional design of racialized Enlightenment thought. First it is assumed that, given the influence and stay-power of these ideas, indigenous peoples who were poorly portrayed in this legacy have two options only: "Seek to adapt these frameworks, principles, and ideals to their own ends, or… attempt to devise alternatives."[36] This position is founded on a false dichotomy. It additionally fails to distinguish between deliberately designed systems and the adoption of principles and ideals to structure a reasoned argument.

Moreover, the idea that Kant's systemic thinking, purged of racism, can serve a positive purpose for the people it injured is utterly superficial, un-labored, and casual. Racism is not an end-goal; rather, it is an instrument that has been used for other, grander purposes. Should that fact stand, then de-racializing the intellectual, education, and knowledge manufacturing systems will have no measurable impact on the schemes of exclusion, interest preservation, and resource hoarding. De-racializing a discourse, as Charles Mills suggests, was indeed a good option for thinkers like Kant once racism was proved to be a limited strategy. If we accept the theory that Kant (and possibly other Enlightenment thinkers) abandoned racist ideas later in their lives, and there is no reason to fully reject it, it becomes clear that Kant de-racialized his own thought.

It is unclear how the ideals of equality are attractive in any meaningful way to "subordinated social groups." It is deeply ironic that, in pursuit of the inclusion and protection of the rights of marginalizable social groups, we must strip individual human beings of all personal identifiers, experiential heritage, and natural distinctions so that they are abstracted as generic human beings who can be said to be equal. Must women gain a Y chromosome to earn equal pay? Must Black men and women find a way to turn the color of their skin white for them to be free, to own property, to seek an education, to reside in a neighbourhood of their choice, to access public services, and to be respected as human beings? Must Native Americans adopt land ownership practices of white men, worship the god white men worship, and adopt the metrics of self-worth that white men devised in order to reclaim their homeland and their autonomy? Must all human beings pursue material net worth for them to have human worth?

Despite subtle differences, the theory and practices of Enlightenment thinkers were set to universalize the values of that generation: *Life, liberty and property*. In pursuit of those goals, social, economic, political, cultural, and artistic systems were carefully designed and calibrated to undertake specific functions and produce specific outcomes. It is possible that none of these systems were deliberately designed to oppress specific social groups, degrade the environment, aggravate poverty, exterminate indigenous peoples, commit mass murder, and inflict other atrocities such as rape, torture, and enslavement. However, there is ample evidence that systems were put in place to augment wealth beyond need and want, exploit natural and human assets, and control and hoard resources—all of which have had the unintended but predictable side effects that caused many human rights abuses. We can see these systems' best work in public life today: The fact that the most affluent cities in the United States have the most severe crises of homelessness.[37]

Some modern philosophers, especially those who are members of historically oppressed social groups and who joined disciplines long dominated by white men, like philosophy, think that they can plug race into "mainstream

Western political theory" to address longstanding social and economic problems.[38] Such an approach, I believe, will result in normalizing and legitimizing these theories before it succeeds in raising awareness about the harm those institutions and theories caused. It is not creative, original, or effective to repurpose the original tools (and agents) of oppression to end oppression. In the words of Audre Lorde: "The master's tools will never dismantle the master's house." Philosophy is more than a discipline; it is a *system* designed to produce and preserve privilege. Philosophers maintain the system, not reinvent it, since they themselves are the product of the system.

By applying systems thinking perspective, the notions that racist Enlightenment thinkers were products of their time and that many of them have renounced their racism[39] reaffirm the main centrality of the general system. If racism and discrimination, at some point, served the general purpose of the ultimate system, then racist discourse must have been implemented as a sub-system. If sexist, racist, and supremacist discourses hindered progress towards the desired goal, then sexism, racism, and supremacy would have been condemned. In the end, racism and other supremacist impulses are not end-goals in and of themselves; they are instruments that galvanize society in a way that makes the overall system work the way those benefit from it desire.

Notes

1. For this work, I am interested in determining what and how Enlightenment thinkers contributed to the discourse of human rights. Given my contention that all human rights abuses are driven by supremacist impulses, I limit my inquiry to identifying the thread of supremacy in determinant Enlightenment thought that might have had a role in the human rights abuses that took place since. As a brief example demonstrating the supremacy of Enlightenment thought itself, any high school graduate from a Muslim-majority country has learned more about Enlightenment thinkers than about Islamic thinkers. That level of systemic privilege, which Enlightenment thought and thinkers enjoy, is the direct result of systems design.
2. I should note that the practice of essentialism, as I understand and apply it in this work, is not inherently limited to Western thinkers. During the peak of the Islamic civilization, Muslim thinkers essentialized other cultures and "geographized" peoples' abilities and capacities. Supremacy is, in many cases, tied to cultural success in hoarding wealth and resources.
3. For more on labels used to identify Muslims, see: Ahmed Souaiaia, "What Is the Difference between 'Muslim' and 'Islamic'?" *Islamic Societies Review* (November 6, 2016). Islamic Societies Review, Available at SSRN: https://ssrn.com/abstract=3013643
4. Roy Porter, "What Was the Enlightenment?" in *The Enlightenment (Studies in European History)*, (London: Palgrave, 1990); Giorgio Tonelli, "The 'Weakness' of Reason in the Age of Enlightenment," *Diderot Studies* 14 (1971): 217–44; Axel Honneth, "Enlightenment and Rationality," *The Journal of Philosophy* 84, no. 11 (1987): 692; and Wei-Ming, *Beyond the Enlightenment*, 19.

5. Monty Agarwal, *Enslavement, Persisting through Our Political Economy* (Newcastle, UK: Cambridge Scholars Publishing, 2018), 209.
6. David Hume, *The Philosophical Works of David Hume* (United Kingdom, n.p, 1826), 3:259.
7. Ibid, 3:281.
8. Naomi Zack, ed., *Oxford Handbook of Philosophy and Race* (Cambridge: Oxford University Press, 2016), 34.
9. It should be noted at this juncture that Kant was not the first to connect geography and anthropology to articulate racialized human beings. More than 500 years before his time, the Islamic collective, known as Ikhwan al-Safa (Brethren of Purity), writing on sciences, philosophy, arts, economics, and politics, also linked geography and culture to people's emotional, temperamental, and reasoning abilities. I will address the legacy of supremacy in Islamic thought in a separate section in this work.
10. Earl W. Count, *This Is Race: An Anthology Selected from the International Literature on the Races of Man* (New York: Schuman, 1950), 704..
11. Some philosophers defend Kant's racist views by arguing that he may have changed his mind later. See Pauline Kleingeld, "Second Thoughts on Race," *The Philosophical Quarterly* 57, no. 229 (2007): 573–92.
12. Immanuel Kant, *On Blackness Without Blacks: Essays on the Image of the Black in Germany*, trans. Sander L. Gilman (Boston, MA.: G.K. Hall, 1982), 87.
13. Kant might be referring to a note attached to David Hume's essay, "Of National Characters," in 1753 in which he stated that

> There never was a civilized nation of any other complexion than white, nor even any individual eminent either in action or speculation... On the other hand, the most rude and barbarous of whites, such as the ancient GERMAN the present TARTARS have still something eminent about them, in valour, form of government, or some other particular. See Zack, *Philosophy and Race*, 31

14. Zack, *Philosophy and Race*, 31.
15. Immanuel Kant, *Observations on the Feeling of the Beautiful and Sublime* (Berkeley: University of California Press, 1960), 109–11.
16. Kant, *Beautiful and Sublime*, 110.
17. Daniel Carey and Lynn Festa, *The Postcolonial Enlightenment: Eighteenth-Century Colonialism and Postcolonial Theory* (Oxford: OUP Oxford, 2009).
18. Kant, *Beautiful and Sublime*, 109.
19. Ibid, 111.
20. For more on race in Kant's reasoning, see Emmanuel Chukwudi Eze, *Postcolonial African Philosophy: A. Critical Reader* (Oxford: Blackwell Publishers Ltd, 1997), 103–31.
21. George Ciccariello-Maher, *Decolonizing Dialectics* (Durham: Duke University Press, 2017).
22. G. W. F. Hegel, *The Philosophy of History* (New York: Dover, 1956), 97–98.
23. Adapted from Hegel's *Philosophie des Geistes*, in Kant, *Blackness*, 94.
24. Kant, *On Blackness Without Blacks: Essays on the Image of the Black in Germany* (Boston, MA: G.K. Hall, 1982), 98.
25. Kant, *On Blackness*, 97–98.
26. Some contend that Kant "changed these views after the mid-1790s." Others tried to reconcile Enlightenment thinkers' contradictory views (condemnation of slavery and colonialism and views degrading non-white peoples) because of theoretical necessities. See Zack, *Philosophy and Race*, 46–47.

27. Bernard R. Boxill, *Race and Racism in Modern Philosophy*, ed. Andrew Valls (Ithaca, NY: Cornell University Press, 2005), 173.
28. Boxill, *Race and Racism*, 174.
29. Jean-Jacques Rousseau, *A Discourse on Political Economy* (1758)
30. Ibid.
31. Ibid, part II.
32. Arthur Schopenhauer, *The World as Will and Representation* (Indian Hills, CO: The Falcon's Wing Press, 1958), 350.
33. Ibid, 358.
34. Edward W. Blyden, *Christianity, Islam and the Negro Race* (London: W.B. Whittingham & Co., 1888), 19.
35. Charles W. Mills, "Black Radical Kantianism," *Res Philosophica* 95, no. 1 (2018): 1–33; 3.
36. Ibid, 1.
37. Seattle and San Francisco, two cities that benefited from technology boom and home to some companies worth more than a trillion dollars, have the largest homeless communities.
38. Charles W. Mills, *The Racial Contract* (Ithaca: Cornell University Press, 1997), 7.
39. Pauline Kleingeld, "Kant's Second Thoughts on Colonialism," in *Kant and Colonialism: Historical and Critical Perspectives*, eds. Katrin Flikschuh and Lea Ypi (New York: Oxford University Press. 2014), and Sankar Muthu, *Enlightenment against Empire* (Princeton, NJ: Princeton University Press, 2003).

5 Islam, supremacy, sectarianism, and human rights

Talbott draws from the legacy of Western European Enlightenment thought, institutions, and events to support his proposal for universal human rights. While the same Western European Enlightenment thought, institutions, and events inform Sachedina, he nonetheless draws on Islamic Enlightenment (post-*Jahiliyya*) thought, institutions, and events to integrate the human rights articulated in the Universal Declaration of Human Rights into modern Islamic thought. Notwithstanding the vastness of Western Enlightenment tradition, my survey of the works of some of the most influential Enlightenment thinkers highlights their connectedness to human rights abuses and the culture of racism. I now turn to classical Islamic thought, or post-*Jahiliyya* era as Muslim historians would call it, to explore the ethical and moral values enshrined in Islamic tradition, and their connection to a legacy of supremacy-driven atrocities, which modern standards would categorize as human rights abuses.

Although the Arabic words "rights" and "human rights" have appeared in classical Islamic texts, the deliberate coinage and function of these words do not support a concept of human rights that can be readily translated into the modern institution of human rights. That said, Muslim thinkers, religious authorities, and political leaders have created and honoured institutions and traditions that provide some protections to life, liberty, and property.

While Enlightenment thinkers are often credited for developing modern human rights discourse, they did not envision a list of inviolable human rights that extend to all human beings. Indeed, the third article of the UDHR states that "everyone has the right to life, liberty and security of person," which is an adaptation of language from the Enlightenment era that asserted "men's inalienable right to life, liberty, and property."[1] The word "men," often interpreted to include women, is unlikely to have been inclusive in the minds of men who uttered them like John Locke, Rousseau, or the drafters of the Declaration of Independence of the United States. These thinkers would want to explicitly reaffirm *men's* right to life, liberty, and property, considering that their land had been ruled by absolute monarchs who, provoked by whim and impulse, could deprive a person of life, freedom, and property. Do those same conditions apply to the culture and geography where Islam was born?

Islam originated in the city of Mecca in the Arabian Peninsula in the first half of the sixth century CE. The city of Mecca, at that time, was a trading outpost, linking Africa, Europe, and Asia. As such, Mecca became a city-State, governed by a tribal council that selected a chief from leaders of its clans, oftentimes the leader of the strongest clan. The economy of Mecca depended on trade and animal herding: Mainly camels, sheep, and goats. Mecca's economy was a market economy involving local and global trade. Residents of Mecca and members of Bedouin clans that lived a travelling distance from Mecca generally traded goods for goods. Caravan owners who transported goods across continents used gold and silver coins, currencies named Dinar and Dirham, to carry out transactions with far communities. Archaeological finds, poetry, and the Quran provide evidence that the inhabitants of Mecca used money and goods for trade. The market form of economy decided the kind of society Mecca could be.

Unlike the people of Madina, a city north of Mecca by nearly 300 miles, the people of Mecca were less attached to their land and more attached to their gold, silver, and camels. A Meccan's material wealth comprised the number of camels they owned and the count of dinars and dirhams to their name. The type of economy in Mecca before Islam, being less dependent on labor and more dependent on exchange (and therefore trust), created specific social values and social relations. The people of Mecca placed a premium on values such as trust, loyalty, honour, and generosity—the kind of traits that emphasize family over the larger community. However, security concerns, mainly the protection of property like caravans and animals compelled clans to enter into treaties with others for mutual security. Quraysh, the umbrella tribal organization that governed Mecca before the rise of Islam, was a coalition of more than twenty clans.[2]

Given their dependence on intercontinental trade, Meccans needed to secure their own caravans as well as their economic interests. To realize both ends, they tolerated and even preserved what might appear as conflicting goals: Transit security, and plunder. People near Mecca made a living through violent raids on distant tribes and caravans. This practice was tolerated, apparently, because it kept traders from distant lands from engaging in cross-continental trade, motivating foreign traders instead to rely on locals to secure trade routes. However, when these raiders attacked clans from their own tribe, that is members of Quraysh, or from a tribe with which Quraysh had a pact, the punishment was severe.[3] These practices created a culture that tolerated and even glorified violence, forging additional social and economic dynamics.

The prevalence of violent confrontations for economic purposes commodified all that was captured during these battles and raids. That included captured people. Under these circumstances, captured fighters of defeated armies and their family members became slaves whom the victorious army owned and distributed as property among fighters or the families of fighters who died in battle. Most enslaved persons were prisoners of war, the captured family members of defeated armies. In addition to a large number of enslaved Arabs, and according to various historical records, we find references to slaves who are listed as Abyssinian (*habashi*; east African), Persian, Copt, Nubian, and Byzantine.[4] Historical sources reveal that the majority of enslaved persons before Islam were Arabs; African slaves constituted about one-third of listed totals. This ethnic or racial composition changed with the establishment of Islam as a State religion and with Muslims establishing their Islamic nation-state and governing institutions.

One of the supportable explanations for the majority of slaves being Arab in pre-*Hijra* times is that the effects of intertribal warfare often resulted in captives being enslaved and their tribe failing to pay ransom to free them. As we can gather from the details of the second war involving Muslims, the Battle of Uhud, fought between the Muslims of Madina and the pagans of Quraysh, it was customary to bring along women and children to the battlefield, apparently to give extra motivation to fighters to win the battle. However, that also meant that when a side lost the battle, their family members, including women and children, would be taken by the victor. Captured women were given to men who took part in the battle. These men either married them or they kept them as concubines. This practice resulted in graded relationships based on a woman's status: A marriage could be one among equals (a free man marrying a free woman), a marriage among non-equals (one free man marrying one—or more than one—captive woman), and concubinage.[5] It was customary to keep captured children with their mothers; a child's status was usually attached to that of its mother. If a captured woman became enslaved, so would her child; but if she was freed, or taken in marriage as free woman, her child would be freed, too.

The establishment of the Islamic state in Madina, and the adoption of Islamic tradition as preached and practiced by the first leader of the community, the Prophet Muhammad, changed some aspects of these practices but did not abolish all of the pre-existing worldview and practices. Among the changes that took place upon the Prophet Muhammad's migration to and settlement in Madina was the new social division he created. He wanted to abolish clan identity and adopt brotherhood among his community.

With Madina still socially diverse, including members of the Jewish community who were not forced to convert to Islam, the Prophet Muhammad created a new default distinction between believers and nonbelievers. The new distinction meant that the believers (who, with the advance of time, would be called Muslims) could not be enslaved, but captives acquired through war were still considered spoils of war, or *ghana'im*. They were distributed among those eligible; but could also be traded in order to free Muslim prisoners held by enemy armies, held and then freed for ransom, or freed when the captive bought their own freedom by performing a specialty service such as teaching illiterate Muslims to read and write. Failing that, they could remain slaves indefinitely.[6]

Violence in pre-Islamic Arabia was not just a result of an indigenous culture and its value systems. It was also an adaptation—the direct result of its environment and circumstances, or what we would now call its geopolitical consideration.

Nowadays, the Middle East is home to violent conflicts and most, if not all, of these conflicts are driven by geopolitical considerations involving parties thousands of miles away. These global actors wish to secure something very valuable to almost everyone's national interest: Energy in the form of oil. Most of these wars are proxy wars fought for access to that oil. The same can be said about Mecca and Arabia in the sixth century.

The Arabian Peninsula, in the century before Islam and during the first half of the seventh century, was a place of dispute over trade routes involving three empires: Persia in the northeast, Byzantium in the northwest, and Abyssinia in the south. Each of those world powers was vying to secure trade routes for their own interests, directly or through proxies. To this end, Abyssinian forces controlled south Arabia, Yemen, and Hadramawt. In 523 CE, for instance, the Negus, the Christian King of Abyssinia, sent 60,000 troops to overthrow King Dhu Nuwas. In 570 CE, the year Muhammad was born, Abraha led a destructive expedition against Mecca; this event, called the Year of the Elephant (*ʿām al-fīl*), was later mentioned in the Quran. When the Persians pushed the Abyssinians back from southern Arabia, and defeated the Abyssinians in 575 CE, they captured and enslaved many of the African fighters, increasing the number of enslaved Black persons in Arabia to about one-third. The clash of empires around Mecca, the alliances Arab tribes made with the Persians, Byzantines, and Abyssinians, and their participation in wars involving these ethnic groups is likely the source of slaves of Persian, Byzantine, and Coptic origins in Mecca immediately before the rise of Islam. Therefore, many of the Black and white slaves in Arabia, referenced in the Arabic sources, were likely enslaved during military conflicts in the second half of the sixth century. Prior to the rise of Islam, enslaved Abssinians in Mecca were primarily a consequence of war, not part of an international slave trade as would be the case in later centuries.

Before we transition to the Islamic era, or to post-*Jahiliyya* era as Muslim historians would call it, I should note another aspect of the social and economic structure of Mecca in the sixth century that is relevant to the topic of human rights.

Since Mecca was primarily a trade city-State, inequality must have been a defining feature of society. To establish a trading caravan, one must have the capital to invest in the resources and connections needed to build a successful trading business. Consequently, the Arabs before Islam must have had some commitment to personal property, life and freedom to enjoy the property they worked to acquire. They must have established and protected customs, laws, and institutions that enshrined and promoted the right to own property and to freely enjoy it. The flipside of that is that the concentration of wealth must have created more need, resulting in the spread of inequity, poverty, exploitation, classism, and elitism. Importantly, concentration of wealth necessarily leads to concentration of power, which creates power differentials among social groups. Indeed, Quraysh did not have princes and princesses, but it had powerful leaders and shrewd businessmen, as narratives chronicling the birth and rise of Islam will reveal. Sources from pre-Islamic and early Islamic times confirm these conditions, circumstances, and realities.

The most important comparison to make between European societies before and after the Enlightenment and Arab society before and during early Islamic times is their sources of wealth and power. In the sixteenth and seventeenth centuries, Europe began to shift its economy towards land and capital instead of the agriculture, due to the population decline after famines and plagues. The land ownership-based economy that produced grain and cereals was labor-intensive. In the following centuries, the industrial revolution was also labor intensive. These economic trends created unique dynamics and a special relationship to land, the most enduring and transferrable form of wealth. Landowners' need for labor created rigid social hierarchies and power gradations in societies.

In contrast, in Arabia in the sixth and seventh centuries, the economy was built on animals and trade. The land, especially since it was mostly desert and not suitable for cultivating grains like wheat and barley, was freely used for grazing. Animal husbandry, consisting of raising camels, goats, and sheep, was more important than agriculture. While sheep and goats provided meat and clothing for the family, camels primarily provided transportation and trade. The same way Europeans were attached to their land and estates, Arabs were deeply attached to their camels, about whom poets composed some of the most moving poems. These economic activities were not labor-intensive and were easily managed by family members. For that reason, families often consisted of one man having multiple sexual relationships—formally, through marriage and informally, through concubinage—producing many children who would help herd sheep or trade goods.

In the rest of this chapter, I will tell the story of Islam and the men and women who spread it to create the culture that embraced it; a global civilization that, in a short time, challenged three major empires, and for the first time in recorded history, brought all of the Arabian Peninsula under the rule of one man: Muhammad. I will provide details useful in gaining proper context and background information necessary to explain significant historical events and institutional developments during his lifetime and after his death that make human rights norms possible or impossible to adopt in Islamic societies.

****

Born sometime in the second half of the sixth century, Muhammad came from humble origins. His clan, Banu Hashim, was neither affluent nor influential. From the day he was born and through his young adulthood, he faced adversity and personal loss. His father, Abdullah, died before he was born. Within his first decade of life, his mother, Amina, died, leaving him in the care of his paternal grandfather, Abd al-Muttalib, who also died when he turned eight. His paternal uncle and the new leader of Bani Hashim, Abu Talib, took him in, and he was raised in the same household as his cousin (and later son-in-law) Ali. When Muhammad was a baby, he was sent to the countryside to live with a female relative who would breast-feed him (*Badiya*), a practice that appears to have been customary for children born in the city. Consequently, his first occupation as a child was as a shepherd. In his late teens, he joined trade caravans connecting Mecca to the Levant region, *Sham*. His honest management of goods and money for the traders who employed him earned him the moniker *al-Amin*—the Trustworthy one—which caught the attention of a thrice-widowed, wealthy woman named Khadija. She hired him in his early twenties to manage her trade business. Soon after, Khadija—at this point in her forties—asked him to marry her; he did. Once married, he continued to manage her trading business for another 15 years or so. From this marriage he had all his children, three sons and four daughters; the sons died as infants, but the girls grew up and later married influential members of the community. His daughter Fatima became a central figure in Islamic history, given her place as the mother of the Imams of Shia Muslims.

Muhammad's ordinary early life did not predict the extraordinary role he would play in human history. However, many of his social and political positions would, in two decades, transform the Peninsula and the lives of billions of people thereafter. Those accomplishments started when he was in his forties, and when he claimed that he was a chosen Messenger, sent by God to all of humanity. But despite such an extraordinary claim, Islamic history did not really start until Muhammad turned fifty and migrated from Mecca to Madina.

Muhammad's claim to divine connections began when he lived in Mecca. At the age of 40, following one of his usual reflective experiences, isolating himself in a cave on a mountaintop overlooking Mecca, he returned home frightened and shaken. He told Khadija about an encounter with a strange being who spoke words to him and ordered him to recite them. It took weeks before he articulated his role and function as the chosen messenger—*Rasul*. These encounters, where new words were taught to him (revealed, according to Muslim scholars), would occur again and again until his death. Muslims believe that through these encounters Muhammad received divine revelations, words, and fragments of recited speech. He taught these words to his followers as the words of God, called the Quran, the Recited Word. After his death, Muslim scholars recorded all of his sayings and deeds, claiming that they too were a form of divine inspiration, just of a lower degree of authority compared to the Quran. Together, the words of the Quran as recited by Muhammad and the narratives associated with his life, became the two primary sources of Islamic teachings and practices that Muslims have adhered to ever since. I will discuss the technical aspects of these texts and narratives later in this chapter.

For ten years, Muhammad, now addressed by his followers as the Messenger, Prophet Muhammad (*Rasul Allah*), or both, preached in Mecca. There he recited the verses of the Quran and interpreted them to nudge Meccans to change their ways, mainly on moral, ethical, and theological matters. He preached that there was no god but the one God, and that he, Muhammad, was a Messenger from *the* God, Allah. He counselled people to honour and be kind to their parents, to respect the poor and destitute, and to spend their hoarded gold and silver to help the poor and needy. After nearly ten years of preaching this message, only an estimated 300 people joined his movement, and most of them were former slaves, laborers, women, and transient travellers. Only five followers were among the tribal elite, including two key figures, Abu Bakr and `Umar. Nonetheless, Muhammad's persistence grew as a threat to Quraysh, the governing authority in the city-state, pushing the leaders to issue a sweeping boycott against him and his followers: No one was allowed to engage in any transaction with Muhammad or his followers, and whoever violated the sanctions would be subjected to the same boycott. Meanwhile the Prophet Muhammad was already in negotiations with leaders from a city called Yathrib, some 300 miles north of Mecca. Yathrib's leaders, interested in the Prophet's skills as a political leader and resolver of disputes, offered him a leadership position in their city. He insisted that he be recognized as a religious leader, a Messenger of God, before accepting their offer. After some negotiation, the leaders of Yathrib agreed to his terms, and on July 16, 622 CE, the Prophet Muhammad and Abu Bakr reached the city of Yathrib, which changed its name to become *al-madina al-munawwara*—the City of the Messenger of God—later shortened to simply Madina: The City.

Upon his arrival in Madina, the Prophet Muhammad established the first mosque, where Muslims would perform their mandatory daily prayers; attached to it was a room for his private residence. He also dictated the terms of a treaty for governing the city-state. Interestingly, while the first institution, *masjid* (mosque) is a place of worship, the second institution—the treaty of Madina—is recognized as a purely secular, civil document. The document laid out guidelines for living in a pluralistic city-state where non-Muslims, including Jews, could live according to their own traditions, but would honour the terms of the larger community by not aiding or conspiring with outsiders. This kind of pragmatism reflected the skills and abilities that enabled the Prophet to bring all of the Arabian Peninsula under his rule in under 12 years. Before his death, he bequeathed to his successors a stable and prosperous community whose frontiers abutted present-day Iran, Iraq, Byzantium, Jordan, Egypt, Abyssinia, and across the Red Sea.

In addition to this vast territory, he also left key institutions and practices that guided his successors to expand their reach.

By the time the Prophet Muhammad died, the Quran had become a source of knowledge, inspiration, and social control. People read it, memorized it, and lived by it. In it, people found ethical and moral guidance as well as legal commands and obligations. Muslims of that time, just like Muslims today, considered the Quran's explicit teachings as obligations. Where the Quran is implicit, vague, or silent, Muslims referred to the example of the Prophet Muhammad, which, with time, gained the technical name Sunna, or Hadith. In fact, `Umar invoked the Sunna, though not by name, to exclude the people of Madina from seeking the position of caliph; this position, according to `Umar, was an exclusive right of the people of Quraysh. That first instance of invoking the Sunna/Hadith became a powerful precedent, which allowed Muslim leaders and Muslim scholars ever since to draw on the anecdotes of the thoughts and deeds of the Prophet Muhammad, or his key disciples, to support a legal opinion, an ethical norm, or a political decision. In short, `Umar's action established the Sunna as Islamic canon law.

Hours after his death of natural causes, during a private meeting in the home of a leader of Madina (*Ansar*), a leadership circle endorsed Abu Bakr to be Muhammad's successor as a political leader, not as the Prophet. This event set the groundwork for the governing institutions and practices that would inform Islamic political theory and practices for hundreds of years. Generally, Islamic political history can be segmented into four eras, each born out of a violent transformation that tested the community's fidelity to the values enshrined in its religious traditions.

What Muslim historians named the Rashid Caliphate spanned from after the Prophet Muhammad's death through the death of the fourth caliph, Ali, in 661 CE. During this period, Muslim leaders struggled to resolve political, social, and economic problems including cronyism, nepotism, mismanagement of public funds, and social and economic inequity. These challenges resulted in one armed rebellion, which the widow of the Prophet Muhammad, Aisha, led; and a brutal, protracted civil war—the first of others to follow—that cost thousands of lives including that of the third caliph, `Uthman. `Uthman was killed by rebels who accused him of violating the Quranic principles of justice (`*adala*). The crises of this era revealed Muslim leaders' failure to deal with political dissent.[7] Because of this failure, marginalized and disempowered social groups rebelled. The government failed to repair the damage, which resulted in the first split along sectarian lines and gave birth to Ibadism, the first social movement that has continuously existed since the seventh century.

During this era, the location, procedure, and level of community participation in deliberating over and choosing their political leaders created a culture of exclusion and elitism that marginalized many social groups simply because of their ethnic and economic statuses.

First, because the first meeting for debating the succession took place in a private home, *Saqifat bani Sa`ida*, the majority of the residents of Madina were excluded, especially women and men outside of the elite. Consequently, no woman has ever formally held the central caliphate position in the history of Islamic civilization. The only exceptions of women rising to political rule happened in distant autonomous regions such as the Fatimid dynasty in Egypt and autonomous Berber regions in North Africa.

Second, when `Umar relayed that the Prophet said his successor should be a member of Quraysh, he set a precedent: Everyone not Arab *and* a member of Quraysh was disqualified for the important political leadership position of caliphate. Predictably, all Umayyad and Abbasid caliphs were Arabs and descendants of the tribe of Quraysh, although some Abbasid caliphs might have been only half-Arabs, since some were born to caliphs from non-Arab mothers including Berber, Persian, and Byzantine women.[8] As caliph, `Umar took additional actions that strengthened Arab supremacy, although his intent may have been otherwise. For instance, under `Umar's rule, Arab armies that conquered distant territories were not allowed to buy homes or live in those distant cities. He did not want victorious Arabs to take the homes, properties, and places of worship of the people they defeated. Instead, he ordered those wanting to stay to build garrison towns and outposts outside of established cities, so that they would not encroach on the lives of the locals. Many of these garrison towns became later major urban centres, including *al-Fusṭāṭ* (*al-Fostat*) in Egypt, founded in 641 CE.

Third, due to this precedent, the process of transitioning political leadership became privatized, decided by the reigning caliph before his death through will and bequest, or by a ruling from a select group of advisors often called the People Who Bind and Unbind (*Ahl al-hall wa-'l-`aqd*) or the Consultative Council (*Majlis al-shura*). This group of individuals, generally men from the elite class, would privately nominate and endorse (*Bay`a khassa*) a person. Only after private endorsement would the nominee stand for a general public referendum (*Bay`a `amma*). In fact, even this limited process became obsolete when the caliphate became a heredity right at the start of the Umayyad rule through the Ottoman Sultans. Arguably, the precedent the first two caliphs established during this period was what authorized Umayyad and Abbasid rulers to appoint their successors—if it was good for the righteously guided caliphs, the rules reasoned, it must be good for them.

The Rashid Caliphate era is the only era during which three different caliphs, from four different clans and unrelated by blood, governed and were succeeded by someone unrelated to them. During all other governing eras (the Umayyad, Abbasid, and Ottoman eras), leadership passed from one person to another within the same family (father-son, father-brother, or brother-brother) or within the same clan. In other words, the caliphate was privatized. Therefore, all Muslims have been denied the right to aspire to political leadership as caliph for the history of the pan-Islamic caliphate. One must belong to a specific clan or ethnic group to have that right.

The transition from the Rashid Caliphate to the Umayyad Caliphate took place in the heat of battle and in the context of civil war. Members of the Umayyad clan used calls for revenge for `Uthman's death—at the hands of rebels from as far away as Yemen and Iraq—to challenge Ali, a Hashimite. The resulting tragic and costly war ended when the Caliph, `Ali, was killed; his son, Hassan, succeeded him but within months offered to settle with his rival Mu`awiyya, the governor of the Levant, in return for peace and security. Mu`awiyya, the son of the last chief of Quraysh and ruler of Mecca before it was taken by the Muslims of Madina, Abu Sufyan, accepted, founding the Umayyad dynastic rule.

From 661 CE to 750 CE, most lands controlled by Muslims fell under control of the Umayyad clan, the leading force within the tribe of Quraysh before Muslims took control of Mecca. Except for one ruler, Umayyad caliphs were not religious and did not care to appear religious or pious. In fact, Mu`awiyya's descendants made a habit of offending religious leaders and religious institutions. According to some reports, one used a copy of the Quran as a shooting target and another paraded through the streets of Damascus after soaking his head with wine.[9] The Umayyad rulers' characters, temperaments, and practices transformed the community, institutions, and society in profound ways.

First, the rulers' lack of religious piety, and their appreciation for knowledge, created a path for independent scholars to fill a void that the caliph traditionally occupied. For the first time, without the Prophet or a caliph spearheading political and religious decrees, Muslims had to obey two separate powers: Political rulers and religious learned men. In a way, these circumstances secularized Muslim society by separating religious and political authorities. During the lifetime of the Prophet Muhammad, Muslims followed him because he told them that God, the Legislator, revealed the proper law to him. The Prophet Muhammad was the judge and executive. During the reign of the Rashid Caliphs, the rulers relied on their recollection of the precedent set by the Prophet, the Sunna, to interpret and apply God's rule (*hukm*) in society. Under the Umayyads, the `Ulama—the learned ones (*ahl al-`ilm*)—interpreted the Quran and the Sunna for the people. The caliph adopted the `Ulama's recommendations. However, caliphs appointed a learned person to a position in the bureaucracy. These palace scholars, as some circles knew them, had to compete against independent `Ulama for their standing. Independent scholars, generally, stood out for their piety and, importantly, for their willingness to rise up or endorse uprisings against unjust caliphs and governors.[10] The divestment of religious authority is the most significant development during this era because it produced an independent institution, the `Ulama', that future political leaders were never able to fully bring back under their direct control. While rulers have had their own scholars and judges as part of their bureaucracy, independent scholars continued to exist, and people often trusted them with religious matters over scholars associated with the caliph.[11]

To replace their lost religious authority, the Umayyads emphasized the bonds that connected clans and ethnic identities to secure loyalty and patronage. Members of the Umayyad clan held key positions within bureaucratic and military leadership. Being Arab earned favorable treatment. This strategy stratified society and created new paths for discrimination. Such social engineering practices designated specific social groups as enemies, disloyal subjects, foreigners, or other social labels that bore economic and social consequences.

Such a government is neither just nor inclusive. People often voiced their disapproval, but the government dealt harshly with public dissent. Indeed, immediately after the death of the founder of the Umayyad dynasty and the rise of his son, Yazid I, to power, a second brutal civil war broke out, which Muslim historians called *al-Fitna al-thaniya* (the second strife), lasting from 780 to 992 CE. Unable to secure uncoerced endorsement from all clan leaders, Yazid sent his security forces to bring them to his palace and required them to publically pledge an oath of allegiance. The grandson of the Prophet Muhammad, Hussain, refused to endorse Yazid, judging him unjust and therefore illegitimate. He opted to leave for Iraq with about seventy members of his family and supporters. Upon hearing of their travels, however, Yazid sent an army to retrieve Hussain dead or alive. This confrontation resulted in what modern standards would qualify as genocide. Yazid's order essentially authorized the destruction of a specific social group—the household of Ali's last living son—and the only living grandson of the Prophet Muhammad.

It is impossible to overstate the significance of this event given its implications, execution, and consequences. First, if the head of a government was willing and able to kill and desecrate[12] the grandson of the civilization's founder, what would prevent him from killing other, less significant, dissenters? Second, for a government to allocate that many resources—five thousand troops—to besiege a travelling crowd of merely 70 people including men, women and children, signals the intent to commit a war crime. These two points help explain the third point related to the consequences of this event: Yazid's intent to inflict cruel acts the way it happened was so traumatizing that it caused the community to convulse and fragment. This event splintered the community and gave birth to the Shia community, who would remember and commemorate the event every year since, sacralising the first ten days of the month of Muharram, reliving the siege and martyrdom of a person who refused to endorse a tyrant.[13] This moment of violence and strife, like the one during the first *firtna* that resulted in the death of the third caliph, `Uthman, created a second sect in Islam, which has endured ever since. In the context of this work on human rights, while these events signify a religious rite for specific social groups, for the general public they memorialize an instance of human rights abuses at the hands of a government. In ordinary history-making, it might be called a *fitna* (strife) or even romanticized it as a civil war. However, in the context of human rights and humanitarian laws, it must be recognized for what it was: A human rights crime and an act of cruelty that no provocation could justify. Because this event, the tragedy of Karbala, is relived and commemorated yearly across the Islamic world, Muslim thinkers must address it and reflect on it not only in sectarian terms, but also in human rights terms.

Although twelve other Umayyad rulers reigned for over sixty-five years since this event, Muslims could not forget the cruelty inflicted in Karbala. Indeed, half a century after the Karbala massacre, another genocide took place within the Muslim community, but it cannot be explained without returning to and referencing Karbala.

The Umayyad dynasty came to an end when members of the Hashimite clan started an underground opposition movement that swore to remediate the grievances of *Ahl al-Bayt*. Once the Umayyad caliph, Marwan II, learned of the movement, he struck as his predecessors had. Marwan II ordered the capture and cruel killing of the leader of the Abbasid clan, Ibrahim. That action only amplified the anger against the Umayyads, and increased empathy and support for the Hashimite clan. In 750 CE, the younger brother of Ibrahim, Abu Abbas, seized the moment and confronted the Umayyad Caliph militarily in a battle near the Zab. Defeated, Marwan retreated to Egypt to rebuild his army, Abu Abbas was declared caliph in Kufa and assumed his functions quickly, mobilizing his troops and rushing them to Central Asia to halt an intrusion of the Chinese Tang Dynasty. After he defeated the Chinese in the battle of Talas in 751 CE, he turned his attention to exact his vengeance on the Umayyads, ordering all Umayyad males killed. Essentially, Abu Abbas ordered and executed the second genocide in Islam, killing all male persons belonging to the Umayyad clan, except for a young boy named Abd al-Rahman, who escaped via North Africa and settled in Spain. Abu Abbas crushed any serious threat with an exacting cruelty, earning himself the title of al-Saffah, the Blood Spiller. Thirty-six other descendants of al-Abbas went on to rule over most Islamic lands, save the autonomous regions in the peripheries, each one of them taking over the reign of government not because they were the most qualified or as the result of a public mandate, but simply because of who they were in relation to the caliph who preceded them. Success and failure, peace and war, and poverty and prosperity were determined by a caliph's whim, temperament, and character, not by an enduring bureaucracy.

For 508 years, Muslims ruled over most of West Asia and North Africa through the institution of the caliphate, over which a man connected to the Hashimite clan presided. In contrast, the Abbasids ruled over an era of prosperity, security, and progress; however, this progress, security, and prosperity came at a significant human and environmental cost. During the Abbasid rule, while progress occurred in the arts, literature, sciences, and technology, many people became disconnected, exploited,

Islam, supremacy and human rights 97

and commodified. Thievery became a way of life, out of contempt for the rich and in sympathy with the poor.[14] Rebellion, like the Revolution of Blacks (*Thawrat al-zanj*) was common due to exploitation and inequity,[15] as was armed rebellion that championed the cause of farmers exploited by landowners.[16] The caliph established financial institutions and guaranteed financial instruments like banknotes and currencies, allowing wealthy Muslims to travel the world for trade and pleasure. In short, during the Abbasid rule, Muslims became the engine of a civilization stretching from Mauritania to Mongolia. With success, however, comes failure and abuse. By the middle of the thirteenth century, the Abbasid caliphate was overcome with the effects of its own laxity and glut, and was overrun by the Mongols. In the span of about ten years, power gradually jumped from the Hashimite clan into the hands of non-Arabs for the first time. People of Turkic descent rose to power, moving up the ranks of a powerful military and eventually moving the seat of the caliphate to Anatolia, signalling the rise of the Ottoman Empire, also called the Ottoman Sultanate.

The Ottoman Empire was, in a way, an inevitable outcome of a civilization that amassed too much wealth and ignored the needs of too many of its subjects. Like any empire, the Ottoman Sultanate focused on building military and administrative institutions that allowed it expansion and control. Coercion became the mode of control rather than persuasion or collaboration. Indigenous communities were forced to assimilate and change how they lived. Previously, caliphs had often appointed locals who converted to Islam to rule over their communities. The Ottomans, on the other hand, preferred to dispatch a Turkish Bey or Dey to govern over indigenous communities. Abuse of power, previously familiar to Muslims of different sects within Islamic societies, became the experience of other faiths. The Armenian genocide is just one example of an outcome of empire rule. All the abuses and the emphasis on military power only increased resentment and lack of faith in a government too distant to connect with local peoples. By the eighteenth century, many Muslims favored European colonial powers over Ottoman rule, leading to the latter's disintegration and shrinking, and opening the door for colonial powers to fill the vacuum and start their own expansion and occupation of Muslim-majority regions.

In this work, a common thread that I would like to make obvious is this: Human rights abuses are crimes the government commits against specific social groups. This does not mean that crimes social groups commit against one another are not human rights crimes. However, even those crimes should be seen as government crimes, since governments allow such crimes to happen or do not bring those responsible to justice. Therefore, all governments are guilty of human rights crimes. Importantly, another government or an international organization would not need to characterize these actions as human rights offenses. Often the abuse is a violation of the laws and policies the government itself recognizes and uses to legitimize itself. For example, when some Muslims rebelled during the rule of the third caliph 'Uthman, these people believed that the caliph's actions were abusive based on the teaching of the Quran, to which 'Uthman had sworn to adhere. When Hussain and others refused to endorse Yazid's rule, they invoked the same principles, values, and rules within Islamic traditions and institutions that judged him to be abusive. Every other instance of dissent and rebellion within Islamic societies throughout the history of Islamic civilization points to the government's abuse of power based on the standards that it swore to uphold. With these facts in mind, it is essential that we understand the nature and functions of the Islamic caliphate and the governing institutions and practices that render it legitimate.

Many modern thinkers, both Muslim and non-Muslim, argue that Islam's problem is with its inability to become secular. They often argue that the interconnectedness of Islamic religious and political discourses makes any Islamic government a form of theocracy and, as such, incompatible with human rights norms. This view is false when we look at the data. The caliphate is different from the modern State in that the caliph is the sovereign but not the institution. It follows, then, that the majority of Islamic governments were more secular than theocratic. Time wise, Muslims have lived under secular governments for far longer than they lived under the rule of a government that one could call a theocracy. This is true even using a very loose definition of theocracy, which normally refers to a system of government where a religious authority such as an *imam* rules in the name of God. In the pan-Islamic caliphate, Sunnism was the official sect to which rulers ostensibly adhered. In Sunnism, there is no infallible religious person who acts as an intermediary between God and the people. Learned persons would qualify as religious scholars, all of whom are equal. The only event that could elevate the status of one scholar (or school of thought) over another is the government adopting it as official. Islamic dynasties and caliphs often did so: Most Ottoman Sultans embraced Hanafism as the official school of jurisprudence, the Islamic Emirate in Spain adopted Malikism at one time and Zahirism at another as official schools of jurisprudence, and most recently, Saudi Arabia adopted Salafism as interpreted by Wahhabists as the privileged school of jurisprudence and theology. Short of such action by the state, any learned person could be considered a religious authority. However, not all caliphs could be recognized as such. Even if we consider piety to be a form of religious authority, not actual knowledge, most caliphs would not qualify as pious.

With all the emphasis on just rule and righteous government, Muslims have been ruled by corrupt and cruel leaders far longer than they have been under righteous leaders. Specifically, since the death of the Prophet and until the formal disintegration of the Ottoman Empire, Muslims lived under 98 caliphs and sultans, excluding autonomous regions. Only six of these would meet the conditions of a just leader according to Muslim legal scholars. In other words, fewer than 6% of the leaders were just, which means that 94% of them have abused the human rights of one social group or another. This underscores the fact that all governments are abusers of human rights or potential abusers of human rights. A plan to universalize human rights must take into consideration these hard facts.

Time wise, the caliphate and sultanate rule covered 1292 years; no more than 55 years were under righteous rule. It would appear that righteous rule is the exception, not the norm, under the Islamic caliphate system.

Developing a human rights-cantered action plan must account for that statistic: What must be done when—not if—governments violate and abuse human rights? The answer cannot be, create a better government. It must be, create a counterbalance to government.

Considering that human rights is essentially a balance between social groups' rights and government overreach, we must consider in this section the institutions of Islam that have the most impact on human rights claims; that is, the people entitled to be caliphs, and the function of the caliph as government.

Muslim religious scholars see the caliph as an executive entrusted with applying the guidelines and rules of Sharia among Muslims to realize justice.[17] This brief definition connects all the foundational elements of the theories of governance in Islam. It identifies the caliph as an executive, not a legislator; Sharia as the source of law; and the goal of the Sharia as realizing divine justice. Muslims scholars developed a list of qualifications required for the job of caliph, some more detailed than others. Summarizing a view held by most Sunni scholars, an eleventh century Shafi`i jurist argued that a potential caliph must meet seven conditions[18] to be considered for the position:

1 Probity (`adala jami`a)
2 Knowledge (`Ilm)
3 Ability to discern (salamat al-hawass)
4 Physical abilities (Salamat al-'a`da')
5 Wisdom (al-Ra'y al-mufdi)
6 Courage (al-Shaja`a)
7 Lineage (Nasab, Quraysh)

The fourteenth century Islamic scholar Sad al-Din Mas`ud Ibn Umar Ibn Abd Allah al-Taftazani, on the other hand, adds being male (Thukura) and being free (not enslaved) as conditions for one to hold the position of caliph.[19]

The idea that the caliph, who since Umayyad times has inherited a powerful position for no other reason than his affinity to the previous caliph, is bound by the terms of another institution, Sharia, is easy to dismiss as pure fiction. It might be, since statistically the majority of the caliphs and sultans do not meet most the conditions established by the `Ulama. The dissonance between reality and theory demands to the logical question: Why is it important to invoke Sharia when it has failed to limit the transgressions of caliphs in the past, and is seen today as the primary force behind human rights abuses? We will examine the meaning and function of Sharia in modern and premodern Islamic times in order to assess Islam's compatibility with human rights norms.

What is Sharia?

The Ottoman Sultanate, which governed over most geographical regions where Muslims were a majority, was the last pan-Islamic political order. With its fall, Sharia gained new meanings and functions in Islamic societies and beyond. By the start of the twenty-first century, Sharia was invoked to contextualize cultural, geopolitical, and religious conflicts. The 2011 protest movements and wars ushered in radical changes, which made Sharia a central topic of debate wherever Muslims existed in significant numbers.

In Muslim-majority countries, where leaders debate and negotiate legal reforms, the persistent question is whether Sharia should be *the* source of law or *a* source of law. In countries where Muslims are minorities, some local and national governments have proposed laws banning the adoption of Sharia.[20] In territories and countries controlled by Islamist armed groups, Sharia courts have been established and self-styled scholars have imposed themselves as chief Sharia judges (sing. *qadi shar`i*). Social movements, violent and non-violent ones, have emerged in many Muslim-majority countries with activists demanding the "implementation of Sharia" in their communities.

These events might give the impression that Sharia is a concrete and well-defined concept, body of law, and legal system. In reality, Sharia—while anyone can invoke it—cannot be found on the bookshelves of libraries and bookstores, in digital archives, or in any other singular standardized storing mechanism. Indeed, there is no consensus, especially among Muslim religious scholars, let alone among scholars specializing in the critical study of Islam, on the meaning and functions of Sharia.[21] However, texts from Islam's formative period, especially during times of dissent and rebellion, provide a glimpse into that generation's understanding of Sharia and its functions in a society. Analyzing this evidence, through lingo-cultural, logical, and teleological lenses, helps reconstruct the social forces that built Islamic civilization.

Today, in Western societies, fear of Sharia might be explained several ways. Prejudice and bigotry drive many people to oppose any idea or action that could mainstream a cultural or religious legacy of an othered community.[22] Established dominant religious communities often work to deny competing religious expressions the opportunity to share the same space. Many people, however, take anti-Sharia and anti-Muslim positions because they do not actually know the meaning and functions of Sharia.[23] Their information about Sharia often comes from reports of harsh punishments in a far-away brutal regime, all because of Sharia.[24] Recently, with Islamist groups seizing control of vast territories and imposing cruel punishments in the name of Sharia law, they have defined Sharia as a concrete legal code of rules and punishments.[25] In all cases, these assumptions, presumptions, and actions were the primary sources of information about Sharia, since individuals cannot consult a Sharia book themselves; no standard book of Sharia exists. What *is* on the shelves of libraries and bookstores or in digital archives are *fiqh* collections, which literally means an *understanding* of Sharia. These collections are always tagged according to their scholars' specific sect (*ta`ifah*; *firqah*), or to a particular school of jurisprudence (*madhhab/mazhab*) within their sect. Theological and political disputes have produced three major historical Islamic sects: Sunnism, Ibadism, and Shi`ism. Meanwhile, purely jurisprudential disputes have produced nine schools of jurisprudence within each sect: Within Sunnism are Malikism, Hanafism, Shafi`ism, and Hanbalism; under the umbrella of Shi`ism are Ja`farism, Zaydism, and Isma`ilism; and Ibadism comes in Eastern and Western forms. Theological arguments and disputes fall in a genre called *usul al-din*, whereas legal arguments belong to the theoretical genre, *usul al-fiqh*. It is in *fiqh* collections in each school of jurisprudence where one can find the body of law.

*****

Both Muslim religious scholars and Islamicists[26] reference Sharia as if it were a concept, instrument, or institution upon whose meaning there is a universal consensus. Despite its ubiquity, Sharia remains a highly ambiguous term. That ambiguity has led to its socio-political use and abuse. In popular non-Arabic narratives, Sharia is often "translated" or explained as Sharia law, the Islamic legal system, Islamic law, religious law, God's immutable divine law, and/or a faith-based code of conduct.[27] Is Sharia any—or all—of these descriptors? And if so, why not simply use the term "Islamic law" and drop the Arabic word Sharia to avoid confusion and fear mongering? To answer this and related critical questions, it will be helpful to examine the ways both Muslim scholars and Islamicist researchers define and use the word Sharia.

Contextualizing Islam in the broader Semitic religious tradition, one could argue that the idea of a Sharia-inspired code, as derived from the Quranic text, is some version of the Ten Commandments. However, this analogy has limits. First, according to Jewish and Christian religious scholars, the Ten Commandments were written on stone tablets, intended as strict rules. Second, the Commandments are commands, appearing in two chapters of the Bible: The Book of Exodus in Chapter 20, and the Book of Deuteronomy in Chapter 5. With the Quran, however, while few of these Commandments are explicitly stated, most of them are implied throughout the Quran. The Quran refers to the tablets but does not list any commandments. If it is the explicitness of rules that determines a religious code's existence (such as Sharia), then textual evidence points more strongly to the existence of a Judeo-Christian Sharia than the existence of an Islamic Sharia.

Considered throughout Islamic history as broad principles guiding law making, Sharia is nebulous because it is derived from Quranic texts. The Quran, compared to the Bible, is not a coherent narrative. It is neither a collection of stories nor clear code of legal injunctions. As far as storytelling is concerned, the Quran depends substantively on Biblical stories for an uninformed reader to make sense of most of its narratives. Not only is the Quran dependent on Jewish and Christian scripture and Rabbinic and Biblical scholars for specific details, each passage of the Quran is dependent on other passages to provide context for its meaning. Muslim scholars rarely, if ever, use a single passage from the Quran to explain a concept. Instead, they cite numerous passages of the Quran to account for the full range of meanings of a word or a law, and determine the proper context in any given case.

There is something else unique about Islamic Sharia as compared to Judeo-Christian Sharia—to wit, the Commandments. In theory, as a basis of law, a central political order consistently and continuously promulgated and implemented Islamic Sharia for nearly 1300 years. Although no central infallible religious figure analogous to the Pope has existed in Islamic lands, the caliph as a person and the caliphate as an institution made Sharia a living legal code. In fact, these caliphs stood in for the Prophet Muhammad immediately after his death and made it their primary function to implement Sharia, legitimizing them in the eyes of the community. Caliphs, in the eyes of Muslims, are God's agents on earth, charged with the singular task of establishing divine justice.[28] However, every time a caliph was challenged, removed, or delegitimized, as cited early in this chapter, his challenger invoked the same claim: He was there to re-establish divine justice as instructed in the Quran and Sunna. In other words, Sharia was where divine justice resides, as claimed by all—those in power and those opposed to them. Indeed, the implementation of the principles and rules of Sharia had fallen into the hands of the caliphs, but the authority to determine Sharia rule concerning a specific event under specific circumstances rested, most times, with `ulamā' (sing. `ālim).[29] The determination of who was `ālim and who was not was also independent from the caliphs' authority and power.

While there were, as is the case nowadays, some `Ulama who were formally educated and trained in government-run institutions, many `Ulama received private educations, were self-educated, or had learned from attending unaffiliated learning courts; these `Ulama had become equally authoritative, and perhaps more influential, than government-certified and appointed scholars. Generally, reputation served a stronger role in the status of a religious scholar than formal education. In a sense, the caliph could help establish the status of the `Ulama both ways: He could legitimize those within the establishment through formalities, and could also legitimize those outside the establishment by their opposition to and watchfulness of him. The authority and standing of scholars within the establishment, and that of scholars outside the establishment, oscillated depending on the public's view of the caliph. When the caliph lacked public trust and standing as a pious and just leader, such as Yazid Ibn Mu`awiyyah, more people revered and trusted scholars from outside the establishment and appreciated their independence. On the other hand, when a caliph was respected and trusted, such as Umar II, the stock of scholars within the establishment rose, perhaps at the expense of those outside the establishment.

The institution of `Ulama is vital to the meaning and functions of Sharia because it is through `ulamā' that Sharia comes alive in society. Some Muslim scholars argue that Sharia is the mathematical absolute sum of individual maxims and principles and the settled determination in learned religious scholars. The whole of the Quran exists in the memories of `ulamā' and the example of the Prophet is in their imaginations, allowing `Ulama', at any single moment, to know the Sharia principle that is most appropriate to the case before them.

Other Muslim scholars contend that Sharia is a set of principles and guidelines that scholars use to derive laws and punishments. However, there is no single authoritative text that lists these principles and guidelines. The Quran does not contain a specific section focused on principles and guidelines of Sharia. Yet, some Muslim scholars assert that the Quran is the primary source of Islamic law. The Quranic principles ostensibly foundational to Sharia are embedded within the Quran's moral and ethical stories; they remain open to interpretation.

Defining Sharia and distinguishing among Sharia, *uṣūl*, and *fiqh* are two of the key challenges that both and Islamicists face.[30] The distinction between Sharia and *fiqh* varies not only between theological sects and jurisprudential schools of thought, but also from one `ulamā' to another within the same school of thought. Scholars of Islamic studies in North American and European educational institutions, too, present radically different explanations of Sharia and *fiqh*. I shall provide a summary of these explanations from classical as well as modern Muslim scholars. The summary will reveal the broad range of opinions and deep disagreement over the definition of Sharia and its related subjects.

Modern Muslim scholars, such as the head of al-Azhar, often qualify something as acceptable or unacceptable in both Sharia and law.[31] This qualification reflects the settled position among Muslim scholars that Sharia *is distinct from law*. Other Muslim scholars contend that Sharia is broader than *fiqh* because of the former's jurisdiction. Sharia rulings, they argue, are those which apply to all peoples and which are supported by unambiguous legal proof[32] in the primary sources (*nass*; Quran and Hadith/Sunna), and not subject to varying interpretations. *Fiqh*, on the other hand, is the body of opinions of legal scholars (*faqih, pl. fuqaha'*) within a specific school of jurisprudence; these opinions may lack legal proof or rely on legal proofs from outside the primary sources. *Fiqh*-based laws are produced through informed legal reasoning, called *ijtihad*, which is specific to its historical and geographic circumstances.[33]

Rules and rulings are also key concepts associated with Sharia.[34] The Arabic root, *h-k-m*, refers to halting corruption in something and restoring it to its wholesome state so that it can fulfill the purpose that *fiqh*, sciences (`ulum`), and wisdom (*hikma*) have determined for it. Therefore, the *hakim* (in the sense of Qadi), halts aggression (*zulm*) and establishes justice.[35] For legal scholars, *al-hukm al-shar`i* refers to the range of rules judging an act as obligatory (*wajib*), recommended (*mandub/mustahabb*), permitted (*mubah*), recommended against (*makruh*), or proscribed (*muharram*). Most know these legal judgments as the five legal rules.[36] For most jurists (*uṣūlis*), however, these are the five legal effects of the legal ruling;[37] for jurists, the legal ruling is the actual text of the Legislator (God) as stated in the Quran and the Sunna.

The Salafist scholar Ibn Taymiyyah proposes yet another distinction between Sharia and *fiqh*. He cites some religious scholars and members of the public who believe that the words *Sharia* and *shar`* apply to acts governed by the science of *fiqh*, and who distinguish between matters of creed (`aqa'id`) and laws (*shara'i`*), or truth and law.[38] He further clarifies that:

> *Sharia* encompasses all matters related to acts of benefit in this world or in the Hereafter. Sharia is the book of God and the Sunna of his Prophet, and that which was the practice of the ancestors (*salaf*) in areas of creed (`aqa'id`), civil law, worship, and politics.[39]

Echoing the opinion of most Traditionalist[40] scholars, Ibn Taymiyyah argues that the Quran and the Sunna contain answers to all possible questions that human beings, anywhere and anytime, might face:

> The opinion of our ancestral authorities (*salaf*) and the majority of legal scholars (*fuqaha'*) and theologians (*mutakallimin*) is this: God has issued a ruling on every event and for every event God has predetermined a specific ruling, be it obligation, proscription, permission, or absence of obligation and proscription, which we called allowance (`afw`). Therefore, no human being can ignore *Sharia* as it relates to all their dealings, because all that would benefit them is found in *Sharia*.[41]

According to Ibn Taymiyya, whose works are considered normative in Salafism, Sharia is one and the same as religious teachings. Sharia is, in other words, Islam. Moreover, the religious teachings, which he considers sacred and divine, would include the consensus (*ijma'*) of the learned ancestors (*salaf*). Sharia, thus defined, is also complete: It contains answers to all possible questions and cases. Lastly, according to Salafism, benefit to human beings is what drives Sharia. However, such benefits are also predetermined in the same source of the law, which is different from Reasonist[42] scholars' understanding of benefit (*maslaha*). For non-Salafist scholars, people may engage in beneficial activities independent of the sources of law. Sharia laws are intended to preserve those benefits. An example can illustrate this difference. Personal property—private ownership of resources—has some benefits in society in that it creates some social and economic order. Most Muslim religious scholars would argue that Sharia-inspired laws preserve and protect personal property rights. Salafist scholars, on the other hand, would argue that individual property rights are Sharia-mandated as being the only beneficial form of economic order. Any other form of property ownership, in their view, would conflict with the absolute, immutable Sharia rule.

Stressing the linguistic meaning of Sharia as the path to the waterway, some Muslim religious scholars draw the following analogy: The same way the physical wellbeing of a human body is dependent on water, the material and mental welfare of a human is dependent on following Sharia. They stress that Sharia, as such, covers all aspects of life. Explicitly or by way of general rule, Sharia determines the proper ruling for every possible event a human might face.

Consequently, Muslim religious scholars agree on one idea: Sharia is general, broad, and principle-driven. Those are the characteristics that distinguish Sharia from *fiqh* and related legal disciplines. Specifically, Islamic legal manuals argue that *fiqh* is an informed determination of the proper ruling deriving from the legal proofs. The legal scholar (*faqih*) is charged with deriving legal rulings from Sharia proofs (Quran and Sunnah) or other sources Sharia empowers, such as consensus (*ijmā`*) and proper analogy (*qiyās sahih*). The legal scholar, therefore, specializes in deriving legal rulings on practical matters, without involving themselves in matters of creed (*al-umur al-`aqdiyya*). Fiqh, in sum, is the acquired knowledge based on legal proofs (*al-dalīl al-shar`ī*), covering legal rulings on practical matters.[43]

As shown in the above discussion, the definition of Sharia is ever-evolving and subject to an emerging understanding shaped by internal and external pressures. The old boundaries are less isolating, allowing for an adaptive understanding of Sharia. Some modern Muslim religious scholars argue that Sharia consists of two types: A general Sharia covering theological matters, socio-economic transactions, and ethics, and a specific Sharia referring to practical cases not theological or ethical in nature. This understanding essentially explains the difference between the general statements and specific legal rulings, both found in the Quran. This position diverges from another explanation some modern Muslim religious scholars have proposed, arguing that both general and specific rulings belong to Sharia. However, Sharia is the specific rulings stated in the primary sources, whereas the rulings jurists have derived through *ijtihād* from the primary sources belong to *fiqh*. The difference between these two definitions is significant. The first definition conflates *fiqh*, as the body of law, with the legal and ethical principles from the Quran and the Sunna. The second definition establishes a body of law derived from the Quran and the Sunna, constituting Sharia, and a second body of law derived from these primary sources through *ijtihād*, constituting *fiqh*. The explicit laws stated in the Quran are Sharia laws, whereas *ijtihād*-based rulings are called *fiqh* laws.

A third perspective further complicates Muslim scholars' attempts to establish a universal definition of Sharia. Some contemporary Muslims scholars define Sharia as all revealed teachings. That is to say that Sharia is all of the Quran and all teachings of the Prophet Muhammad. *Fiqh*, on the other hand, is the all-encompassing legal discipline that reflects humans' understanding of the religious teachings and consists of jurisprudence (*uṣūl*) and law (*furū'*). This understanding presents Sharia to mean the religion (*al-din*) and *fiqh* as the jurists' understanding of the religion. The domain of Sharia is broad, covering theological, ethical, and practical matters. *Fiqh*, on the other hand, covers only practical matters. In other words, *fiqh*, as defined here, is not human understanding of the whole, it is part of the whole. *Fiqh* thus conceived is different from a *fiqh* defined as the informed judgment of the jurist, regardless of the judgment being correct or erroneous.

The imminent Sunni institution al-Azhar provides yet another distinction between Sharia and *fiqh*. According to al-Azhar, Sharia is all the divine teachings as revealed to the Prophet Muhammad. *Fiqh* is the human understanding of these teachings and their application to produce legal norms and legal decrees. Such legal norms and decrees consider not only the legal proofs (*dalīl*) found in the primary sources (Quran and Sunna), but consider also the circumstances involving place, time, event, and actors. Having said this, it becomes evident that a direct statement from the Quran, even if it is clear and explicit, is not part of the *fiqh* because, for something to be part of *fiqh*, it must be processed through intellect and contextualized by the specific circumstances.[44] This characterization clarifies that *fiqh* is not and cannot be Sharia, because only Sharia is unbound by time, place, and circumstances—that is, universal.

Notwithstanding the lack of consensus on the relationship between Sharia and *fiqh*, Sunni Muslim religious scholars do agree on Sharia's character. They conclude that Sharia is broad, consisting primarily of general principles. These principles then guide Muslim legal, ethical, and theological scholars in producing the practical and detailed rules in each of these areas. Subsequently, legal scholars produce *fiqh*, and such a *fiqh* is—unlike Sharia—limited. Sharia thus defined is intimately connected to religious texts and traditions, whereas *fiqh*, by definition, is mere humans' understanding of Sharia. Even in places with rulers who adhere to the most conservative interpretations of Islam, like Saudi Arabia,[45] religious scholars tend to equate Sharia to Islam and *fiqh* to law. In the case of Saudi Arabia, members of the cabinet (*majlis al-wuzara'*) endorse law. In this context, *fiqh*, not Sharia, is of two kinds: Judgments gleaned from primary sources and judgments derived from religious primary sources through *ijtihad*.[46]

In summary, religious scholars do not distinguish between Sharia and content of the Quran and the Sunna. According to the majority of Sunni scholars, there is no distinct body of law called Sharia law because Sharia is more than law. Law, for them, is found in *fiqh* collections, which jurists produce through the process of informed independent reasoning, *ijtihad*.

From this brief overview of Muslim scholars' opinions on the meaning and functions of Sharia and *fiqh*, it is clear that there is no authoritative consensus. However, they agree on this: Sharia is broader in scope than *fiqh* and Sharia, as provided by the Lawgiver (God), is the source of the principles that guide lawmakers who produce the body of law (*fiqh*). Despite this consensus, Muslim jurists and Western experts in Islamic law do not identify a catalogue of Sharia principles or a hierarchy of such principles. Each scholar can use a principle from the primary source to justify their ruling on any given case. Some argue that the degree of explicitness and implicitness of a principle's legal proof (*dalīl*), not its nature, decides its potency. In theory, such distinctions seem reasonable. However, they lose all meaning when actual cases present themselves. For example, Sharia ruling on theft (*sariqa*) is well-known to Muslim jurists from all major theological and jurisprudential schools, because the Quran contains an explicit statement respecting the male and female thief.[47] Yet the Quranic text prescribed the punishment for male and female thieves, not for the act of theft; there is no explicit definition of theft. Consequently, the definition of theft fell to the jurists and, as expected, they did not agree on a single definition. Clearly, the presence of explicit text in a primary source does not establish a class of cases for which Sharia ruling is predetermined. Some Muslim religious scholars' distinctions, between Sharia as a body of law explicitly addressed in the primary sources (Quran and Sunna) and *fiqh* as a body of law derived through *ijthad*, are unsupported by facts and logic. First, there is no collection of Sharia law that stands independent from *fiqh* collections. Second, even explicit texts of the Quran dealing with transactional legal matters (*mu`āmalāt*) are a subject of deep disagreement among Muslim scholars on aspects including definition, scope, and circumstances.

Indeed, the body of legal and jurisprudential legacy Muslim scholars have produced is complex and diverse, the result of their sectarian and methodological differences. That diversity aside, the majority of Muslim scholars do not consider the body of law found in the various *fiqh* collections to be equivalent to Sharia. Quite the opposite: Most Muslim scholars, including those affiliated with the most conservative tendencies, emphasize that Sharia is that which is stated in the Quran and the Sunna, and that anything else is mere interpretation. However, even the most unambiguous passages of the Quran need human qualification in the form of definition, scope, and circumstance.

Confusion about the meaning and function of Sharia is often the outcome of uninformed commentators or reductionism: Simplicity-driven theories. Abuse of Sharia in Muslim communities is also prevalent, in part due to wilful ignorance of the first three centuries of Reasonists' contributions to law and jurisprudence, and in part due to the privileging of Traditionists' interpretations and applications of Islamic legal heritage. Traditionists claim that the Sunna and the Quran are the twin sources of Sharia. The first four caliphs, and Muslim jurists of the formative period, are unlikely to have regarded the Sunna as the source of Sharia. Their practices and precedents suggest that they understood the Sunna as part of the body of *fiqh*, the same way they knew that their practice, too, was building the body of *fiqh*, not defining an immutable Sharia. Sunna, thus understood, is interpretive, not legislative. Sharia, on the other hand, is legislative because it is rooted in the Quran.

Another general thought regarding Sharia is about its intimate connection to the political order during the Islam's formative period. Many of the legal rules and rulings were made part of the body that informs Sharia because they were enacted or enforced by key political figures, not because of sound legal reasoning, an established textual basis, or consensus among independent legal authorities. The first four caliphs especially played an unmatched role in defining and shaping Islamic law (*fiqh*), which Sharia reflects. For example, the rule of `awl, which is central to Sunni inheritance law, a fundamental institution with implications on property rights, became a legal principle not because it was based on explicit Quranic or Sunnaic text or broad consensus among jurists of that era, but rather because the second caliph, `Umar, imposed it. Therefore, one cannot understand the legal texts and legal theories that define Sharia without understanding the origins, evolution, and functions of Islamic political order and political theory.

From the above discussion, I would propose a working definition of Sharia, which will allow the reader to identify the events and practices that make the Sharia what it has been throughout the history of Islamic thought and societies. A definition of Sharia that is useful must account for events and ideas from both the caliphate and post-caliphate era.[48]

Sharia is an oral[49] legal system rooted in the belief in a creator, and it derives its authority and power from this creator. The belief ensures the compliance of its adherents and subjects, is boosted by enticements and threats, and is empowered through reciprocal coupling of ethical and legal norms. Sharia is a multi-filter lens through which Muslims view and explain the world at any given moment, capturing judgements for any given occurrence. Muslims apply this multi-filter—including social, ethical, religious, psychological, political, and economic filters—to a specific case producing a legal judgment, augmenting the body of *fiqh*. Sharia, thus framed, is guideline-oriented where select cases represent the minimum entitlements when dealing with rights (e.g., inheritance rights) and maximum punishments when dealing with crimes (e.g., killing). Sharia is akin to an instrument residing in the minds of jurists, whereas the content of *fiqh* is the outcome produced using Sharia, residing in the various collections of law. Therefore, *fiqh* is a catalogue of Sharia-aided snapshots related to theoretical cases, such as events occurring under normal circumstances, and abstract cases, such as fatwas. Sharia is adaptable filters through which jurists pass information about any given case at any given time and in any society to determine the best judgment. Such a judgment may end up being purely moral, requiring no punishment; legal-related matters of worship—requiring no government policing or enforcement; or legal-related to interpersonal transactions—requiring societal or government intervention in determining the form of redress and punishment (*ta`zīr*).

Sharia is often explained as a strict and harsh code of law. Human rights advocates often point to Sharia as a source of abuse in Islamic societies. They argue that Sharia allows torture, uses threats of torture, and sanctions punishments too harsh for modern times. Some Muslim thinkers and religious leaders challenge this assessment of Sharia as cultural imperialism; others call to reform Sharia, aligning it with norms of modernity and enlightenment. Both positions are flawed.

There is ample evidence that the West has, and continues to, pursue an imperial agenda when interacting with the rest of the world. The West is intent on preserving the dominance of its worldview. The question is not whether the West practices cultural imperialism; the question is whether Muslims believe in some form of human rights, independent of what the West does and wants. If Islam establishes a path towards greater respect for human dignity, then Muslim scholars and thinkers need to articulate that vision and those principles independent of any Western position or action.

Those who wish to reform Sharia to align it with the imperatives of the modern era are reactionaries. They wish to create a hybrid system that has elements of Sharia and elements of Western legal systems, and hope that this will solve the problem. Such a reform will not take hold, because any reformed system built on incompatible systems is compatible to neither. Western legal systems are built on norms that make them work. Sharia is also built on features that are necessary for it to work. Most importantly, Sharia is a system that combines both religious and secular aims, but the secular aims depend on the religious imperatives, practices, and doctrines. Sharia is a system, and if it is changed to adopt foreign elements and divest of original elements, the result is a new system, not Sharia. Sharia's force is not in the harsh sanctions and rigid punishments. Its force is in the threats and enticements not linked to any actual punishment or reward in this world. Sharia works because of its delayed punishment and reward, not its immediate swift justice. Any attempt to separate the two realms of Sharia would result in ending Sharia as a legal system. Therefore, Western ideas and instruments cannot vaccinate Sharia against human rights abuses. It either stands on its own as a system or is side-lined all together.

Sharia differs from modern legal systems. The latter are based on the power of the State, which is derived from society's norms and is dependent on strict enforcement of the law through coercion and financial incentives. Being a system, Sharia cannot be fully or partially implemented in a foreign environment. It requires all the elements that ensure its success, the same way a European legal system could not be successful in an environment designed for Sharia. A system, in this context, is a social environment containing all the forces and factors whose effects—without factoring in any outside forces—can generate an intelligible, quantifiable, and qualifiable social dynamic equilibrium.

Recalling the proposals of the two "moral philosophers" we relied on as expert witnesses on universal human rights, we come back to answer the critical question: Under what conditions can human rights norms thrive? Talbott suggests that a government providing legal guarantees to respect a package of nine basic rights will create the kind of liberal society and liberal governments necessary for human rights norms to thrive. Sachedina, on the other hand, suggests that through an ethical and moral interpretation of religious tradition, Sharia, all of the human rights enshrined in the Universal Declaration of Human Rights can be respected and accepted. Based on 300 years of liberal society experiments in Western societies and more than one thousand years of caliphs entrusted with just application of Sharia, we know that human rights are more likely to be abused than promoted. I submit that more work is needed to refine the theoretical and institutional frameworks that might have some success in universalizing human rights and reducing the harm that results from human rights abuses.

Relevant to the human rights equation I emphasize, governments exert power limited only by the law. In the case of classical Islamic political order, the caliphate, the Sunni pan-Islamic government, in theory[50] and in practice[51] has been built on a legitimacy extracted by dominance (*al-ghalaba*), not through a social contract. The dominance came from clan solidarity (*asabiyya*), grievance claims (*mazlumiyya*), or institutional military power (*askar;* recall, *mamluks*). Such a government cannot be trusted to promote the rights of the vulnerable or the rights of all. The classical forms of government, notwithstanding their rootedness in a model of dominance, lacked the power to legislate, a void filled with Sharia, an elastic institution that is the domain of independent scholars employing *ijtihad* and guided by settled precedent (*ijma'*). In other words, Islamic societies have too many systems geared toward producing different outcomes than their counterparts in Western societies. The question of compatibility of Sharia with modern human rights norms is irrelevant because the modern human rights discourse, as articulated in the UDHR, was designed for a different social system with an overarching worldview that is aimed to achieve different outcomes through different mechanisms.

Notes

1. See, for example, the writings of John Locke, Jean-Jacques Rousseau, and the text of the Declaration of Independence of the United States.
2. Because some clans were too small and were not all represented in the governing tribal council, historians are not sure about the exact number of clans within Mecca. The historian al-Mas'udi lists 25 clans as being part of Quraish. Others list fewer or more than that. We should name few of these clans because they will be relevant to our discussion of the Islamic governments. These are some of the influential clans, members of the tribe of Quraysh: Banu Hāshim (Muhammad, `Ali), Banu Zuhra, Banu Taim (Abu Bakr), Banu 'Adī (`Umar), and Banu Umayya ('Uthmān, Mu`awiyya).
3. Arabic culture authorized discretionary punishment for those involved in highway robbery (*qat` al-tariq*), which was later termed by Islamic law as *ḥirabah*, and made punishable by death according to some Islamic schools of jurisprudence.
4. See, for example Ibn Qutayba, *Kitab al-Ma'arif*, 63; Ibn Sa'd, *al-Kitab al-Tabaqat al-Kabir*, 1:2:179–80; al-Tabari, *Kitab al-Rusul*, 1778, 1779, 1780, 1781, 1940; Ibn Sa'd, *al-Kitab al-Tabaqat al-Kabir*, 3:1:26, 3:1:167, 8:153; and Ibn Hisham, *Kitab Sirat Rasul Allah*, 486, 999.
5. Because anyone could fall into slavery by simply being part of an army that loses awar, slavery in Arab society did not carry the kind of stigma attached to slavery in Western and US societies. For instance, a slave girl, due to the various terms of marriage in Arab society, could become a powerful political force. Al-Khayzuran, a slave girl in the house of the ruling Abbasids, became the wife of al-Mahdi when he became Caliph and the mother of his two sons who also became caliphs. As such, according to some historical records, she was the de facto caliph during the reign of her husband and two sons.
6. See, generally, Zaydan, *al-Tamaddun al-islami*, and 5:39 and 5:139; al-Bayhaqi,*al-Mahasin wa-'l-masawi'*, 613 and 609; and al-Baghdadi, 1:51.
7. Dissenters, especially social groups expressing dissent who are not connected to the ruling elite, were labeled as outsiders, khawarij. When `Aisha, the widow of the Prophet and daughter of the first caliph, led an armed rebellion against the fourth caliph, she and her followers were not considered khawarij. Those unattached to the ruling elite who asked for fairer distribution of resources were labeled so and pursued militarily. See, generally, Ahmed E. Souaiaia. *Anatomy of Dissent in Islamic Societies: Ibadism, Rebellion, and Legitimacy* (New York: Palgrave Macmillan, 2013).
8. According to Islamic historical accounts, only three out of 37 Abbasid caliphs were born to free mothers: al-Saffah (d. 136/754), al-Mahdi (d. 169/786), and al-Amin (d. 198/813). All others were born to former slave girls (*Jawari*). Cross references were derived from Ibn al-Jawzi's *al-Muntazam* and Ya`qubi's *al-Buldan*.
9. Justin Marozzi, *Islamic Empires: Fifteen Cities that Define a Civilization* (UK: Penguin, 2019), 36.
10. With the start of the Umayyad rule and through the Abbasid rule, scholars consistently showed their independence by taking part in or endorsing armed rebellion. For instance, the armed "Rebellion of Scholars" marked the first organized armed opposition to the Umayyads and consisted primarily of religious scholars. They fought in a series of battles that ended in 83 AH. See, generally, Thahbi's *Syar A`lam al-Nubala*. Abu Hanifa, the founder of one of the main Sunni schools of jurisprudence supported Zaydi rebellion against the Umyyad caliph, Hisham Ibn Abdul Malik. Zayd Ibn Ali Ibn al-Hussain Ibn Ali rose up in 122 AH. He framed his rebellion this way: to

follow the book of God and the practice of his Messenger, to fight against oppressors, to protect the oppressed and disempowered, and to return the right of the exploited. See, generally, Ibn al-Athir's *al-Kamil*. Malik Ibn Anas (d. 179 AH) also supported another armed uprising led by al-Nafs al-Zakiyya (Muhammad Ibn Abdullah Ibn Hassan Ibn al-Hassan Ibn Ali) against the Abbasid caliph, al-Mansur. Malik was arrested, tortured, and imprisoned for this. Lastly, al-Shafi`i (d. 204 AH), also was imprisoned by the Abbasid caliph, al-Rashid, for refusing to condemn armed rebellion against rulers.

11. Information about `Ulama's action to preserve the independence of the institution and their rejection of wages and grants from political rulers is chronicled in a number of sources including *Ihya' `ulum al-Din* (Ghazzali (d. 505 AH), *al-Dhakhira fi mahasin ahl al-jazira* (al-Shantiri al-Andalusi, d. 542 AH), *Siyar a`lam al-Nubala* and *Tarikh al-Islam* (Dhahbi, d. 748 AH), *Tabaqat al-shafi`iyya* (Sabki, d. 771 AH), *Kifayat al-akhyar fi hal ghayat al-ikhtisar* (Taqiyy al-Din al-Hasni, d. 829 AH), *al-Durra al-gharra' fi nasihat al-slatin wa-'l-quda wa-'l-umara'* (Mahmud Ibn Isma`il al-Khayrabayti, d. 843 AH), *Ma rawah al-asadin fi `adam al-maji' ila al-slatin* (Jalal al-Din al-Sayyuti, d. 911 AH), *al-Farq bayna al-firaq* (Abdul al-Qahir al-Baghdad, d. 429 AH). To preserve their independence, scholars often engaged in trade to make a living; when they were criticized for their involvement in trade, they justified it by claiming that "if it were not for these dinars from trade, scholars would have been used by kings and emirs. When you see a scholar seeking the company of caliphs (sultans), know that they are thieves; if they seek the company of the rich, know that they are pretenders; they claim that they are doing what they are doing, to help the poor; it is the devil's trick used by some scholars as ladder to riches." See Hilyat al-awliya (Ahmad Ibn Abdullah al-Asbahani (d. 430 AH). In addition to trade, scholars engaged in manual vocations like carpentry, artisanry, tannery, jewelry, etc. For more on the occupation of scholars, see *al-Ansab* (Abu Sa`d al-Sam`ani al-Maruzi, d. 562 AH) and *al-Sunna` min al-fiquha' wa-'l-muhaddithin* (Muhammad Ibn Ishaq al-Sa`di al-Harawi). Public trust (waqf) also played a major role in fostering the independence of educational and learning institutions in Islamic societies. Some of the longest and continuously operating learning institutions are Islamic waqf universities, like al-Qarawiyyin University, founded in 859 CE in Fez, Morocco.

12. Yazid ordered the head of Hussain displayed at one of the gates of Damascus

13. It is often stated in secondary sources that the Shia split occurred immediately after death of the Prophet Muhammad. A close reading of the facts of that time period would reveal that to be false. It is true that disagreement occurred early on. But since Ali remained attached to the ruling class, becoming a caliph himself, it would be a mistake to think that Shia, as a distinctive sect and movement, was born at this time. The seeds for splitting may be connected to this time period, but it was only after the brutal killing of Hussain that we can see the formal emergence of a distinctive school of thought and political movement we can call Shia.

14. Muslim historians reference a social movement they called *Lusus, Shuttar*, and `Ayyarun (thieves, hustlers…) that appeared in Basra and Baghdad in the second and third Islamic centuries, during the Abbasid rule, that stole from the rich and handed to the poor. They grew popular and strong, at some point consisting of an army of more than one hundred thousand troops. This movement was focused on protesting extreme poverty and extreme wealth and took up arms to work against the extreme inequity. See al-Tabari's *Tarikh al-rusul wa-'l-muluk*, 3:872, 882, 889, 900, 1552, 1566, 1587; al-Mas`udi's *Muruj al-dhahab*, 6:446, 468, and 470.

15. The armed "Rebellion of the Blacks" was a long struggle that lasted more than fifteen years (255–270 AH/769–883 CE). It involved thousands of people enslaved from east Africa and employed in harsh conditions without meaningful compensation. See al-Tabari's *Tarikh al-rusul wa-'l-muluk*, 3:1745–1773.
16. See Qaramite rebellion, 261–282 AH/874–899 CE, as described by Muslim historians, Ibn al-Athir, 7:137 and al-Tabari, 3:2130; this movement, based on their teachings, are seen as the first communist movement that accused religious figures, including Muhammad and Jesus, of tricking the people with promises of salvation to be lived in another world, which resulted in enslaving the people in this world by their religious dogma. See, al-Baghdadi's *Tarikh baghdad*, 281–288.
17. See Abd al-Razzaq Ahmed al-Sanhuri, *Fiqh al-khilafa* (Cairo: Muassasat al-risala, 2008), 79.
18. Al-Mawardi (Abu al-Hassan Ali Ibn Habib al-Basri), *al-Ahkam al-sultaniya* (Cairo: Dar al-Hadith, 2006), 20.
19. Taftazani explains that *al-nisa' naqisat aql wa-din mamnu`at mina al-khuruj ila al-mashahi wa-mughawarat al-hurib*. See, al-Taftazani, *Taqrib al-maram* (Beirut: Dar al-Kutub al-Ilmiya, 2017), 356.
20. See, generally, Anna C. Korteweg and Jennifer A. Selby, eds., *Debating Sharia: Islam, Gender Politics, and Family Law Arbitration* (Toronto: University of Toronto Press, 2012).
21. A recent work dedicated to answering the question, What is the Sharia?, concluded that Sharia "does not have an intrinsic meaning accessible to, at any rate, human understanding… mot classical scholars did not evoke the Sharia and did not claim to know it." Baudouin Dupret, *What is the Sharia?* (Oxford: Oxford University Press, 2018), 7–9.
22. Dominic McGoldrick, "Accommodating Muslims in Europe: From Adopting Sharia Law to Religiously Based Opt Outs from Generally Applicable Laws," *Human Rights Law Review*, 9, no. 4 (2009): 603–645.
23. Sarah M. Fallons, "Justice for All: American Muslims, Sharia Law, and Maintaining Comity within American Jurisprudence," *International & Comparative Law Review*, 153 (2013).
24. See, generally, Anna C. Korteweg and Jennifer A. Selby, eds., *Debating Sharia: Islam, Gender Politics, and Family Law Arbitration* (Toronto: University of Toronto Press, 2012).
25. It must be noted that some Muslim politicians' inclination to impose Sharia law is not limited to the twenty-first century and is not a result of the 2011 social change movements and wars. In the twentieth century, many authoritarian Muslim rulers imposed Sharia law (selectively imposing harsh punishments in the name of Sharia) to acquire legitimacy. In Sudan, in September 1983 Jaafar Nimeiri imposed a form of Sharia law throughout his country, amputating the hands of thieves to win support from religious groups. Omar al-Bashir, too, embraced a form of Sharia regime to distract people from the fact that he grabbed power through military coups and to appease opposition groups. In Pakistan, since 1977, General Muhammad Zia-ul-Haq took steps to introduce Sharia laws and establish Sharia courts.
26. An Islamicist is a secular university-trained scholar of Islamic civilization specializing in classical Islamic thought and institutions. The qualification "secular" distinguishes a scholar on Islam from a scholar of Islam. A Muslim scholar may attend an Islamic university that teaches traditional disciplines as part of its curriculum to train Imams. But such a person would not be one we would label as Islamicist.

27. For sample definitions of Sharia by Islamicists, see Baudouin Dupret, *What is the Sharia?* (Cambridge: Oxford University Press, 2018), Patricia Sloane-White, *Corporate Islam: Sharia and the Modern Workplace* (Cambridge: Cambridge University Press, 2017), Maurits Berger, ed., *Applying Sharia in the West : Facts, Fears and the Future of Islamic Rules on Family Relations in the West* (Leiden : Leiden University Press 2013), A. Kevin Reinhart, "Islamic Law as Islamic Ethics," *Journal of Religious Ethics*, 11, no. 2 (1983): 186–203, N. Coulson, "The State and the Individual in Islamic Law," *International and Comparative Law Quarterly* 6 no. 1 (1957): 49–60, Irshad Abdal-Haqq, "Islamic Law - An Overview of Its Origin and Elements," *Islamic Law & Culture* 27 (2002), and Yvonne Yazbeck Haddad and Barbara Freyer Stowasser, *Islamic Law and the Challenges of Modernity* (Lanham, MD: Rowman Altamira, 2004).
28. Hugh Kennedy, *Caliphate: The History of an Idea* (New York: Basic Books, 2016), 1.
29. It should be noted that scholars would often, if not always, refer to the opinion (*ra'y*) of the `ulamā', using the plural form of the word, rarely if ever, the singular form. This suggests at least two things: `ulamā'is more of an institution then a group of scholars, and individual opinion by a single `alim lacks precedential authority until it is independently confirmed by other scholars.
30. See this sample definition of *fiqh* by Orientalists: "Fiqh is a system of rules and methods whose authors consider it to be the normative interpretation of the revelation, the application of its principles and commands to the field of human acts." Baber Johansen, *Contingency in a Sacred law: Legal and Ethical Norms in Muslim Fiqh* (Leiden: Brill, 1999), 1. See, also, Korteweg, *Debating Sharia*.
31. *shar`an wa-qanunan*.
32. *Dalil*.
33. *al-ijtihad ibnu zamanihi wa-makanih*.
34. *al-hukm al-shar`i*.
35. see, *Lisan al-arab*, h-k-m entry.
36. *al-ahkam al-shar`iyya al-khamsa*.
37. *al-hukm al-shar`i*.
38. See Ibn Taymiyyah, *al-Fatawa al-kubra*, 4:231.
39. Ibid.
40. I employ the term "Traditionists" in reference to *Ahl al-hadith*.
41. Taymiyyah, *al-Fatawa al-kubra*, 9:307.
42. "Reasonist" is used to denote the Arabic phrase, *Ahl al-Ra`y*.
43. See al-Amidi, *al-Ihkām fī al-Ahkām*, 1:5.
44. Based on public remarks delivered an al-Azhar official Mohammed Kamal al-Din Iman, archived at https://swaana.integr8d.org.
45. Daryl Champion, *The Paradoxical Kingdom: Saudi Arabia and the Momentum of Reform* (New York: Columbia University Press, 2003).
46. R. Hrair Dekmejian, "The Rise of Political Islamism in Saudi Arabia," *Middle East Journal* 48, no. 4 (1994): 627–43.
47. See *wa-'l-sāriqu wa-'l-sāriqatu…*5:38.
48. I must admit that I have struggled to find meaningful demarcation points that allow for the distinction between circumstances and environments influencing the development of the idea and institution of Sharia. I am comfortable separating two distinct periods: the time during which Muslims lived under a pan-Islamic government that covered most Islamic lands, which is the time since the migration to Madina until the dissolution of the Ottoman Sultanate,

as being the caliphate era. Even this distinction is imprecise, because Muslims' attitudes toward many Islamic institutions began to change much earlier than the formal dissolution of the Ottoman Sultanate.
49. It might be asked: If Sharia is derived from the Quran and the Sunna, and both the Quran and the Sunna are now written works, how can Sharia be oral? To answer that, the reader must recall that although the Quran is written down in collections called *muṣḥaf*, the Quran, for Muslims, is the recited (oral) tradition with all the elements that spoken words and gestures add to written words. The fact that Muslims refer to the written Quran as *muṣḥaf* instead of the Quran supports this conclusion. As for the Sunna, it should be recalled that Hadith was preserved and used orally for nearly three centuries before producing the various collections of hadith.
50. Ibn Khaldun, *al-Muqaddima* (Beirut: Dar al-kutub al-`ilmiyya, 195), 220.
51. With the exception of the first thirty years, the majority of Islamic dynasties that governed over the pan-Islamic caliphate came into existence and preserved their rule on the basis of dominance—*ghalaba*.

Part III
Globalism, history, and human rights today

Among the critical ideas relevant to human rights norms and institutions is the significance of the theoretical framework and the universality of human wrongs. For the former, I contend that systems thinking is the most appropriate lens through which we can explore human rights because human rights abuses are not accidental; they are the product of deliberate value systems designed to produce specific outcomes. Such systems may not be intentionally configured to yield the human rights abuses that we have witnessed throughout history, but those abuses were reasonably predictable outcomes, on account of the desired outcome's excesses. For example, societies may not have designed social and economic systems with the intent of producing extreme poverty—poverty being the underlying cause of many denied rights—but societies did design systems that enabled people to pursue happiness, as enshrined in many of Western societies' bills of rights, through hoarding resources. The mechanisms by which hoarding resources is secured, most involving violence, further aggravated human rights abuses.

The latter idea, the universality of human wrongs, is both connected to and independent from the idea of systems. As the evidence in the first two chapters support, human wrongs have happened and continue to happen in every society, irrespective of it being liberal or illiberal. The occurrence of human rights abuses are predictable because they are a result of conditions and circumstances more than merely incidental.

The most recent wave of human rights atrocities resulting in severe injuries, murder, torture, disappearance, mass displacement, the use of weapons of mass destruction, loss of property, genocide, ethnic cleansing, and terrorism has been taking placing before us since 2011 in Southwest Asia and North Africa (SWANA). These events, including uprisings, civil wars, and proxy wars, involve actors from across the globe and are motivated by claims and counterclaims of grievances that have been festering for hundreds of years within and across Islamic and Western societies. The 2011 SWANA conflicts not only involve national, regional, and international State actors, but are motivated by sectarian, racist, and supremacist impulses nourished by value systems, some unique to—and others ubiquitous across—cultures and communities connected only by geography.

Among the 2011 SWANA conflicts, the war in Syria is a powerful case study that establishes the connections between historical, religious, cultural, political, and societal systems across time and space proving that human rights abuses can neither be addressed within national borders nor in isolation from dominant value systems.

Moreover, human rights are at risk most during violent conflicts and social change movements. By any standards of measurement, the transformative events that started in 2011 in Southwest Asia and North Africa are more consequential than any other social movement around the world. These transformative events might have even inspired other significant movements outside their region, including the Occupy movement in the West. Radical change often leads to social dislocation and increased risks for marginalized social groups. In this section, we present key facts about these events and then analyze these facts to prove that human rights abuses do not occur in vacuum. Human rights abuses result from accrued attitudes, justifications, and motives that are both historical and global.

In short, this section is an account, and analysis thereof, of historical actors and global actors that drives people to commit, incite, tolerate, and justify atrocities; and States' instrumentalization of human rights to inflict injury, death, destruction, and starvation in pursuit of political and economic goals.

6 The case of the 2011 wars in SWANA

The idea of war narratives is a key element in the justification and sustaining of wars: that is, the narratives states and other actors create in order to justify their involvement in war and motivate individuals to support it through resources or actions. The author explores this concept through the lens of various actors in the Syrian war, breaking down how countries such as the U.S. built a war narrative to justify their involvement; how Syria explained its measures; and how individual sects, religions, and groups came to view their role and circumstances within the conflict. He additionally interrogates media outlets across a broad spectrum of sources to analyze how actors in the Syrian war framed their involvement to their supporters and audiences.

The idea of *universal* rights, as developed in this work, is a commitment to certain norms and practices that should exist throughout time, across cultures, and under all circumstances. Whether such a commitment was honored in all times and places is less important than its mere existence, because its application is dependent on the strength of societal institutions and the compliance of governments. Thus far we have looked for human rights across more than 1400 years, in Islamic and Western societies, and in times of peace and war. To introduce a broad range of perspectives, I have interrogated the works of two expert "moral philosophers" who are passionate advocates for universalizing human rights. To understand the backgrounds that inform their discourse, I examined the intellectual and ideological heritage on which they drew—Western Enlightenment thought and Islamic ethical and legal traditions, respectively. In this chapter, I enter data into evidence for a case that, I believe, combines all elements present in the opinions of the two experts and in the historical legacy they invoke: the 2011 uprisings and wars in Southwest Asia and North Africa (SWANA). The similarity between the European wars of religion and world wars that culminated with the UDHR and the 2011 SWANA conflicts is striking. In chronological order, here are some of the elements critical to human rights norms present in this case.

The first armed rebellion against the sitting caliph, and the first Islamic civil war, involved key actors from Mecca and Madina and the Levant, or present-day Syria. Specifically, the seventh century wars—in which the third and fourth caliphs, `Uthman and `Ali, were killed—involved the then-governor of modern-day Syria, Mu`awiyya.

The war in Syria today involves Saudi Arabia, Iran, Turkey, and other governments allied with them; these governments recall sectarian themes from previous clashes. Today, Saudi Arabia's governing system mimics that of the Umayyads of the seventh and eighth centuries, the dynasty whose actions shaped the development of Shia Islam. Iran is the first Imami Shia-run and Shiism-inspired country in the history of Islamic societies. Turkey was the seat of the Ottoman Sultanate, the last Sunni pan-Islamic government. According to Shia scholars, Zaynab, the Prophet Muhammad's daughter and Hussain's sister—who was with Hussain when he was killed by Yazid's army—was buried in Syria. The seventh and eighth centuries' wars resulted in the first breakup of the Muslim community into sects; in the twenty-first century wars in Syria, Iraq, and Yemen, followers of these sects are key actors. In plainer words: The twenty-first century sectarian war is an echo of the unresolved tension created by the violence and wars of the seventh century.

All major world and regional powers have been directly or indirectly involved in Syria's 2011 war. The United States and Russia both have combat troops on the ground in Syria, the U.S. supporting armed opposition groups and Russia fighting alongside and supplying Syrian government troops. When the United Nations Security Council saw resolutions condemning the Syrian government, both China and Russia vetoed them. France went as far as recognizing a Syrian opposition coalition as the sole representative of the Syrian people, essentially delegitimizing the Syrian government. The Arab League, the intergovernmental organization representing Arab-speaking countries, froze Syria's membership and, during several sessions, invited representatives of the opposition forces to take Syria's seat. Turkey, a member of NATO (and formerly the seat of the Ottoman Sultanate, with open claim to parts of Syria based on that era), launched armed operations in three regions in Syria to support Sunni fighters and create safe zones for them inside Syria. Iran sent weapons and recruited fighters to support the Syrian government and to protect Zaynab's gravesite.

The war in Syria, to some extent, is a continuation of the war in Iraq, in which the US administration justified an illegal invasion by falsely claiming that Iraq's leader, Saddam Hussein, possessed weapons of mass destruction. The invasion and subsequent occupation that deployed American and Western troops to Iraq resulted in the loss of more than 650,000 Iraqi lives[1] and created the conditions that allowed the Salafist armed group, the Islamic State in Iraq and the Levant (ISIL), to flourish and export its ideology and resources into Syria. Iraq's destabilizing was so great that its ripple effect destabilized Syria, Jordan, and Lebanon, creating new tensions along sectarian, religious, ethnic, and racial fault lines. Amplifying the tension was Western-specific narratives of racism and Islamic-specific narratives of sectarianism, which disturbed the stability of societal institutions and threatened peace across communities.

The escalation in Syria of an unarmed protest movement into an armed rebellion, which quickly turned into a global proxy-war, diminished any potential of the unarmed uprising that started in Tunisia. It also dimmed the hopes of Arab people for social and political change, change that was needed to address corruption, abuse of power, economic disparity, systemic torture of political prisoners, and poor management of human and natural resources.

No other case provides a context that brings to the fore the historical legacies of sectarianism, racism, colonialism, crimes against humanity, genocide, war crimes, and human rights abuses—and highlights the West-Islamic connections—the way the 2011 SWANA war does. In many ways, this case is a microcosm of the conditions and events that led to some of the cruelest human rights abuses across Western and Islamic societies. It is an opportunity to examine facts of war, violence, abuse, cruelty, deprivation, exploitation, arrogance, racism, and supremacy before they are varnished, edited, and reproduced. Thanks to advancement in technology for archiving, sharing, and analyzing digital content, we have access to a large body of raw, unfiltered data, rendering battle fields and meeting rooms open-access laboratories. In the rest of this chapter, I will present information to background the 2011 events in SWANA and offer an interpretation that contextualizes them within the discourse on human rights.

Just before leaving office, President George W. Bush was asked this question: Knowing what we now know, did he think that invading Iraq in 2003 was a mistake? He defended his decision to invade, claiming that the world was a better place with Saddam Hussein gone. Beyond that, he left it in the hands of history, which he had confidence would vindicate him: "History will ultimately judge the decisions that were made for Iraq and I'm just not going to be around to see the final verdict."[2] Some believe that history is an objective account of what has happened. Reading about the European wars and documenting the 2011 wars in Southwest Asia and North Africa, however, I have become less certain this is true.

Human rights abuses have immediate emotional, psychological, and physical impact on their survivors, witnesses, and on those who informed of them. History cannot capture everything, even if its historians are eager and willing. That said, what the tragic events which started in December 17, 2010 as a protest movement in Tunisia and mutated into proxy-wars in Syria and other countries teach us is that history is built on narratives. War narratives are never objective. Each side produces its own narrative. By war's end when the victor gets to continue writing and editing the narrative, the vanquished is often silenced. Preservation of raw data of events as they happen, not after the fact, counteract history's editorial processes. I intend to de-emphasize the narratives of winning and losing wars and battles, and emphasize the impact of specific events and actions on the human rights discourse and on the subjects and objects of human rights abuses.

Before escalating into a global proxy war, the protest movement that started in Tunisia was a cyclical protest against government corruption and abuses. Tunisians are familiar with social activism when injustice and abuse of power become unbearable. In the seventies and eighties, Tunisians protested against their first president, Habib Bourguiba. In 1987, their protest and labor strikes ended Bourguiba's tenure. He was replaced by his prime minister, Zine El Abidine Ben Ali, in a bloodless dawn coup. Ben Ali, aware of the power of the masses, promised not to make the same mistakes as his predecessor. He promised to lift restrictions on political opposition, amend the constitution to ban lifetime presidency, introduce economic development plans that brought balance between coastal and the inner regions, deregulate economic and educational institutions, and fight corruption and cronyism. However, neither Ben Ali's constitutional amendments nor his public policies improved the economic, social, and political conditions in the country. By 2010, Ben Ali was still president, far beyond his two-term limit, having won four sham elections by 95%, 99%, 94%, and 89% since 1994. Corruption was rampant. More than a quarter of the work force was unemployed, political opponents were tortured and imprisoned, the press was muzzled, and the wealth gap between people living in the coastal cities and elsewhere was staggering. Again, people rose up, and this time they forced Ben Ali out of the country; he escaped to Saudi Arabia.[3] The difference between this protest and previous ones was that Qatar's Al Jazeera broadcasted the 2011 protest for the entire world to see. Those who could not see it on Al Jazeera were able to follow virtually on Facebook and Twitter; many travelled hundreds of miles to the capital, Tunis, to join it in person.

Digital technology allowed the energy of the Tunisian uprising to spread to other countries where people lived under similar conditions. This connection between the Tunisian uprising and the wave of protests in other Arab countries led some commentators to coin the phrase "Arab Spring" to historicize and narrate these events. Seven years later, however, it became evident that it was only a Tunisian spring at best. The rest of the Arab world fell into chaos. The uprising of the Tunisian people, transformed by powerful actors into a global proxy-war, impacted almost every country in Southwest Asia and North Africa (SWANA).

Although each country has its own circumstances, it was evident that the protest movement in Egypt was not like that in Tunisia. Egypt, unlike the smaller Tunisia, is a country with serious regional and global significance. Therefore, Egypt's protesters, its government, and regional and global actors were mindful of the effects of an independent Egypt. That knowledge informed these outside actors' involvement and strategies. The same can be said about Yemen and Libya. Events in Syria represented all these factors and more. Syria's location, demographics, government system, and alliances made it the most important country in the region and for these reasons, all regional and global actors committed resources to influence the direction of the Syrian crisis. That taken into account, and taking into account the issues inherent in being representative of issues in Bahrain, Yemen, Libya, and Egypt, the initial Syrian political crisis and its subsequent war will be our main case.

After the fall of Hosni Mubarak in Egypt, the social media- and satellite television-driven protest movements spread quickly, impacting the majority of the countries of SWANA. The unifying chant was: "The people want to bring down the [political] order."[4] In addition to Tunisia and Egypt, widespread and sustained protests took place in Libya, Bahrain, Yemen, Morocco, and Iraq. The uprising in Libya turned violent, resulting in the regime fall and brutal murder of Muammar Qaddafi. In Bahrain, Saudi rulers sent in troops to crush the peaceful but persistent uprising and to erase its iconic symbol, the Pearl Roundabout, the protesters' encampment. In Yemen, a Saudi plan forced out Ali Abdulla Saleh and brought his vice president, Abdrabbuh Mansur Hadi, to power; but when this failed to end the violence, the Saudi rulers launched a war on Yemen, turning Hadi's rule from time-limited to permanent. In Morocco, the shrewd king, Mohammed VI, sensing danger if he ignored the protesters' legitimate demands, ordered a constitutional amendment that offered political parties more power-sharing privileges. The Iraqi government, still struggling to stabilize a country traumatized by the US invasion, failed to manage sectarian tension and lost many of its Sunni-majority territories to resurgent al-Qaeda remnants operating independently as the Islamic State.[5] In other countries, including Algeria, Lebanon, Jordan, Kuwait, Oman, Sudan, Djibouti, Mauritania, Palestine, and Saudi Arabia, protests slowly died out after regimes made cosmetic changes, or as a result of demoralization from Syria and Libya's escalating violence and destruction. Given the similarities and connections between the rebellions across SWANA, the data from Syria and its analysis can be generalized, with minor caveats, to explain the other wars across the region during the same time period.

Just like protesters in other Arab countries, some Syrians began demonstrating on March 15, 2011, in Syrian cities in the south such as Daraa and north including Aleppo and Idlib. Just days before protests reached his country, Syrian president Bashar al-Assad downplayed the potential of such an uprising. He justified his prediction by arguing that his government's policies and ideals were in harmony with the demands of the Arab masses. He might be right on that account. His government, generally, took a more populist position on major issues relating to the Arab world at large. His government's support for the Palestinian people earned him high marks among Syrians and non-Syrians. Not only did his country take in a large number of Palestinian refugees, but it also offered shelter to political leaders of radical political movements, which no other country was willing to host. Hamas, the movement that had won the last round of elections in Palestinian-controlled territories, and which represented the backbone of the political wing opposed to the Oslo initiative, was headquartered in Damascus. Likewise, Syrian government had opposed military interventions in Iraq in 2003. Overall, Syria's stances on most regional and international issues were closer to the Arab street's views and appeared independent of Western dictates, which often characterized decisions so-called "moderate" Arab rulers made. However, Assad neglected to consider that people's goodwill has limits. His government, notwithstanding its populist and Western dictates-free policies, was a carbon copy of all other Arab regimes: a president for life, a single party dominating political life, a clan monopoly on political power, rampant corruption, widespread cronyism, and a flawed constitution. By the time President Assad realized the legitimacy of the protesters' demands, his security forces had already used their heavy-handed tactics against them, giving those on the side lines a reason to join the demonstrators or to withdraw their open support to the government.

When, on March 18, 2011, police and security forces confronted protesters with water cannons, tear gas, and killed four with live fire, shocking images of the clash eroded a larger segment of the Syrian people's goodwill toward the rest of the government. Soon afterward, more deadly clashes took place. The government claimed that armed protesters shot at and killed demonstrators to enflame tension. We have collected evidence supporting that claim in a number of instances. However, there is also evidence that government forces fired at peaceful protesters. By the end of March, nearly 70 people were reported killed in Syria. A month later, the number jumped to about 1,050 persons, including security forces and armed soldiers staffing check points.[6] With the increased violence, some police and military officers began defecting and forming "protection units" to resist the government's use of force. In most cases, defectors took their weapons and ammunition with them. In other cases, defectors joined other armed groups that were receiving support from foreign governments. On July 29, 2011, some of the high-ranking officers who defected, most of whom now reside in Turkey and Jordan, formally announced the formation of the Free Syrian Army (FSA), and the new entity dedicated itself not to the protection of civilians attacked by government forces, but to the overthrow of the Syrian government. A month later, on August 23, the FSA formed a political arm, the Syrian National Council (SNC), which some governments—including Qatar and France—immediately embraced as the sole representative of the Syrian people. With this event, the stage was set to uproot the standing Syrian government and all it represented, and to replace it with a new one under a new flag of three green, white, and black stripes with three red stars at the center.

Representative of regional actors' eagerness to take sides in the Syrian conflict, Turkey's government famously offered the Syrian government fifteen days, from the formation of the SNC, to meet the protesters' demands or face de-legitimization measures. Other countries followed: The Arab League, now under Qatar and Saudi Arabian control, gave the Syrian government three days to end "the violence" or find its membership in the League stripped and handed to the SNC. Parallel to these political steps, Turkey, Jordan, and Qatar had already begun equipping Syrian opposition forces with military hardware, finances, and fighters. Turkey in particular opened its borders to allow fighters from all over the world to enter Syria and join armed groups, especially al-Qaeda derivatives. By the end of 2011, Syria was effectively a battleground between the Syrian government and fighters with the support of a coalition calling itself "the Friends of the Syrian People," nominally comprising 63 countries when the group first met in Tunis,[7] but effectively of five states when they met at the end of 2017 or early 2018: the United States, the United Kingdom, France, Saudi Arabia, and Jordan. The FSA was the channel through which this coalition distributed weapons to all armed groups. The FSA's backers did not care, at this point in time, who as affiliated with the FSA, as long as the end result—which was is the overthrow of Assad—was achieved. The unity in purpose and aim among all armed groups survived for nearly six months after the formation of the FSA. However, that unity began to unravel in early 2012.

On December 23, 2011, two suicide bombers attacked the military intelligence facilities in Damascus, killing 44 people and injuring more than 150. Within days, a group calling itself *Jabhat nusrat ahl al-sham* (later shortened to, al-Nusra) took credit for the attack.[8] The FSA and the SNC did not condemn the attack. Rather, some of their leaders openly welcomed it. It later emerged that al-Nusra was a cell of al-Qaeda, created by order of Abu Bakr al-Baghdadi, the leader of al-Qaeda in Iraq (QIA), and led by a Syrian operative with the nom de guerre Abu Muhammad al-Julani. The new group, with a flag distinct from the FSA's, began to attract fighters from all over the world, and in some cases siphon fighters from other FSA groups. Al-Nusra continued to operate in Syria as a branch of al-Qaeda with a reporting line to al-Qaeda in Iraq. However, the al-Nusra's success moved al-Baghdadi to order al-Nusra to fold into al-Qaeda in Iraq under the new name, the Islamic State in Iraq and the Levant (ISIL; *al-Dawla al-Islamiya fi-'l-Iraq wa-'l-Sham*). Al-Julani rejected the move and continued to operate independently, under a number of names and within a number of coalitions, most recently (as of spring 2020), as Hayat Tahrir al-Sham (HTS). Meanwhile, ISIL expanded in both Syria and Iraq, to the point that it declared itself the pan-Islamic State (IS, 2014); this continued until its expansion and attacks forced members of the UN Security Council to authorize military and financial actions against it in 2015. The would-be decade-long war in Syria must be back grounded by these major events, as the actions of other players largely depended on regional and global actors.

Table 6.1 State and non-state actors in the Syrian war

	Syrian gov. and allies	Anti-Syrian gov. and allies
State actors	Russia, Iran, Iraq*, and China* (al-Duwal al-Sadiqa)	Qatar, KSA, Jordan, Egypt*, Turkey, U.S.A., U.K., France (Friends of the Syrian People)
Non-state actors	Allied Forces (al-Quwwat al-Halifa): 73 armed groups	Free Syrian Army (al-Jaysh al-Hurr): 101 armed groups
Hybrid groups	National Defense Forces (NDF), [al-Quwwat al-radifa]	Syrian Democratic Forces (SDF, Qasd): 73 armed groups

* Countries that did not formally send troops to Syria

Note. Compiled from 2011 War in SWANA: A Primary Sources Repository, https://swaana.integr8d.org/documents. 2019.

Before committing human rights crimes, they create war narratives

The 2011 war in Syria confirms the importance of narrative. In order to prepare for and execute a war, one must not only build a strong army and vast armament, but, importantly, one must compose a convincing story. A war narrative is crucial not only to absolve those who declare war from its financial cost and responsibility, but also to justify its human toll to the families of its fighters. If armed service is voluntary, a narrative is also critical to motivate more people to join and stay in the armed forces during wartime and to fight with zeal. One side may be able to wipe out the other militarily; however, winning a war requires a war narrative to keep a positive image of the war for future generations.

Each side must explain to its fighters and supporters why they are fighting. Regional and international actors generally justify an intervention to their citizens by linking it to a national interest. The meaning of national interest varies not only from one country to another, but from one administration to another. In all cases, national interest is often defined along security, economic, ideological, and/or political lines. In most cases, the stated justification differs from the actual motiving interest. Stated interests generally appeal to both domestic and global audiences. To appeal to the broadest audience possible, the justification for going to war emphasizes shared values and near-universal principles and norms. In the case of the Syrian war, justifying intervention in the affairs of a sovereign state required an appeal to virtuous motives. Governments of the U.S.-led coalition justified their involvement through the need to overthrow a government they accused of violating human rights and ruling without the consent of their citizens. Leaders of the Russia-led coalition justified their intervention through the need to preserve world order and defend Syrian sovereignty. The real motive behind all of these actors' intervention, though, is to defend national interests in Syria. We must look elsewhere for significant narratives that help to explain the real forces that drive groups of people to kill, in the most horrific way, other groups of people. We must look at the narrative that sustains the people and groups fighting on the ground.

The first step to building a war narrative is identifying the enemy by name. It is the most important, and telling, step. The actors coin specific names for themselves, but the other side assigns a new name for its opponent. Even journalists adopt a specific name, or qualify a name with their own description, to lead readers in the direction they want the narrative to take. When faced with detrimental political or legal circumstances, groups change their names to escape legal sanctions, rebrand, create new alliances, and/or appease sponsors. The Islamic State was the last name that al-Qaeda in Iraq took since the start of the war in Syria.[9] However, most commentators, politicians, media outlets, and opponents of the group adopted the Arabic acronym, Da`esh,[10] which is the Arabic abbreviation of *al-Dawla al-Islamiyya fi al-Iraq wa-'l-Sham*.

ISIL and al-Nusra were especially adept at rebranding, creating coalitions, and assigning labels to others. The labels they took signalled their political and social agenda for the communities they conquered. ISIL was especially committed to erasing the cultural and demographic presence of communities they deemed condemned on the basis of religious and sectarian identity. Their cultural purge was retroactive in that they purged cultural icons created thousands of years before the start of Islam in the territories they controlled, such as the ruins of Palmyra. In fact, twice ISIL attacked the city of Palmyra and threatened its cultural heritage, and the US coalition did not act to prevent the destruction of historic ruins,[11] focusing instead on building a militia to control oil and energy fields in nearby Deir Ezzor.

The most powerful and militarily effective armed groups in Syria espoused Salafist ideologies. Initially, ISIL, al-Nusra, Jaish al-Islam, Ahrar al-Sham, Failaq al-Sham, Failaq al-Rahman, and other similar groups identified their enemy as *nusayris* and their *rafidi* and cross-worshippers backers. They adopted the term *nusayri* as early as 2012 and carried out purging campaigns in Alawi, Shia, and Christian neighborhoods, towns, and cities. Their genocidal crimes forced these communities to move to safer areas, or to resist and live under siege for years. The fate of the towns of Ma`lula, Nubl, Zahra, Kafriya, Fu`a, and other besieged or destroyed towns where sectarian and religious communities lived under stress and threat is well documented.

In 2013, with guidance from leaders of Hezbollah, these communities adopted the label *takfiri* for their threatening enemies. The government of Iraq adopted the acronym Daesh to refer to ISIL and *dawaesh* (the plural of Da`ish) to refer to all those who embrace ISIL's ideology and practices. The word Daesh was received as so diminutive that many governments around the world, including that of Saudi Arabia, the birthplace of the Wahhabi religious doctrine espoused by al-Qaeda derivatives including ISIL and al-Nusra, adopted it as well.

War narratives are stories that answer questions around why and how one should fight. While national armies and armed groups have their own media outlets to tell these stories, it enhances the stories' credibility if other outlets, independent or otherwise, become conduits for them. Therefore, one must examine sources and consider who is telling a story in order to form a fuller picture of reality and distinguish facts from propaganda. It must be noted that news media in Arab countries, like their counterparts in the United States of America,[12] have struggled with a trust deficit. News media in all Arab countries are either under the direct control of governments, limited by strict laws informed by the ministries of information, and/or controlled by special interest groups.

For this work, I relied on more than one hundred media outlets from all over the world, storing data of their online coverage—or lack thereof—of the events of these case studies, and tracking them over the span of 8 years, resulting in a more than 77,000 data points. The data includes evidence produced by the warring parties themselves, by third parties, and by governments involved or uninvolved in the conflict.[13]

From a systems thinking perspective, media and news organization are part of national and international systems. They are not independent systems designed to carry out their own functions. Media outlets are formally or informally connected to other systems, and their functions are designed to produce outcomes in harmony with other systems. The evidence emerging from the Syrian war confirms this systems thinking analysis. Media outlets signal their bias in many ways. The choice of words in a headline, the location of the story on the website's main entry page, the illustrative photograph that accompanies or does not accompany the news story, or even the absence of a news story about a significant event communicates a clear position of the media outlet. For this work, it suffices to cite several examples to highlight some editorial decisions that signal a political position relevant to political events.[14]

Qatar played a major role in Arab Spring events in general, and in the war in Syria in particular. The rulers of this geographically small but natural gas-rich country can exert immense political and diplomatic power. They can do so partly due to their alliances with influential political groups in several Arab countries, and partly due to their leveraging the power of the Al Jazeera satellite channel and its accompanying digital media resources in shaping public discourse in the Arabic-speaking world. From 2011 to 2013, Al Jazeera's coverage of the war in Syria was prominent: an average of three news stories occupying the immediately viewable space of the channel's website, with at least one story enhanced through graphic images showing the death and/or destruction caused by what they consistently called "the forces of the Syrian regime" or "Assad's forces." Then, in the summer of 2013, the Emir of Qatar stepped aside and his son, Tamim, took over. With that political change, the news channel and its associated assets dialed down the tone and frequency of their coverage of the war

Table 6.2 Ownership of media outlets used in this study

Ownership Kind	Code	%
Government-owned media	GO	29.0
Corporation-owned media	CO	7.9
Private corporation-owned media	PCO	29.0
Political Party-Owned Media	PPO	11.3
Private Individual-owned media	PIO	11.3
Non-profit-owned media	NPO	11.9
Media with unknown ownership	UKO	0

Note. Compiled from 2011 War in SWANA: A Primary Sources Repository, https://swaana.integr8d.org/media/, 2019.

in Syria, although the language remained broadly unchanged. Al Jazeera continued to refer to the Syrian Arab Army (SAA), the official name of the armed forces of Syria, as the forces of the regime (*quwwat al-nidham*), but referred to the armed opposition groups by the name they took for themselves: the Free Syrian Army (*al-jaish al-suri al-hurr*). The editorial policy Al Jazeera adopted to report on the war in Syria did not create much conflict for it within the GCC. However, the war in Yemen increased pressure on Al Jazeera to accommodate the Saudi narrative of that war, by resonating with other state-owned media outlets like Sky News and Al Arabiya, which were broadcasting out of the United Arab Emirates. For instance, while Al Arabiya used the word *qutila* (killed) to refer to the deaths among forces opposing the Saudi coalition and *istushhida* (martyred) to refer to deaths among Saudi troops, Al Jazeera insisted on using *qutila* to refer to deaths on both sides. That policy forced the rulers of the U.A.E. and K.S.A. to accuse Qatar of supporting Houthis, or of not being supportive of Saudi troops and the troops of its allies.

The large number of armed groups, their divergent loyalties, their ideological and religious backgrounds, and the shift in political climates for their backers made it difficult for all of these groups to converge on one mission and align under one slogan. Nonetheless, we will identify the most common features among the majority of, or most influential, armed opposition groups.

Since taking up arms from 2011 through 2018, all armed fighters opposing the Syrian government, Syrian and foreign, committed themselves to one goal: the overthrow of the Syrian government. On that point, there was no disagreement and it was not open for negotiation. The main backers of the opposition forces also embraced that position. The governments of France, the United Kingdom, the United States under the Obama administration, Turkey, Qatar, and Saudi Arabia have maintained that Assad must be removed as a prerequisite for peace in Syria.[15]

Members of all armed groups fighting in Syria concluded audio and video statements and actions by shouting, "God is great" (*allahu akhbar*) three or more times. They used the chant when they fired their weapons, when they executed prisoners, when they abused civilians accused of sympathizing with the government, and whenever they undertook any act associated with their cause. Over 91% of the videos released by the various armed opposition groups affiliated with the FSA or the Salafists have framed their battle against the Syrian government as a battle against the Nusayris and the Safawis. All Salafist groups identified Shia (*rafida*) and apostates (*murtaddin*) as their main enemy.

Qatar and Saudi Arabia framed the war in political and ethnic terms. First, they insisted that Bashar Assad lost legitimacy because he killed too many of his own people. Second, and most importantly, they blamed the war in Syria on Iran, accusing Iran of interfering in Arab affairs. This might explain their original enthusiasm for weakening Syria's government and subsequent actions to overthrow it by force. Saudi Arabia and Qatar did not like Syria's friendly relations with Iran; they thought the war in Syria was the best opportunity to end Iran's influence in the region. Turkey, though less sectarian, was also driven by Recep Tayyip Erdogan's aspiration to be both a pan-Islamic leader for Sunni Muslims and a Turkish nationalist for Turkish people. Erdogan was hostile to both non-Sunni religious groups and to Kurds. Those sentiments shaped his regional, foreign, and national security policies.

The non-state actors supportive of the Syrian government can be divided into two main groups. Secular Arab nationalists from Syria and its neighboring countries like Lebanon, Iraq, Jordan, Egypt, and Palestine; and religious minorities like Shia, Druze, Christian, and Assyrian communities. The Shia were among the earliest to join the battle in Syria, mainly motivated by Salafists' threats to Shia shrines. Salafist armed groups had already destroyed many religious sites, spurring Shia Muslims to go to Syria to protect their religious shrines. Hezbollah initially sent fighters solely to protect Shia shrines near Damascus. With the war engulfing all of Syria, and with many Shia towns threatened by armed Sunni groups, Shia presence in Syria expanded and soon became full partner to the Syrian government forces, the Syrian Arab Army (SAA). Despite the sectarian motives compelling Shia fighters to enter the Syria war, Hezbollah leaders took care framing their participation. The leader of the movement, Hussain Nasrallah, coined the phrase *al-irhab al-takfiri*, and his fighters and supporters used that designation ever since.

In general, most opposition groups adopted names and slogans that appealed to their supporters and funders. Historically, financial support to religious groups has come from the rich Arab states of the Persian Gulf: mainly Saudi Arabia, Qatar, Bahrain, and Kuwait. Saudi Arabia often supports Salafists while Qatar generally supports groups associated with the Muslim Brotherhood. That trend persisted in Syria. However, the urgency with which they wanted to overthrow Assad forced them to channel money and weapons to all groups powerful enough to help achieve that goal. The most zealous fighters were generally Salafist, and Saudi Arabian support went to those groups. The growth of Salafist groups and their ability to win battles reduced the level of resources going towards the secular FSA groups. By 2013, the influence of the FSA was drastically reduced, forcing many of its fighters to either quit or join other groups with more resources and influence. Consequently, the Salafist groups combined managed to control nearly 60% of Syrian territory by the end of 2014.

The Syrian government, led by an Arab nationalist party, is secular, with a history of hostility towards religious political parties. During the war, that history became a liability for the Syrian government. It was easy for religious armed groups to attack government officials' and party members' lack of religious commitment. The Syrian government badly needed an actor with religious credentials to take its side and provide some balance.

Most governments of nations belonging to the Arab League, lacking legitimizing democratic authority through free and transparent elections, rely on historical religious institutions for legitimacy. Those institutions are limited. Today, there are six influential religious institutions in Islamic societies: four Sunni and three Shia. The Sunni institutions consist of the learning centers of Hijaz located in Mecca and Madina,[16] the Azhar learning center in Egypt, the Hashemite authority in Jordan and Morocco, and the Ottoman legacy in Turkey. The learning centers in Najaf in Iraq and Qom in Iran represent the Shia institutions, along with the Zaydi legacy in Yemen. These are either ancient institutions or ones that sprung from ancient institutions. Governing systems and individuals throughout the Islamic world have used these institutions to legitimize themselves, regardless of whether they are the institution's host country. Throughout Islamic history, these institutions competed for influence and control over resources—human and otherwise. They played a major role in the 2011 war in SWANA as well.

The Hijaz institution is controlled by Salafism, the creed which a large number of the armed opposition groups in Syria follow, including al-Qaeda and its derivatives. Salafism, as interpreted and applied by Wahhabists, is also the dominant sect in Saudi Arabia and Qatar. Al-Azhar represents the "moderate" Sunni Islam and, since falling under the control of the Egyptian government, has lost much of its influence. However, al-Azhar is believed to have been inspirational to the Muslim Brotherhood, the seventy-year-old religio-political movement with global influence. In other words, however real or perceived, the loss of independence al-Azhar suffered was recouped through the Muslim Brotherhood and its derivatives. The blood bond that ties the ruling families in Morocco and Jordan to the Hashemite clan, from which the Prophet Muhammad descended, provides those two monarchs with much-needed stability and legitimacy for countering extremists within their countries. Turkey being the seat of the last pan-Islamic political authority inspires grandeur in Turkish leaders like Erdogan and a measure of respect and nostalgia among Sunni Muslims outside Turkey. Imami-Shia learning centers in Najaf and Qom have played critical roles in Iran and

Iraq and commanded influence over millions of Shia Muslims around the world, including Hezbollah, whose leaders were inspired by Najaf-trained and Qom-educated scholars. Moreover, the fatawas of grand Ayatollah Ali al-Sistani since the 2003 US invasion of Iraq have played a stabilizing role in Iraq. Lastly, the heirs of Zayd Ibn Ali, the fifth Shia Imam, continue their legacy of challenging unjust rulers today, which has been a driving force in Yemen's war. Importantly, all of these institutions have direct or indirect influence on the war in Syria and they will play a role in formulating human rights norms at the conclusion of the conflict. The authoritative standing of these institutions has forced governments to pay close attention to them and, in many cases, to coopt them—making them part of the overall system. The Syrian government, understandably, needed their influence to craft a winning narrative for a very brutal and divisive war.

The Syrian leadership hoped that Hamas, a very popular movement in the Arab world and an affiliate of the Muslim Brotherhood, would provide the Syrian government with a religious endorsement and dispel the charge of Alawi control over Syria. Hamas, at that time, was enjoying wide support from Qatar and Egypt, then-ruled by Mohamed Morsi, the first president belonging to the Muslim brotherhood. Hamas chose to leave Syria instead of siding with the secular Syrian government. It is safe to project that, without open support from other Arab governments, which did not materialize, and without support from popular religious movements or institutions, the Syrian government would have lost the war to the religious groups. When a respected religious scholar, al-Buti, refused to condemn the government and endorse the armed opposition, a suicide bomber targeted him in a mosque, killing him with scores of students and worshippers. That event underscored the importance of religious authorities providing cover to one side or another. In short, the Syrian government, without any endorsement from religious authorities or religious groups, would be seen as a militantly secular regime controlled by an offshoot religious sect committed to oppressing Sunni Muslims. That narrative was one which all armed opposition groups embraced and used because they believed it to be a winning narrative.

Religious leaders like al-Qaradawi in Qatar and al-`Ar`ur in Saudi Arabia not only condemned the Syrian government, but also called upon their followers around the world to either join the war in person or send money to those fighting against the Syrian government, which they dubbed infidel. So, when Hezbollah decided to openly join the war on the side of the Syrian government, that moment must be seen as a turning point—not because of the military edge it added to the war, but, importantly, because of the narrative it injected. The Syrian government's war narrative, abbreviated in "*allah, suriyya, bashar, wa-bass*" was a losing narrative by itself.[17] It badly needed a winning narrative and a legitimate argument for fighting this war.

Hezbollah, even though it is a Shia movement and armed group, is widely respected by many Arabs and Muslims, regardless of sect. The movement decided to invest that political capital in the Syrian war and, in doing so, it forced a new conversation on inclusion, on the place and function of religion, on the rights of minority social groups, and on universal values. Importantly, Hezbollah (which translates to "the Party of God"), which was seen by its admirers as moral actor, needed to articulate a narrative for fighting a war against other Muslims: If they were killing other Muslims to avenge and protect a sectarian creed, how far would they go to achieve that goal? The Party's answer had the potential to add fuel to the already burning fire or extinguish it. Importantly, the Party's narrative could shape the nature of discourse on human rights within Islamic societies. Hezbollah's intervention, besides adding a new narrative to the war in Syria, helped the Syrian government refine its own narrative and make it more compatible with that of its current and future allies.

For the Syrian government, the official narrative was very simple: The Syrian government, led by President Bashar al-Assad, is legitimate and sovereign. The government interpreted sovereignty to mean that no group of people within its border can use violence against the state or its citizens. Therefore, anyone taking up arms against the state is a criminal terrorist and the government had the responsibility to fight them until they submit, move out of state-controlled territories, or face the armed forces of the state. Moreover, representatives of the Syrian government argued that fighting terrorism, which may lead to killing unarmed bystanders, does not delegitimize the government because such a loss of life occurred while agents of the state were discharging their duties to protect its citizens. The chants of the soldiers of the Syrian Arab Army in the battlefield were: "God, Syria, Bashar. Period" (*allah, suriyya, bashar, wa-bass*). As to the government's enemy, government officials consistently said that their war was on terrorists and terrorists' backers, and that war would continue until they "cleanse the homeland from the filth of the terrorists" (*tathir al-watan min rijs al-irhabiyyin*). The government's slogan and declaration of war on terrorism remained consistent for the duration of this study.

Armed opposition groups used slogans and committed acts that threatened minority religious and ethnic groups. The narratives and actions became real to these communities, especially since many of the armed groups committed crimes of genocide and documented themselves doing so. Consequently, these groups were either prepared to escape and relocate to government-controlled areas or establish Community Protection Units to repel attackers or die trying. After eight years of active war, Kurdish, Ayzidi, Shia, and Alawi villages and towns were besieged by armed groups, but they did not surrender because doing so would mean imminent death, torture, and enslavement. It was not difficult, then, to frame the war as sectarian (Shia-Sunni) and ethnic (Arab-Kurd-Persian-Turkmen) conflict. The data supporting this reality was abundant: shocking and repugnant images of cruelty, desecrating dead bodies, cutting off internal organs and chewing them, placing POWs in metal cages and burning them alive, and forcing

134 *Globalism, history, and human rights today*

Table 6.3 The various actors' descriptions of their opponents. The use of labels by the warring factions include these tags: Rafida, Nusayri, Persian, Crusader, Apostate, `Ilmani, Regime, Assad Regime, and Daesh

Actor	Label used to identify the opponents
Syrian Government	Terrorist, Takfiri, Daesh, Regime, government
U.S.A.	Regime, militia, ISIS, government
Russia	Terrorists, opposition, "Friends"
Hezbollah	Takfiri, Daesh, government
Iran	Takfiri, Daesh, Wahhabi, Terrorist, government
al-Qaeda	Crusaders, Apostate, Atheist
ISIL	Rafida, Nusayri, Persian, Crusader, Apostate, `Ilmani,
HTS/Nusra	Rafida, Nusayri, Persian, Crusader, Apostate, `Ilmani,
Jaysh al-Islam	Rafida, Nusayri, Persian, Crusader, Apostate, `Ilmani,
Ahrar al-Sham	Rafida, Nusayri, Persian, Crusader, Apostate, `Ilmani,
FSA	Nusayri, Persian, Daesh, Regime, Assad Regime

Note. Compiled from 2011 War in SWANA: A Primary Sources Repository, https://swaana.integr8d.org/documents/, 2019.

children to witness or participate in public executions and mass killings. In short, it was easy for any party to frame the entire conflict as a civil war or a sectarian war and build a narrative to sustain such strife.

Although the wars in Libya and Yemen were no less brutal, it was in the war in Syria that the stakes were so apparent, the alliances were extensive, and the justifying narratives were so clear. In Syria the sectarian, ideological, and political rhetoric was scripted and choreographed to shocking levels. The toll and suffering that civilians in Syria endured is captured in many contexts and through numerous tools. Thousands of videos released by all parties provide raw statements on why they fought and how they fought, giving us, researchers and observers, a glimpse of the horror and cruelty of other armed conflicts. The level of access to that spoken and practiced cruelty was sickening, but once taken in the context of the cruelty of European wars, it offered hope—hope born out of humans' recoil from savage instinct and naked racism.

The hopeful, low-violence uprising in Syria lasted several weeks before external self-serving forces took over and directed it into a sectarian war, then a regional war, and then a global proxy war. During each transition, the war narratives and slogans changed, flags were replaced, and alliances were rebuilt. But cruelty and violence remained constant. Social media allowed researchers like me to remotely access battles and outcomes of battles, and to view and listen to the most graphic images and the most obscene statements. In most cases, this social media-enabled access was authored by the conflict's very actors. The content is raw, uncensored, unfiltered, and unapologetic—things historians and theoreticians thought were impossible.

The 2011 wars emerged out of rebellions motivated by political injustices and social grievances that cut across racial and ethnic boundaries.

Specifically, the war in Syria was framed along racial, ethnic, and sectarian fault-lines. The majority of armed groups, especially the better armed, trained, and supported ones, used coded words and phrases, *nusayri, rafidi,* and *farisi* to frame the war as a war in which the builders of the Islamic civilization face threats from deviant racial groups intent on corrupting the true Islam—Sunni Islam—and the race trusted with Islam: the Arab race. Without providing actual evidence, these groups accused Persian Iran and its mercenaries in Syria, Iraq, and Yemen of "raping Muslim women" and altering the "demography of Arab cities and lands." They conflated Shiism with being Persian and considered it an attack on Arabs and Sunnis for Shia Muslims to publicly practice and preach in historically Sunni communities. The murder and cruel treatment of Shiite worshippers in Egypt during Mohamed Morsi's presidency was an example of this narrative in action.[18] The marginalizing of the Shia majority in Bahrain and the push to assimilate Shia minorities in Saudi Arabia point to a systemic and supremacist impulse in some Arab societies to demean other social groups on the basis of ethnicity and sectarian identity. Even when the Shia communities' mosques were attacked in Saudi Arabia and Kuwait, rulers came out to speak against the violence, but they consistently refused to acknowledge the victims as they were—Shia—and as equal citizens. The rulers of Saudi Arabia, for instance, insisted that the communities in the eastern parts of the country were part of the fabric of Saudi Arabia and as such they should be protected. In other words, the rulers of the kingdom indirectly blamed these communities for the violence they endured because they may have identified themselves as something other than Saudi. Placing the burden on the victim is a common practice of states with a legacy of supremacy.[19] Such practices were ever-present in the 2011 wars in SWANA. The evidence is overwhelming.

Notes

1. In 2006, researchers at the Johns Hopkins Bloomberg School of Public Health and al-Mustansiriya University in Baghdad found that as many as 654,965 Iraqis may have died since hostilities began in Iraq in March 2003. See Gilbert Burnham et al, "Mortality after the 2003 invasion of Iraq," *The Lancet* 368, no. 9545(2006): 1421–8.
2. George Bush, interviewed by John King, *Bush 43,* CNN, April 25, 2013, last accessed at www.cnn.com/2013/04/24/politics/bush-interview-king/index.html 7/15/2020:"History will ultimately judge ... I'm a content man."
3. Interestingly, facing public outcry from the families of the people Ben Ali's regime killed and/or tortured, Saudi rulers justified their offering him asylum and protection through their commitment to the institution of *ijara* (or *istija*), the pre-Islamic Arab and Islamic norm that requires leaders to offer protection to offenders (or those simply accused of committing an offense) facing harsh retributions. This is a very good example of the continuity of custom and tradition and how they can be used or abused dependent on the circumstances.
4. *al-sha`b yurid isqat al-nizam.*"

5. While al-Qaeda sympathizers may have existed in parts of Iraq prior to the US invasion and subsequent occupation of Iraq, al-Qaeda organizing an armed presence in that country was initiated by the invasion and overthrow of the Iraqi government. Initially, al-Qaeda-inspired and -affiliated groups took many names and often changed names to adapt to changing political and military conditions in Iraq and neighboring countries. The Islamic State was the last name adopted by fighters who espoused the same ideology and religious creed as al-Qaeda and who splintered for strategic and operational reasons.
6. This is the number of deaths as reported by the end of the day on May 24, 2011.
7. The first Conference of the Friends of the Syrian People was held in Tunis on February 24, 2012. The participants called for restrictions and sanctions on the Syrian government including travel bans on members of the government, freezing their assets, ceasing the purchase of Syrian hydrocarbon products, stopping infrastructure investment and financial services in Syria, reducing diplomatic ties, banning shipment of arms and related materials to the Syrian government, and considering means of restricting the Syrian government's access to fuel and other supplies used for military purposes. By the time the group met again in Paris, France (July 6, 2012) the number of participants jumped to 107 countries and organizations. The United States, Saudi Arabia, France, Jordan and the U.K. met in Europe and drafted a political plan, which they presented to the UN Syria envoy Staffan de Mistura, to counter the Sochi meeting organized by Russia for the same purpose. The unannounced meeting could be the last meeting of the Friends of the Syrian People, signalling the demise of the group.
8. Al-Nusra formally announced its formation on January 23, 2012.
9. As of June 2020.
10. The author of an article in *the Boston Globe* suggested that what we call the opponent, in this case ISIL, could predetermine their defeat. "The Obama Administration should switch to this nomenclature [Daesh], too, because how we talk about this group is central to defeating them." www.bostonglobe.com/opinion/2014/10/09/words-matter-isis-war-use-daesh/V85GYEuasEEJgrUun0dMUP/story.html; accessed Dec. 21, 2014. It must be noted that there is no linguistic Arabic root for the derivative Daesh, which makes the abbreviation even more powerful: Instead of being recognized as the Islamic State, with all the glory and reverence that term may invoke, Muslims opposed to ISIL preferred to use a meaningless word to rebut the group's claim of legitimacy in name and actions.
11. Eventually, ISIL invaded Palmyra, killed the caretaker of the heritage organization, Khaled al-Asaad, and destroyed most of the ancient ruins in August, 2015.
12. According to Gallup, Americans' trust in mass media has steadily declined from 55% in 1999 to 32% in 2017.
13. This research benefited from the collection of documents including news media records, videos, maps, and files made part of a repository of primary sources documenting the 2011 SWANA War. The collection of primary sources can be accessed by other researchers and students online: https://swaana.integr8d.org.
14. This work is part of a more comprehensive research project consisting of broad categories of primary sources including a media coverage quantitative study based on a database of screen capture of media outlets over the span of a decade. Interested researchers may examine the associated website linked to from the author's.

15. Initially, the armed groups and their backers wanted a total and complete regime change. However, after three years of pursuing that goal without much success, some of the regional and global powers reduced that goal to the removal of Assad. By the end of the seventh year, Saudi Arabia at least, perhaps encouraged by its allies, tried to negotiate a deal would allow Assad to stay in power on the condition that he break his alliance with Iran.
16. It must be noted that the Hijaz institutions do not necessarily derive their power and authority from the kind of scholarship and credibility of the scholar but from geography and economics. Mecca and Medina are two of three of the most revered cities in the world for Muslims. They are controlled by the Saud Clan, which turned the custodianship of the two mosques in those two cities, coupled with the huge wealth generated from oil, into a source of authority and power.
17. Statements by al-Qaradawi and other religious scholars, in relations to rebellion and political legitimacy are archived in this repository: https://swaana.integr8d.org.
18. The cruelty of this event was captured on video and played on main television stations, most of which are still loyal the Mubarak regime, and on social media, creating much of the sympathy that supported the coup against Morsi and his Muslim Brotherhood party.
19. Explaining racist attitudes by pointing to the identity of the abused social group helps perpetuate racism rather than defeat it. Parallel to the war in SWANA, Muslims in Western societies were targeted with hate speech, physical attacks, and destruction of property. To explain these events, some scholars coined the term "Islamophobia" as a mental condition embedded in perpetrators of hate and violence. In other words, the same way a person may have an irrational fear of spiders, these individuals have an irrational fear of Islam and Muslims. This theory, in a sense, blames the victim, not the victimizer. The perpetrators are the problem: Their hate being targeted against Muslims is circumstantial, for hating Muslims is tolerated and even enabled by the current US administration. When it becomes more convenient to hate another social group, they will do so, because racism is rooted in supremacy and supremacy directs one to feel and believe that they are better than all others.

7 Actual and instrumentalized human rights

The 2011 wars in SWANA bring to life all the forces, tensions, inconsistencies, impulses, and conditions that shape discourse on human rights and allow for human rights abuses to persist. The most persistent forces that weaken the drive for respecting human rights echo throughout history: supremacy, racism, greed, and hubris. On their own, these impulses are not destructive to human rights norms. However, they are consequential when the State (government) enables them through action or inaction. In this case, we see how the West instrumentalized the proscription against weapons of mass destruction to achieve a political goal. Yet the West, and all other nuclear countries, possess and threaten use of these weapons. From a logical standpoint, the mere possession of nuclear weapons is a statement of willingness to commit war crimes, with a necessarily supremacist justification: Some people are prepared to kill everyone in another country if such a country threatens their people. This is not an equation of mutual destruction; it is a statement of intent to commit a crime within a set of circumstances.

The 2011 wars in SWANA present new challenges and new realities relevant to human rights discourse and to the institutions entrusted with mitigating human rights abuses. The wars expose weaknesses in the current world order and the failure of world leaders to address changing practices of the State including the State's adoption of hybrid wars to shrink their own responsibility. Since the invasion of Iraq and subsequent extended occupation, Western governments realized that to win the war on terror, as they called it, the rules of engagement had to change. Part of this change meant inventing new legal vocabulary, such as *illegal combatant*, *enhanced interrogation*, and *pre-emptive war*. Some practices were too cruel to be captured by the phrase *enhanced interrogation*. Western governments engaged in rendition, through which captured fighters are sent to countries run by governments that torture people. These loopholes allowed Western governments to circumvent their obligations under human rights treaties they ratified and which prohibit them from torture, indefinite detention, and extrajudicial killing. The precedents set during the occupation of Iraq became normalized, including in countries that used to fear criticism and sanctions from the US administration in defense of human rights.

Governments resigned to fighting asymmetrical wars adopted a new strategy: the hybrid war. In hybrid wars, states enhance their combat and control operations through hiring private mercenaries and affiliate armed groups. These affiliate forces, called *Quwwat radifa* when Arab armies use them, operate in the shadows and are not bound by the laws of armed conflicts even when governments pay them. The data collected over the past eight years shows that the majority of human rights abuses were committed by non-state actors who were either affiliated with states or allowed by the state to operate in areas under their control.

The case presented here also provides evidence that the colonial powers do not recognize colonialism as a crime. Invasion of other countries, occupation of other people's lands, and imposition of harsh sanctions designed to cause famine and disease are reaffirmation of colonial practices. These actions reveal that colonial countries' support for freedom and self-determination is mere posturing, not policy or ethics. Muslims' propensity for sliding into sectarian wars and sectarian hate speech show that they have not addressed or resolved their collective past crimes. They have not learned from the years of caliphs committing genocides and war crimes. Tunisian politicians' inability to avoid political binaries of civil versus religious, and Muslim versus *kafir,* points to their willful ignorance," and of the mindset that resulted in excluding dissenters through *khawarijism* discourse and the inquisition (*Mihna*) under the Abbasid rule.

The case of the 2011 wars in SWANA confirms that human rights abuses occur when the State unleashes violence, or allows it to take place, to achieve political goals. Importantly, in this case, we see that human rights abuses are more likely to happen when historical tensions align with present conditions. Here, we have the Western legacies of racism, genocide, and colonialism intersecting with Arab and Islamic legacies of sectarianism, ethnicism, supremacy, genocide, and intolerance to dissent. The result is amplified hate speech, human rights crimes, widespread destruction, and normalized death and abuse.

The events of the 2011 wars in SWANA prove that human rights crimes and abuses are exclusively State crimes. States may commit abuses directly, through proxies, or by creating conditions where non-state actors can commit crimes. The data show that the cruelest and most brazen human rights abuses occurred when armed groups either had open support from regional or world governments, or when world governments did not care that such groups committed human rights crimes. Once governments withdrew their open support to these armed groups or condemned their practices, instances of open abuses decreased and brazenness disappeared.

Importantly, we have also learned that many of the armed groups changed their names to adapt to different conditions, to maintain the support of their sponsors, or both. With the same ease they can change their names, they can also cease to exist after committing human rights crimes and escape punishment. With responsibility placed squarely on the State, governments would have no incentive to use proxies to commit crimes; they would still be held responsible for crimes committed by groups they supported or allowed. Human rights crimes should not be subject to a statute of limitations when they are State-only crimes, and if non-State actors are held responsible for crimes they committed instead of the governments that support them, it creates a backdoor statute of limitations, which will further weaken the struggle for bringing those responsible for human rights abuses to justice.

Saying that human rights crimes are State crimes only does not mean that only the State can be held responsible, which would limit legal action to civil action. Agents of the State must be held personally responsible, too. This would require that the doctrines of sovereign immunity and qualified immunity must be revoked or, at minimum, redefined to make them inapplicable to human rights crimes.

The outcome of the war in Syria (though still ongoing as of this writing) will confirm a historical fact that cuts across cultures and through time: Armed rebellion against one's own government is the least sure path to achieving social and economic rights. In the context of Islamic societies from the seventh-century caliphate to the twentieth century sultanate, only two armed rebellions—out of 112 major armed insurrections—succeeded in overthrowing the established political order. And if we exclude outside military intervention in support of armed rebels, then no armed uprising has succeeded in overthrowing a government. The success rate of *unarmed* uprisings in changing rulers, or forcing them to make critical changes, is much higher. It should be noted that unarmed, un-militarized rebellion does not necessarily mean peaceful protest. It simply means that the main instrument of resistance is not the power of the sword or the gun. In the SWANA region, and since 2011, more governments were overthrown or forced to reform by unarmed uprisings than by armed rebellion. Importantly, even in the rare instance when an armed rebellion succeeds in overthrowing its own government, such success comes with a devastating price in terms of human, economic, health, and environmental costs. In the majority of cases, the country and the community end up fractured for generations. These facts underscore the basic principle related to human rights: Struggling for human rights should never be built on the assumption that the next government will not abuse human rights. Rather, it should be built on the fact that every government, especially since the adoption of the modern nation-State paradigm, is a violator of human rights or a potential violator of human rights. Therefore, using the single instrument of the State on which it has a legal monopoly—violence—to replace one regime with another, is ultimately authorizing the State to use violence and abuse human rights in the process. The strategy for human rights advocacy should be about creating the systems that reduce harm and abuse at the hands of the State, not establishing a utopian State that, against all odds, might promote human rights.

More relevant to the discourse on human rights, the war in Syria exposed the instrumentalization of human rights for political purposes when armed groups claimed that they were fighting to protect civilians, when their actions turned urban areas into battle grounds. All armed groups were launching their attacks from densely populated areas, which is a war crime. Unlike the Kurds, who have been fighting Turkish armed forces by launching attacks from the mountains and other sparsely inhabited areas, Syrian armed groups occupied towns and cities and tuned mosques, schools, and community centers into command and control centers, drawing bombardment from government forces, resulting in total destruction of civilian areas. The data show that most of the armed activities took place within densely populated areas, causing loss of life and injury among civilians and destruction of civilian infrastructures.

Generally, as the 2011 SWANA events show, the concept of human rights has become political modeling clay in the hands of the governments of powerful nations, invoked whenever they have a need for intervention, and ignored when it is inconvenient to speak up against wanton abuses. Through military occupation and political, economic, and cultural influence, and at times coercion, Islamic societies are made to relive the atrocities of the European wars in the dawn of the twenty-first century.[1]

To understand the genesis of the human rights discourse in Western societies, we must recall the so-called War of Italian Unification. On June 24, 1859, Franco-Sardinian armed forces clashed with Austrian troops near the town of Solferino in northern Italy. Henri Dunant, a Swiss businessman who came to the area to meet Napoleon III, witnessed the aftermath of this battle. Dunant described that war's horror this way: soldiers missing limbs packed on church floors, bodies of dead soldiers covering battle fields, and civilians displaced by violence. The images had a profound impact on him and in 1862 he wrote a monograph entitled *A Memory of Solferino*.[2] After describing scenes burned into his memory, Dunant concluded his book with a series of questions and wishes. Specifically, he wondered if it would be possible, "in time of peace and quiet, to form relief societies for the purpose of having care given to the wounded in wartime by devoted and thoroughly qualified volunteers?"[3] He wished for a time when "some international principle, sanctioned by a convention and inviolate in character, which, once agreed upon and ratified, might constitute the basis for societies for the relief of the wounded in the different European countries?"[4]

Henri Dunant's book was a transformative and motivating work. It was translated into many European languages and read widely. One reader was a lawyer from Geneva, Gustave Moynier, who chaired a small charity called the Geneva Public Welfare Society. Moynier asked his society to read the book and use its suggestions to come up with practical plan to limit the horror of militarized conflicts. On February 9, 1863, a five-member committee, including Dunant, Moynier, General Guillaume-Henri Dufour, Dr. Louis Appia and Dr. Théodore Maunoir, was established. Preliminarily, they called the committee the International Committee for Relief to the Wounded. Later, the name was changed to the International Committee of the Red Cross (ICRC).

On August 26, 1863, the International Committee convened an international conference in Geneva. Thirty people (fourteen government delegates, six NGO representatives, and seven unaffiliated individuals) attended the event. This meeting laid the foundation for what would later become the International Conferences of the Red Cross/Red Crescent. The conference adopted ten resolutions, which provided for the establishment of societies, the Red Cross/Red Crescent, for relief to wounded soldiers.

Less than a year after the founding of the Red Cross Societies, Austrian and Prussian armies invaded Denmark. On February 1, 1864, the International Committee sent two delegates to the battlefield to care for the wounded, a first test of the 1863 conference resolutions. The ICRC provided a praiseworthy service as a neutral party in the war, which motivated the Swiss government to call for an international conference, inviting 18 countries. On August 22, 1864, the 16 states in attendance signed the Geneva Convention for the Amelioration of the Condition of the Wounded in Armies in the Field, which was drafted by the International Committee.

It was during the Austro-Prussian war of 1866 that the International Committee established the first Information Agency for families of wounded or captured soldiers. Subsequent armed conflicts between 1875 and 1878, the Serbo-Bulgarian war (1885–1886), and the Balkan wars (1912–1913) tested the resources and commitment of the Red Cross/Crescent. It was these bloody conflicts that produced the first seeds of human rights norms.

When Archduke Franz Ferdinand, heir to the Austro-Hungarian throne, was assassinated in Sarajevo on June 28, 1914, it ignited the fuse of the First World War. Ferdinand's death at the hands of the Black Hand, a Serbian nationalist secret society, set the stage for two devastating global wars that took the lives of more than 98 million people.[5] Before Western societies were ready to ink the Universal Declaration of Human Rights, their governments collectively produced the most horrific events in the human history: deadly ethnic and religious wars in which weapons of mass destruction were used on large scale,[6] an indescribable holocaust that persecuted Jews, genocidal campaigns that targeted religious and ethnic minorities, and exploitative colonial expansions that subjugated native peoples in Africa, Asia, and South America. With such a record of brutality, Western societies had no option but to improve their humanitarian record. In this context, the Universal Declaration of Human Rights was a bright chapter that meant to end a dark history of brutality motivated by nationalism, sectarianism, and racism. It was not an act of empathy born out of luxury and enlightenment. The more horrible the acts of brutality, the more possible it was to embrace human rights norms. The same way judicial torture shocked Enlightenment rulers into abolishing it,[7] the catalog of cruelty the two world wars produced compelled Europeans to proscribe abuses of human dignity.

The post-wars narratives associated with the UDHR are important. But equally important are the narratives that preceded the wars and armed conflicts in European societies. They must have been moving and powerful narratives that justified the cruelty and horrors of war and motivated those directly involved. Therefore, it is imperative to examine pre-war, war, and post-war narratives in order to understand the origins and evolution of human rights norms. The ongoing events in Southwest Asia and North Africa offer an opportunity to understand these events with more data, more access to events, and documents produced by all sides.

The circumstances that produced human rights norms in European societies[8] resurfaced in Southwest Asian and North African societies. However, the outcome will not be an indigenous discourse on human rights as derived from the UDHR. Rather, it will be a refinement of these societies' own understanding of the idea of human dignity. The brutal violence that the US and the UK governments unleashed in Iraq in 2003, the repugnant display of cruelty and disregard to human dignity following the NATO-assisted removal and killing of Muammar Qaddafi in Libya in 2011, and the opportunistic militarization of the pro-democracy movement in Syria to overthrow Bashar al-Assad amount to nothing short of another world war.

After failing to secure UNSC authorization to attack Iraq, the Bush administration created an alliance to shield itself from, and spread the blame of, charges of aggression against a sovereign state and launched its illegal war anyway. Similarly, France led the campaign to secure a vague UNSC legal cover before starting their bombardment campaign against Libya. While Western governments controlled the skies over Libya, Qatar and some of the Gulf States supplied opposition groups, including al-Qaeda affiliates, with money and weapons.[9] The global nature of these conflicts was most evident in Syria, when, by 2015, two distinct coalitions were launching daily bombardment from the air and transferring weapons to their allies on the ground. The United States led one coalition consisting of some European and Arab allies who called themselves the anti-ISIL coalition. Russia led the second coalition that included Syria, Iran, and Hezbollah, who justified their presence in Syria as responding to a request from the legitimate government of Syria to help it in its fight against terrorist organizations. Without doubt, this is a world war-level conflict in which Syria represented the most active battleground. The similarities between the European wars and the 2011 war in Southwest Asia and North Africa are compelling, notwithstanding the existence of two radically different narratives.

One narrative, the anti-Assad one, is based on the emotional appeal of the Tunisian and Egyptian revolutions to instigate and justify the violent removal of regional foes. Another narrative, pro-Syrian government, appealed to international order to oppose foreign interventions in the internal affairs of sovereign nations. Specifically, the US coalition, which included some of the least democratic regimes in the world, claimed that military intervention was necessary when a government used violence to silence opposition groups. Russia, on the other hand, argued that only UNSC-authorized intervention is legal, no matter how harsh a regime might be. Meanwhile, the Gulf States flooded Syria with sophisticated weapons and gave a free hand to religious leaders and media outlets to provide moral, economic, and political support to rebel groups, all rebel groups, including the ones designated by the UNSC as terrorists. This mixture of weapons and ideologies produced devastating results. By the end of 2018, nearly quarter of a million people died, and Syria had sustained more than $180 billion dollars' worth of damage.

In the case of movements-turned-wars in Syria, Libya, and Yemen, it was clear that some states intentionally conflated desire to act for dignity and self-serving appeal to human rights to achieve ideological and political objectives. In this work, advocating for human rights is not considered an ideological or political position. In fact, many human rights abuses have happened because human rights were treated as partisan, political positions. It is essentially an ethical and moral position with basis in law in a universal context. By revisiting the evolution of human rights discourse in Western societies and the birth of dignity uprisings in Arab societies, we might be able to produce new philosophical and legal frameworks for human rights in Islamic societies and beyond. The dual reality stemming from the aspirations of the Tunisian and Egyptian revolutions, and the post-revolution power structure, should remind us of the critical moments that produced the culture, documents, and treaties that enshrined human rights norms in European societies.

The similarities between the conditions that led to the European wars and the 2011 wars are stunning. In both cases, racial groups that enjoyed a prolonged monopoly on power and resources had grown entitled to those privileges. When previously suppressed and oppressed communities and ideologies became significant, the empowered social groups acted to enforce the social and economic hierarchies. When they failed to achieve those goals through State agencies, they resorted to State-enabled violence and economic sanctions.

If Henri Dunant were to visit Aleppo, Afrin, East Ghouta, Deir Ezzor, Mosul, Raqqa, Fallujah, or any of the towns and cities devastated by the 2011 wars in SWANA and write down his observations, this is what those observations might include: soldiers missing limbs packed on mosque floors, bodies of dead civilians laying unclaimed on the roadside, neighborhoods reduced to rubble, ancient ruins erased, and religious and ethnic communities displaced by violence. That description would be the clean, less graphic description of what can be witnessed in person or what is depicted in thousands of videos and images.

There is a simple explanation for the cruelty individuals and groups commit in wars like these. A fighter cutting open the body of dead soldiers and chewing on their internal organs is both a reaffirmation of what it is to be human and a manufacturing of a psychology that could survive the trauma. The person committing these horrors needs to justify to themselves that what they are doing is the absolute good. It cannot be the absolute good if it is done to a person who shares something with the perpetrator. Therefore, they must totally strip their opponents of any trait that reminds them of those opponents' humanity. They must debase them; demean them beyond any reminders of shared characteristics. The demonizing of the other takes many forms. Societies can identify the "other" as a biologically defective person or group of persons who cannot be reformed, improved, or made whole. Therefore, they must be destroyed. Alternatively, the "other" is often demonized through the claim that the person or the group of persons would, could, or have committed cruel acts against "our innocent people." Therefore, they must pay for their crimes or be frightened so that they would not even think of committing such cruelty. In this case, their acts are pre-emptive. In Syria, all forms of demonizing the other were used on a large scale, as the thousands of videos and documents these groups released show.

The demonization and retribution continued for as long as regional and global state actors were willing to allow it to happen. However, when left to internal dynamics of power, displays of cruelty diminished. In fact, displays of cruelty galvanized society to act against them, mostly by building political and legal safeguards. The violence and resistance created a dynamic, a cruel equilibrium that forced involved parties to rethink their ways. Such a dynamic equilibrium can be established only when all involved actors are accounted for within a system. That is, when all the forces are internal. The active actors in the Syrian crisis cannot be called internal. Most of the actors on the battle fields may have been Syrians; however, the real forces behind them came from outside.

First, by "cruel equilibrium" I mean that respect for human rights and dignity occurs at the edge of an abyss. On one side, actors empowered by values rooted in racism systematically work towards the maximum disempowerment or complete eradication of the "other." The other side reacts, totally determined to fight back with every means available, and with the singular aim to stop the aggressor from achieving their goal or die trying. The aims of each side are mutually exclusive, dictated by the fact that one side wants the complete eradication of the other, while the other side establishes a very high cost for the former to achieve its goals. Such a conflict often ends in a dynamic equilibrium in which one of three things must happen: (1) One side completely destroys the other or render it powerless to constitute a perceived threat, (2) the two sides fight to a stalemate, forcing both of them to work towards a negotiated settlement without resolution of the conflict's causes, or (3) the violence teaches the two sides—or one side at least—that the harm is too severe to persist on the path of destruction and one or both sides opt for resolution on the basis of shared values. The resisters may feel the hopelessness of their conditions but their desire to mark their very existence by fighting on until there is no one left to fight reaffirms their claim to continued existence as beings with dignity. No real human rights are preserved without the willingness to counter the cruelty with undiminished resistance. No human rights are earned without the settled disposition that death is a better option than life without dignity. No true human rights come freely granted; they are always earned.

Second, the cruel equilibrium refers to the fact that human rights are necessarily born out of an equational conflict. On one side of the equation we find the State, the primary violator of human rights, potential violator of human rights, or responsible for creating the conditions for human rights violation. On the other side, we find disempowered individuals, social groups, and communities.

Third, human rights abuses occur in an environment that lacks a balance of power. Power, here, is defined as the ability to constantly create and impose unfair social conditions, cause harm, inflict violence, and/or create an event or an environment hostile to individuals or social groups shortly after issuing the command. Power, thus conceived, is proportional. In other words, not everyone is devoid of any power, but all persons and institutions do not enjoy the same level of power. One's power is strongest when one's commands are realized in the shortest time. We can formulate social power through the following equation:

$P = t\,(C)$; where P is power, C is command (constant), and t is time for a command to be executed.

Based on this definition, we are able to understand the reason behind the State enjoying more power and, as a more specific example, how an executive officer could be said to enjoy more power than a legislator.

The State, with its monopoly on the legal use of violence, is positioned to be the primary abuser of human rights. Therefore, State power is greater than the sum of society's individual and group power. The balance of power is brought to equilibrium through legal and practical separation of the legislative and judicial branches from the executive branch of government, the legal protections to civil society institutions, and cultural shifts in the mind of individuals. That is, the equilibrium occurs when a country establishes ground rules in the form of constitutional and legal regimes that limit the power of the executive branch of the State. The equation is balanced by inserting, on the side of disempowered communities, legally protected and empowered civil society institutions. Civil society institutions are broadly defined in various layers with independent judiciary and legislature and independent press as the primary layer; NGOs, clubs, religious institutions, and advocacy organizations as the tertiary layer. The secondary layer is occupied by institutions that are government-funded or both private- and government-funded, and that provide public services such as universities, special services government agencies, public radio and televisions, and similar entities. Human rights abuses are likely to occur more often in countries where the imbalance of power in favor of the State is greatest.

Nations without civil society institutions:

$$s > d$$

Where s refers to State power and d refers to power of persons (individuals and communities).

In nations with strong civil society institutions, the equation of power is brought to balance through the collective action of civil society institutions:

$$s \rightleftharpoons d \times \Sigma i$$

Where Σi is the sum of civil society institutions.

This model is, generally, predictive. Human rights abuses are more likely to occur in nations with absent or weak civil society institutions. If persons or regimes with authoritarian inclinations and aims ascend to power, they would embark on a course that would allow them to silence the press, terminate the independence of the judiciary, and roll back the constitutional and legal safeguards that protect other civil society institutions. Once these steps are successful, human rights abuses will certainly occur and, in many cases, no one will be able to report about them. Because of the constant changes and shifts in power, the equation is never static; it is a dynamic equilibrium.

This model offers a predictive tool to learn about when and how human rights abuses happen. It is also prescriptive. Once it becomes clear that the State, or something that acts like it such as a large corporation, is the sole actual or potential abuser of human rights, it becomes imperative that no one should expect the State, any State, no matter who is leading it, to promote human rights or act against the abusers of human rights.[10] Human rights abuses are prevented or remedied through civil society institutions, not through State intervention—represented in the executive branch and its agencies with executive privileges, that is. Human rights abuse is remedied through limits to State power, not through added power freely given to the State.

This framing of the human rights struggle is applicable domestically and globally.[11] Asking one State, especially a powerful one, to intervene on behalf of human rights victims in another nation amounts to empowering a potential human rights abuser to confront an alleged perpetrator of human rights abuses. If a State which enjoys a significant power differential is asked to intervene in another country, there are no guarantees that its intervention will be limited to dealing with human rights abuses. It may end up subjugating the people of the nation in which it intervened. One State's intervention on behalf of the citizens of another State is almost impossible to reconcile with governing charge. A government is established with the single aim of protecting and furthering the interests of its own citizens, not those of another country. All powerful countries intervening ostensibly on the behalf of human rights victims in another nation must be domestically justify themselves as being done to defend vital national interests.

It is true that in some cases, defending citizens of another nation purely as a matter of ethical and legal responsibility may create friendship ties to people who would in gratitude open their markets to goods and thereby augment the wealth and prosperity of the citizens of an intervening nation. However, there are no guarantees that the opening of those markets would ameliorate the lives of both nations' citizens equally, let alone the possibility that other communities' overall goal is the constant augmenting of wealth and material possession. In any case, such humanitarian intervention is commodified and made subject to economic forces. That is not a comforting reality for people who aspire to have their rights protected, rather than commodified or instrumentalized.

This approach to human rights advocacy highlights the organic connections between rights abuses, racism, and power. Moreover, it helps create a stable strategy to combat human rights abuses in both national and international contexts, as well as single instances of human rights abuse within society or wide abuses during times of international conflict.

The same way human rights abuses are connected to racism and supremacy in Western societies, human rights abuses in Islamic societies are connected to the colonial legacy of Europe and Western European leaders. Western governments mostly honored their commitments to respect the rights of dominant of influential social groups within their borders. However, all colonial nation-states have committed war crimes, crimes against humanity, genocides, aggression, or other forms of exploitation and abuses against communities in Asia, Africa, and the Americas. In the post-1948 era, France killed more than 1.5 million Algerians in pursuit of subjugation and control of that resource-rich country. White European settlers created the most obscenely racist system in South Africa. The United Kingdom continued its control and subjugation of indigenous communities on at least three continents. The United States used indiscriminate weapons of mass destruction in its wars in Vietnam and Korea. Even after the retreat of European colonial regimes, and as recently as the 1990s and the first decade of the twenty-first century, the US government formed coalitions, mainly consisting of other Western states and some corrupt Arab and Muslim regimes, and launched brutal wars in Iraq and Afghanistan that resulted in the killing of hundreds of thousands of civilians and the revival of torture regimes and practices. With just these events in mind, it becomes evident that human rights norms were meant to benefit European societies, not to impose limits on themselves to protect the rights of vulnerable social groups at home or abroad, or to empower people on other continents.

Western governments often use the occurrence of human rights abuses in other countries as a pretext for intervention, regime change, or as means to preserve their own societies' interests. Many of the authoritarian regimes in Asia, Africa, and South America that were friendly to the West—but abusive to their own peoples—the West shielded from intervention. Regimes hostile to Western policies faced sanctions, pressure, and even removal through military interventions, coups, or sabotage. This global order appeared to come to an end with the start of the 2011 series of uprisings across SWANA. The first regimes to fall, those of Ben Ali and Mubarak, had been propped up by Western governments. The uprisings in Bahrain, Jordan, and Morocco, if successful, would have demonstrated a rejection of three more Western-propped regimes. Sensing a danger in that pattern, Western governments and nervous Arab regimes directed the flood of social change to regimes they did not like. Peaceful and hopeful protest movements turned into armed conflicts in Libya, Yemen, Iraq, and Syria, resurrecting the horror of the first two world wars.

Evidence does not support the theory that the origins of, and motives for, human rights are by products of European Enlightenment or higher values which civilized people of the modern world *discovered*. Governments born out of the Enlightenment have perpetrated too many war crimes, crimes against humanity, and genocides to give credence to the *discovery* theory of human rights. The horror that decimated 60 million people in Europe and forced a dynamic equilibrium of cruelty is the real impetus that forced Western societies to commit to norms of coexistence, lest they perish killing one another. These same cruel conditions, which delivered the West from the throes of destruction, have now been playing out in many Arab societies since 2011.

The wars and uprisings in SWANA were a unique opportunity to help us understand human rights as an aspiration and human rights as an outcome of violent conflict. It is a rare social experiment in which historians and analysts can observe, in real-time, the processes of protesting, rebelling, revolting, and rebuilding. Digital technology, social media, and unprecedented access now allow us to document and analyze events better than we were able to do it in the past. From these social experiences, we have augmented our knowledge with a few truths, including the following:

1 Today we can identify the actual actors in each event without being solely dependent on inductive and deductive reasoning. Retroactive analysis of outcomes to understand the role of some social groups in the initial events may seem tenable. However, capturing events as they happen provides us with a fuller picture of evolving logic, purpose, and goals than edited or censored historical records.[12] What we know for a fact about the protesters in Tunisia and Egypt, and those who rose to power after the revolution, speaks to the limitations of inductive and deductive reasoning. Specifically, Ennahda and the Muslim Brotherhood, respectively, did not initiate the Tunisian and Egyptian uprisings. In fact, they did not participate until they were certain that

the revolutions would succeed. Yet they reaped the political benefit of the revolutions. Looking at that end result alone, years after the fact, it is easy to assume that they initiated the uprising and saw it through. That is far from the truth. To deduce that they must have played major roles during the actual events is besides the facts. Therefore, it is unlikely that regimes that take over after the uprisings will fulfil the aspirations of those who rose up and risked their lives and freedom.

2 Human rights are valued and embraced when they are imbued in society culturally and psychologically. Human rights are imbued in society when they are linked to human dignity, not to ideology, religion, or nationalism. We learned that from the Tunisian revolution. Mohamed Bouazizi, and those moved by his plight, rising to overthrow the corrupt regime, were not interested in righteous politics or in democracy. They stood up to end fear and claim their dignity. Tunisians collectively respected that and they created a better system than the one that was. It was an indigenous movement that produced genuine improvement in the way Tunisians treat one another, and, in the way their political leaders govern them.

3 Embracing human rights happens under fire. Human rights norms are not the product of a state of developed intellect or morality, or a condition of evolved civility. Emotional commitment to human rights norms is embraced during moments of brutality, horror, aggression, and manifest violence. Human rights norms are not discovered in university libraries or classrooms, decided in the halls of legislatures, or pronounced from atop courts' benches. Commitment to human rights norms is formed out of the thunders of war, the echoes of the torture dungeon, the cries of orphans, and the screams of children separated from their parents. Human rights are the catalog of acts judged by a simple involuntary utterance: That is not right.

4 Human rights abuses persist because the narratives that record them are racialized, ethnicized, or ideologized. When people are told that they are victimized because they are Sunni, Shia, Druze, Alawite, Christian, or Ayzidi, it fragments sympathy and relativizes brutality. Alawite Syrians are victimized not because they are Alawites, but for the same reason many other vulnerable communities were victimized before them. It is not who they are, what they believe, or what they do that causes their suffering. Rather, they are victimized because of who the offenders are, what the offenders believe, and what the offenders do.

5 Many brutal scenes of Sunni Salafists killing Alawites, cutting their bodies open, and chewing on their internal organs are tools of shock and fear that help propagate a false narrative that says "we are doing this because they are doing it to us," since there was very little evidence otherwise to support their claim. This pattern of manufacturing horror to manipulate people into following them and embracing their claims

has been commonly practiced throughout history. Sunni extremists in Syria, in the absence of real evidence of religious or ethnic genocide, committed their own genocide against members of the community they are fighting and claim that it is justified, preemptive retaliation. This perverted practice has been present especially in Syria because it was made possible through the complicity of the States that opposed the Syrian government more than they valued human rights.

6 Human rights abuses are systematic and methodical. We use the term systemic to refer to the space within which human rights abuses occur. Such a space must account for all the forces that are internal, contributing, directly or indirectly, to the protections and abuses of human rights. Human rights abuses are active and advocacy for human rights protections is reactive. With that being the case, human rights abuses must augment the resistance side of the equation to reestablish balance and counter the actions of the powerful—the State.

What are the broader implications and contexts?

Many Western scholars who write abstractly about human rights assert that these rights should be universal. However, some of the actions of Western governments are the clearest and most convincing argument against human rights' universality. Elected governments often reflect the attitudes and values of the people they govern. In this context, the United States government twice used weapons of mass destruction in Japan, killing hundreds of thousands of non-combatants, injuring many more, and causing biological and physiological damage to future generations. When President Barack Obama visited the sites upon which atomic bombs were dropped, he did not apologize for it. Thus, he upheld the argument that killing unarmed, non-combatant civilians of one country to force its political and military leaders to surrender and shorten the war is acceptable.

The superficial, convenient embrace of human rights is not common just among politicians, but also widespread among people in the West. Three-quarters of a century removed from the passion of wars in which the atomic bombs were dropped, nearly fifty percent of Americans justify the use of such weapons of mass destruction. In Europe, during a debate in the House of Commons, the person who would become Prime Minister, Theresa May, was asked whether she was "personally prepared to authorize a nuclear strike that could kill 100,000 innocent men, women and children." May's answer was an unequivocal "yes." In this, she was contrasting herself to Jeremy Corbyn, who had previously said that he would never launch a nuclear strike. May took the position of many people whom she governs: Sixty-six percent of surveyed people in the U.K. agree with her.[13] This deeply rooted belief that some people's survival should be secured through the total and complete destruction of another people is the reason behind the spread of chemical and nuclear weapons. Around the world, governments of other countries are adopting the same view. Nearly a dozen countries hold on to nuclear weapons and each one of them is prepared to use them, not only against other nuclear nations, but against anyone who threatens them, even with conventional weapons. The possession of and threat to use indiscriminate weapons of mass killing reflect a belief that not all human beings are entitled to life. Human rights cannot be universal and violable at the same time.

The universality of human rights, while championed by Western elites, is also undermined by Western governments' selective appeal to it. They often invoke human rights abuses to accuse unfriendly regimes of violations. However, when Western countries or their allies face accusations of human rights violations, the reports are either rejected or purged. For instance, Saudi Arabia is essentially the most notorious abuser of human rights. Not only do its leaders persecute minorities and exploit foreign workers, but the kingdom has archaic laws that clearly and explicitly discriminate against people on the base of sex, gender, and religious affiliation. The only country in the world where women were until recently barred from driving cars is less often cited as a human rights violator than countries with better human rights records, including Syria before the recent war. Moreover, when the UN included Saudi Arabia in its blacklist of entities that kill children because it was responsible for 60% of child fatalities in Yemen, the rulers of Saudi Arabia threatened to declare the UN an "anti-Muslim" organization and withhold support from its relief work. The UN was forced to remove the Kingdom's name from the list pending a joint examination of the records that was never made public.

Western governments invoke the universality of human rights as pretext for aggression against countries that work against the global system which Western governments created and imposed, and to justify invading sovereign states for political and economic aims. One cannot be in favor of absolute human rights and in favor of unbridled power of the State at the same time.

When hundreds of thousands of Tunisians revolted against one of the most authoritarian regimes in the Arab world, they carried a wide variety signs and chanted diverse slogans. But among all the handwritten signs and shouted chants, one cannot find the phrase "human rights." Yet after the fall of their dictator, Western media and politicians as well as some Tunisian political parties' leaders attempted to write a new narrative that centered human rights as the primary motive and drive for the Tunisian revolution.

The 2011 protest movements that started in Tunisia shed new light on rebellion, revolutions, and dissent movements. Importantly, these movements provide us with an environment to observe and study the social forces that motivate people or a group of people to break the chains of fear and rise up to demand that their civil, political, economic, and social rights are respected. However, if we look at the demands of the people in the street separate from the politicians and activists who inherit the outcome of the revolution, we find that people are moved to act for reasons which political leaders and activists do not necessarily articulate. This difference constitutes an opportunity to provide a new critical perspective on human rights discourse.

Compared to Western societies, especially US society, Arab societies have a fundamentally different view of concepts and institutions such as nation, government, and politics. In American society, political views and inclinations are deeply personal. Also, in the United States, elections and public participation in electing political leaders is sacralized. These subtle factors are present in the minds of American scholars and politicians as they project their own views and beliefs onto Arab communities. The reality is radically different. The lack of participatory governance in Arab countries separates the idea of a nation from the institutions of governance. It is simple for a Tunisian citizen to be both deeply pro-country and deeply anti-government. Tunisians, like many Arabs due to political cultures and practices, are essentially cynical about politics: All politicians are corrupt or will soon be corrupt and therefore there is no need to compete for such a corrupting vocation. This attitude towards government institutions makes citizens naturally on the side of the disempowered, and effectively pro-human rights. Western governments have immense influence over most of governments of the Islamic world. However, their influence, by design or by accident, is rarely informed by the culture and politics most effective for introducing human rights norms to Islamic societies. Importantly, Western governments' military interventions to address human rights abuses often have the opposite effect.

When the government of an economically underdeveloped country commits human right abuses within its territory, it does so because of an imbalance of power: The State is too powerful, and its citizens and the civil society institutions representing them are too weak. When human rights advocates appeal to a more powerful State to act against a less powerful state, the imbalance of power increases because once that State intervenes, the citizens of the invaded country come under the rule of a powerful State unleashing the violence associated with war. That does not serve the cause of human rights, as it creates the very conditions under which human rights abuses are likely to take place. That explains why foreign interventions in the affairs of developing countries often result in more severe human rights abuses and there is no higher power to which one can appeal to stop the crimes committed by an invading all-powerful country. The US invasion of Iraq in 2003 is a strong case in point. Saddam Hussein was a human rights abuser. However, human rights abuses, during the occupation and during the rule of the regimes the occupying forces installed, increased. Not a single high-ranking person, American or Iraqi, was ever tried for war crimes, crimes against humanity, torture, or other crimes that took place.

In the Syrian case, there is a clear need for dynamic equilibrium to safeguard human rights in a principled way. When many Syrians, without resorting to arms, protested in Syrian cities and towns demanding political and economic rights and stronger civil society institutions, and when the government responded with violence, the imbalance of power was obvious. The place of the advocates of human rights is on the side of the protesters. If a segment of the Syrian people were to resist the government crackdown with violence, though it is an unwise and unproductive choice, the advocates of human rights should be on the side of the resisters still because the imbalance of power favors the Syrian state. However, if richer and more powerful governments, like Qatar, Saudi Arabia, the United Kingdom, the United States of America, France, and Turkey took the side of the armed resisters, who have become armed rebels, and provided them with political, financial, and military support, the place of the advocates of human rights cannot remain in support of these armed groups. The imbalance of power has shifted.

Critics of this position would argue that excluding superpowers from being recruited to defend human rights abuses in weaker countries would give a carte blanche to such governments to violate human rights norms and laws. The case studies cited in this work, and other similar cases, point to the fact that foreign interventions rarely end human rights abuses. In fact, they make abuse more severe and add different levels and aspects of abuses. Instead of ending human rights abuse, armed interventions amplify them.

Powerful countries can play roles in helping citizens of another country overcome cruelty and hold those who violate the rights of their own citizens accountable. First, they must provide humanitarian assistance in all its forms. Second, they must support civil society institutions and court systems to counteract government abuse of power. In other words, powerful nations have the responsibility to help (R2H), not the responsibility to protect (R2P) via destructive military actions. Systemic thinking tells us that the true R2P falls on the shoulders of the national government not on foreign governments, which encourages invasions of vulnerable nations. Where responsibility to protect is uttered to encourage powerful nations to invade weak nations, it becomes an endorsement to imperialism, which is the greater threat to indigenous peoples.

Throughout the duration of the first seven years of the war in Syria, Western governments threatened, and acted on their threat, that they would use force against the Syrian government if or when it used weapons of mass destruction. This was an eerie echo of the United States' invasion of Iraq, in which the existence of weapons of mass destruction served as pretext for American involvement. US President Obama and later French President Emmanuel Macron considered the use of chemical weapons a red line which, if crossed, would require an immediate and unilateral action—meaning an action outside the authority of the UN Security Council. The use of chemical weapons and all forms of weapons of mass destruction should not be tolerated. However, who is to stop Western powers from developing and using weapons of mass destruction? When it comes to the use of weapons that cause mass casualties, the US government's record is damning, and no one has ever been held accountable for their use of weapons of mass destruction which have resulted in documented civilian deaths and ecological and biological harm. Many US-waged wars, some launched under false pretexts, resulted in the premeditated killing of civilians because of the use of weapons of mass destruction, including the firebombing of Tokyo in which 100,000 civilians lost their lives, the nuclear strikes on Japan in 1945 that killed 120,000 civilians, the 1952 Korean War that killed 2.5 million civilians, the Vietnam War that killed 1.1 million civilians, and the 2003 Iraq War that killed 1.5 million civilians. The US government has erected memorials on the National Mall honoring American sacrifices in foreign wars. Unmentioned in these memorials are the people of those foreign countries who perished in the conflicts.

The major wars the United States has fought have produced colossal carnage. It is not by accident that the casualties' figures are mere estimates. Following the Vietnam War, it has been US policy not to do a "body count" of civilians in attacked countries. Months after the start of the US war in Afghanistan, Secretary of Defense Donald Rumsfeld said: "I don't do body counts. This country tried that in Vietnam, and it didn't work. And you've not heard me speculate on that at all, and you won't."[14] A few days later, General Tommy Franks told reporters who wanted to know about "enemy" casualties: "You know, we don't do body counts."[15] Because of this, many people in Islamic societies are skeptical of Western appeal to protecting human rights as justification for their interventions in other countries. Human rights norms are, to some extent, aspirational, but the aspiration must be driven by internal forces, not outside dictates and posturing.

Nearly 400 peaceful protesters lost their lives in Tunisia, and twice as many were killed by the police and security forces in Egypt before the long-ruling authoritarians, Ben Ali and Mubarak, were forced out. However, a few years after the passion of the revolutionaries died out, Tunisians elected a president, Beji Caid Essebsi, who was almost the same age as Bourguiba when he was forced out. The same happened in Egypt. A year after the election of the first post-revolution president, Mohamed Morsi, a second revolution was launched which resulted in Morsi's overthrow and the rise of a Mubarak-like authoritarian, Abdel Fattah el-Sisi. These events suggest that, contrary to claims by Western politicians and commentators, political reforms including constitutional term-limits and representative governments were not the motivating force for Tunisians and Egyptians challenging their oppressors. The abuse of human dignity and open abuse of power were the crossed lines that moved people to act. After generations of political corruption, the Arab masses had grown accustomed to corrupt politicians and corrupt political processes. However, they also expected such corrupt politicians to keep their abuses under control. Corruption and abuse of power in Tunisia, as in most other Arab countries, were out of control and out in the open the same way they had been during the late 1980s under Bourguiba, which had brought Tunisians to the street. This fact suggests that discourse on human rights is about fundamental rights of the most vulnerable social groups and about the abuse of the essence of being a human being.

There are stark differences between, and serious implications of, theories of rights born in the battlefield or in the dark dungeons of prisons and detention centers and theories of rights born out of academic discussions at educational institutions. Similarly, there is a difference between a claim to rights invoked by someone who has experienced human rights and someone who has reasoned about them. The difference between human rights in the minds of those who are driven to die for such rights and human rights in the minds of those who catalogue human rights is vast. Those who fight and die for human rights represent what is universal in human rights. Those who codify and articulate human rights represent the particular cultural and philosophical ideas of human rights. Ultimately, reasoned human rights claims are a list of abstract claims, whereas lived human rights experiences are rooted in the dignity of being. Therefore, if a claim to a right is not intimately connected to dignity, it is a different kind of right.

One of the key recommendations of this work is the importance of research that takes into consideration, with equal emphasis, the theoretical and the practical aspects of human rights. Thus framed, human rights research focuses on the executive branch of the government as the actual or potential abuser of human rights. What separates the actual abuser from the potential abuser of human rights is the condition of civil society institutions. The modern entity known as the State has at its disposal the levers of soft and hard powers. It is unlikely that the State would give up its monopoly on the lever of hard power: armed forces, police, national guards, and armed marshals, among others. However, in the interest of protecting citizens from the State's abuse of power, soft power must be checked and made independent from the executive branch of the government. Even democratically elected leaders with authoritarian ambitions, as opposed to those who grab power by force, often work to undermine the separation of institutional power and authority and weaken civil society institutions' influence. Authoritarians, rising to power in democratic countries, bent on grabbing more power, often take specific steps to achieve their goals: They work to bring the judiciary under their control, restrict the freedom of the press, establish legal regimes to shut down media outlets that refuse to conform, impose limits on academic institutions, and subject non-government organizations and social institutions to extreme scrutiny. Once they create these conditions and achieve such goals, abuses of the rights of individuals, disempowered social groups, and dissenters will occur and there will be no court that will stop or remediate the abuses and no press that will expose the crimes. The goal of human rights advocates should be to reverse this path if it is occurring, or to build safeguards that prevent the executive branch of government from taking such a path. Specifically, the primary aim of human rights advocates should be to ensure that the judiciary is totally independent from the executive branch of government, that the media is not beholden to any party or interest group, that academics are free from political pressure, and that the right of thought and expression are guaranteed.

The mapping of the road that authoritarians take toward human rights abuses, described above, is not a hypothesis. The events in SWANA since 2011, and the specific case of Turkey's transformation since 2002, are illustrative examples and resounding reminders of how easy it is to radically transform societies and countries through both democratic and undemocratic practices. The rise of Recep Tayyip Erdogan cannot be fully understood without referencing the practices of the Turkish leaders prior to 2001.

Before 2001, secular Kemalists in Turkey engineered a system that allowed them to control the judiciary, the media, the army, state universities, and even mosques. Since 2001, conservative Erdoganists have used the same system to reconfigure the courts, the media, the army, the state universities, and the mosques to their benefit. Erdogan stands today where Mustafa Kemal Atatürk stood a century ago: one man shaping the republic to his liking. Evidently, both secular Kemalists and conservative Erdoganists followed the same path to achieve the same goal: total destruction of civil society institutions and the creation of the most powerful executive branch of government, the presidency. Turkey is only one example; many other leaders in the Americas (including now North America), Europe, Asia, and Africa have followed the same playbook of rules to grab more power and destroy civil society institutions, which enables them to commit human rights crimes. The path to the throne is often paved by the skulls of the vulnerable.

While editing the full draft of this work and listening to an international satellite channel covering the 2018 elections in Egypt, Russia, Tunisia, Lebanon, and Iraq, the words of an Iraqi politician, Ali al-Allaq, unknown to me at that time, confirmed one of the main arguments of this work:

> The rise of Daesh changed the idea and the practice of citizenship in Iraq. Because of it, we have entered the era of upright citizenship. The people of Iraq have realized that the path of animosity and rage is exhausting to all (*munhikun li-'l-jami`*)… We will all lose unless we all change our ways in dealing with one another.[16]

Based on the arguments and the evidence presented here, the outcome of Iraq's election was not in favor of those in power (Prime Minister Haider al-Abadi and his allies). Importantly, for the first time in the history of Iraq, a religious cleric established a coalition with secular activists, including communists, to win the largest number of seats. Still, even if the people had not embraced candidates with views like al-Allaq's, the fact that a candidate representing a major political party used such inclusive views as a platform signals a fundamental shift in some conservative Muslims' attitudes towards pluralism, religious and ethnic identity, civil society institutions, and citizenship—the cornerstones of any human rights initiative.

The idea of universalizing human rights norms is particular and conceptual. The abuse of human rights is universal and tangible. Even the most zealous advocate for universal human rights would concede that throughout history, and in every culture and society, some social group had suffered an abuse of human rights at the hands of a dominant social group and that the State has enabled that abuse. Despite the editorial touch of history, we are able to reconstruct a legacy of abuse of rights in both the Islamic and Western contexts throughout the last 1400 years of history. Western European governments have a legacy of cruelty and so do Islamic caliphs. The 2011 wars in SWANA exposed both Western and Islamic governments as producers of abuse of rights, not promoters of human rights. Therefore, a proposal intended to promote human rights should not be contingent on producing a specific kind of government; it should be built on limiting the power of government to abuse the most basic rights of the most vulnerable social groups.

Some may argue that bringing Western governments to an exploration of the state of human rights in Islamic societies absolves Muslim leaders and Muslim thinkers of responsibility for the atrocities of their own doing. However, given the level of direct and indirect Western interference in Islamic societies, human rights within them must be always addressed while taking into consideration European history. To omit Western influence is to imagine Islamic societies as isolated systems. It is to ignore the constant armed conflicts Western armies waged in Muslim-majority countries throughout the second half of the twentieth century,[17] and to deny the pervasiveness of Western influence not only on the origins of modern human rights discourse[18] and the drafting of the UDHR, but as a globally dominant force. Lastly, it is impossible to leave Western governments out of this conversation because human rights abuses are universal, occurring both in Western and Islamic societies.[19]

The West must own its failure to universalize human rights norms. The leaders of the West failed when they protected the human rights of their own while engaging in the most horrible abuses of human rights in Africa, Asia, and the Americas. They failed because they lacked either the morality or courage and foresight to apologize and accept responsibility for the crimes of genocide inflicted on indigenous peoples in Africa, the Americas, Australia, and Asia. They failed when they refused to take responsibility for both slavery and colonialism during an international meeting on the matter in South Africa.[20] They failed when they produced and used weapons of mass destruction and continued to possess these weapons while asserting moral authority to deny others nuclear technology, much less nuclear weapons. They failed when they resisted calls asking them to apologize and redress forced sterilization. They failed when they did not apologize and redress running experiments on Black men and women.

Human rights institutions were necessitated by acts of European states and they must be examined in European systems of governance, social engineering, and economic instruments of disparity, not just as an isolated issue within a single community. Moreover, Western states enjoy overwhelming power, allowing them to set the agenda for the entire world. The burden of achieving universal respect for human rights norms falls on Western powers. Their military interventions make them directly responsible as well. In the case of the war in Syria, the outcome of the military confrontation is a binary outcome, but its impact on the future of human rights in Islamic societies is universal.

Events and ideas borne out of the 2011 wars in SWANA do not support the notion that Islamic societies and Islam are incompatible with modern human rights norms. For that to be true, Islam must be deliberately designed as a social system and institutionalized in modern Islamic societies. In Syria, as is the case with all the other countries affected by the wars and uprisings in SWANA, the governing structure and the socioeconomic systems are Western designs. Ba`thism, the form of nationalism and ideology espoused and practiced by the government of Syria, is of Western origin. There is nothing Islamic about Ba`th nationalism in Syria and Iraq, Constitutionalism (Dusturism) in Tunisia—the birthplace of Arab Spring— or any other nation-state in the Islamic world. Islam has been processed through Western systems, and reduced to mere culture, to make room for the Western value systems to shape and control societies in the region. The reasons and motives behind the abuse of human rights are the same reasons and motives behind the abuse of human rights in Western societies: a highly differentiated global system designed to achieve specific outcomes—none of which promote or safeguard human rights.

Notes

1. Rashid Khalidi, *Resurrecting Empire: Western Footprints and America's Perilous Path in the Middle East* (Boston: Beacon Press, 2005); P. J. Henry, Jim Sidanius, Shana Levin, and Felicia Pratto, "Social Dominance Orientation, Authoritarianism, and Support for Intergroup Violence Between the Middle East and America," *Political Psychology* 26, no. 4 (2005): 569–84; and Sina Ali Muscati, "Arab/Muslim 'Otherness': The Role of Racial Constructions in the Gulf War and the Continuing Crisis with Iraq," *Journal of Muslim Minority Affairs* 22, no. 1 (2002).
2. Henri Dunant, *A Memory of Solferino* (The American National Red Cross, 1959).
3. Nicholas O. Berry, *War and the Red Cross: The Unspoken Mission* (New York: Palgrave Macmillan, 1997), 8.
4. John Buckley and George Kassimeris, eds., *The Ashgate Research Companion to Modern Warfare* (New York: Routledge, 2016).

5. During the First World War, the Allies mobilized about 42 million people. When the war ended, nearly 52% of them had been killed (22 million). The other side (Germany, Austria, Bulgaria, and Turkey) mobilized 22.8 million people to fight the war, of who 15 million lost their lives. The total number of people killed was a staggering 37 million people. The Second World War almost doubled in its number of casualties. More than 61 million people lost their lives, not counting the wounded.
6. In addition to the use of nuclear weapons during WWII, during WWI, warring parties in Europe developed and used chemical weapons. Between 1915 and 2019, the German army and the Allies, combined, used 120,000 tons of chemical agents, killing and injuring nearly 550,000 soldiers.
7. Talal Asad, "On Torture," *Social Research* 63, no. 4 (1996): 1088.
8. I use the "European" designation to refer to both European societies in Europe and in North America, excluding the Native Peoples of the Americas.
9. German and US intelligence have concluded that Saudi Arabia and Qatar were either complicit or did not do enough to stop the flow of terrorists into war zones and the financing of violent extremists. In 2017, Saudi Arabia and three other Arab countries accused Qatar of supporting terrorism and slapped it with sanctions.
10. Perhaps one of the most illustrative arguments that heads of State, no matter their background, abuse human rights or fail to protect the rights of all citizens is the case of Aung San Suu Kyi, who projected herself as a champion of human rights, earning the Nobel Peace Prize in 1991, but when she became prime minister (formally State Counsellor), she presided over and justified the systemic genocide of Rohingya Muslims.
11. The creation of the Human Rights Council, attached to the UN, which is, a sense, a club of the executive branches of governments from around the world, has not stopped or even limited abuse. In fact, it politicized human rights causes and became a platform for human rights abusers. It is a matter of time before it will disintegrate. Human rights causes would be better served by creating an agency that does not represent or report to the executive branches of world governments.
12. The New York Times held back the publication of their dossier on US torture programs for a year and a half, after receiving notice from the administration that publishing the story would risk the safety and security of US personnel still serving in Iraq and Afghanistan. Most of the damning photos the New York Times had, and later the US Senate committee investigating torture, were not made public and the government moved to classify such evidence still under its control. Only about 700 pages out of just under 7,000 pages of documents were made public; the rest of the documents remain classified despite numerous lawsuits initiated under FOIA that reached the USSC, which refused to hear the case.
13. Matthew Smith, "59% of Brits would Push the Nuclear Button," YouGov, July 28, 2016. https://yougov.co.uk/news/2016/07/28/59-brits-would-push-red-button/
14. Donald Rumsfeld, *CBS News*, CBS, March, 2002. See, also, Roger Stahl, *Militainment, Inc.: War, Media, and Popular Culture* (New York: Routledge, 2010), 26.
15. Neta Crawford, *Accountability for Killing* (Oxford: Oxford University Press, 2013), 88.
16. Ali al-Allaq, Almayadeen, April 9, 2018. The interview is also archived under the URL, www.youtube.com/watch?v=LZJiB13581o, accessed April 10, 2018, 8 am. Al-Allaq is an elected member of the parliament of Iraq, a candidate in Nasr Coalition, and a leading figure of Dawa Party.

17. Since the signing of the UDHR, 87% of these wars took place in lands inhabited by Muslims, resulting in more than 26 million people in Muslim-majority countries killed and more than 150 million peoples displaced. The longest wars are still ongoing in Muslim lands: in Kashmir (since 1947), in Palestine (since 1948), and Afghanistan (since 1978). Involvement of global actors was profound: The war in Afghanistan in 1978 involved the two superpowers of the era, the United States and the Soviet Union, as well as Saudi Arabia; the United States—and again, its ally Saudi Arabia—bankrolled the Iran-Iraq war (the first Gulf War), and two years after its end, the U.S. and its allies intervened in what was dubiously called the Persian Gulf War; the first decade of twentieth century saw American involvement in increased war atrocities in Afghanistan, Iraq, Qatar, and Syria, and a brutal war on the most vulnerable in the poorest Arab country, Yemen.
18. The conditions and events that made it necessary to produce legal regimes and institutions that promote human rights norms are entirely of European origin.
19. Mere weeks after start of the uprisings in SWANA, the Occupy movement picked up across the Western world. Months later, in cities across the United States, Black protesters rose up against institutional, systemic State violence. As I write these words, the second wave of Black Lives Matter protests is underway, only stronger. It should not require deep thinking to connect targeted killings in the streets of Syria to targeted killings in the streets of major cities in the United States, where—in both places—uniformed and heavily armed American officers are present. Human rights abuses occur in every corner of the earth that the arm of the State can reach.
20. World Conference Against Apartheid, Racism, and Colonialism (Durban, South Africa; August 31 to 7 September 2001).

8 Conclusions: Human rights, civil society, and the state

Succinctly and directly answering Talbott's question, as stated on the cover of his book, *Which Human Rights Should be Universal?*, I submit that two basic rights should be universal: freedom of thought and freedom to publicly express such thought. In the context of Western thought, the basis for these rights is well established. In the context of Islamic history, though Islamic tradition is imbued with values and principles that could be used to support these rights, it will suffice, in my view, to point out one historical event and a singular institution[1] connected to it in support for universalizing these two rights. To define this institution, we start where Muhammad started.

As indicated in Chapter 3, when Muhammad reached his forties, living in Mecca during the Jahiliyya times, not yet recognized as prophet by anyone except his wife, he started preaching that God had chosen him to deliver a message to the people. Over time, we learned that this message was all-encompassing and radical. By that time's standards, and many of the today's standards, his message was blunt, antagonistic, disruptive, heretical, and offensive. He told the people of Mecca that they were worshipping false gods. He accused the Meccan elite of abusing the dignity of the poor, slaves, and women. He equated the humanity of a slave to that of slave masters. He told the rich that gold and silver would be melted and poured over them for hoarding their wealth instead of spending it on good causes. While in Madina, he told Jews that the Rabbis corrupted their Jewish scriptures and he told Christians that Jesus was not God. In any society, such a person would end up committed, tortured, imprisoned, or dead. For over ten years, Muhammad was called crazy, a magician, a rebel, and a troublemaker; he was insulted, spat on, and threatened. But he was not imprisoned or killed. He continued to live in Mecca among the people he deemed corrupt, abusive, hypocritical, and arrogant. Why?

Muhammad was able to preach and express his opinions thanks to an institution to which the Arabs of Jahiliyya, untouched by the Enlightenment, adhered: *Ijara*. The term *ijara* is often translated to denote asylum; and is simply defined as a public declaration by a leader of a clan that someone is under their protection. In a way it is more powerful than asylum, because the beneficiary of *Ijara* does not have to leave their hometown, city, or tribe to enjoy such a protection. In a sense, *Ijara* is a mobile shield that protects the person anywhere where the institution is honored. In other words, a person protected by *Ijara* can continue to live where they are and, importantly, continue to do what they were doing. In this case, Muhammad was able to continue to preach his radical views in Mecca for as long as his uncle, the head of the Hashimite clan, extended to him the protection and it was in effect.

In addition to the critical role of this institution in allowing Muhammad to preach, one cannot ignore the fact that Muhammad insisted on preaching his message despite the resistance he faced from his community. Ten years of persistent preaching was met by ten years of rejection. It is reasonable to assume that a person who insists on speaking despite broad opposition would recognize the rights of others to do the same: to express their thoughts and beliefs with the same zeal, passion, and persistence. This assumption is confirmed: The Quran adopted the institution that had protected him when he was vulnerable:

> If one amongst the polytheists (*ahad min al-mushrikin*) ask you for protection (*istajarak*), grant it to them (*fa'ajirh*) so that they may hear the word of God, then deliver them to where they can be safe and secure; for they are people who do not know.[2]

The fact that Muhammad insisted on his right to express his thoughts in public and the fact that he recognized the right of others who do not share his views and beliefs to seek protection, indicates that he would endorse a universal freedom of thought and freedom to publicly express one's thoughts. One does not have to believe in Muhammad's teachings or in the source of his teachings to hold that the protection and rights one claimed must be extended to others.

While proposing a much shorter list of basic rights that should be universal than my two colleagues, I must emphasize two things for this list of rights to be meaningful and functional. First, I submit that the right to hold thought and the right to publicly express thought are necessary but not sufficient. Second, these rights, when adopted as law and public policy, must be adopted in a way that does not reproduce the inequities that already exist in society. A guiding principle that could help achieve the proper adoption of these rights is to be mindful of the power dynamics among social groups and the power differential between the people and those holding power over them.

These two rights must be universal because without them no other rights can be discussed and debated between "moral philosophers" like Talbott, or negotiated between social groups and their governments. No truth can be spoken, no crime can be reported, and no right can be invoked without absolute protection of freedom of thought and freedom of expression. Of the rights my colleagues propose, be it the full list Sachedina recommends derived from the Universal Declaration of Human Rights, or Talbott's proposed limited package of nine basic rights, none could be universalized without universalizing, or at least prioritizing, the two fundamental rights. Indeed, it has been over seventy years since the signing of the UDHR and more than half a century since the ratification of the first few key treaties derived therefrom, and all countries have limitations on freedom of thought and freedom of expression, while bragging about protections or guarantees of other rights that are ultimately violated under some pretext or another. The reverse would have been more effective. If the freedom of thought and freedom of expression were absolutely guaranteed, other rights might have been made more secure in more countries.

Additionally, human rights are born in moments of crises and challenges; they are the byproduct of circumstance. What might be thought of as a universal right in one time or one culture might not be so in another time and another culture. Human rights are dynamic processes, not end results. Every law can be circumvented through loopholes; legal guarantees are often suspended under some pretext or another; and the State, through its agents, will always find ways to grab more power enabled by the powerful interest groups who sustain it. The changing circumstances and the constant shifting of power trends must be met with strong and absolutely protected voices that are able to express dissent. The fluidity within society and the elasticity of ideas and norms require absolute protection of thought and expression of thought.

These two rights do not need bottom-up processes to discover them or a natural disposition to acknowledge them. They are universal not by fiat or reason but by willpower of everyone irrespective of culture, politics, or form of government. Every social movement, every rebellion, and every revolution starts with an idea, a declaration of thought and subsequent action to implement such thought, without waiting for king's consent, government authorization, or society's tolerance. It is practiced across history and across cultures. What is needed is to strengthen the right of thought and the right to expressing thought, and to weaken the burden and the cost experienced by those who express their thought. What is needed is institutional guarantees that no limits or restrictions are imposed on these rights to make it easier for human rights advocates to focus on other rights instead of relitigating and refighting for these rights.

I started my concluding thoughts with my own list of rights that I contend should be universal. That list should not be the main takeaway of this work. Proposing a list of basic rights that should be universal without connecting theory to practice does not advance the cause of human rights. Therefore, I must emphasize some of the other ideas and objections highlighted throughout the previous chapters and in the context of the work of the two experts on the discussion of primary sources from Enlightenment and Islamic thought.

Human rights, civil society, and the state 165

Talbott is a builder of rights on the legacy of Enlightenment, and I suspect that he accredits many thinkers of that time period with *progress* made in the area of human rights. To be sure, his book started with a discussion of the words of the US Declaration of Independence, echoing Locke's declaration that men have inalienable right to *life, liberty, and property*. These rights were not a declaration of human rights; they were a reaffirmation of what was thought to be natural rights of *men* of that era, not human rights in all times and all places. Taken in the context of that time, when kings claim ownership of the land and then parcel it out to others for use and profit from the labor of land users, it becomes clear that these rights were not intended to be human rights. Considering that land ownership is the most durable type of property, and knowing that the king or queen of England is the legal owner of all the land under their rule,[3] the property rights European settlers had in mind could not be understood to signal their commitment to universal human rights.

We also know that it could not have been a declaration for *human* rights because Black people, Indigenous peoples, and women were denied these rights. Even after they were legally granted these rights *pro forma*, they were curtailed by other measures and practices. The right to life, liberty, and property, therein reaffirmed, are the rights of men who already had freedom. The declaration is therefore a reaffirmation of their right to enjoy liberty, life without restrictions imposed by authority (such as a king, government, or church), and right to property without the government seizing it or taxing it.

These rights could not have included women, because women were considered the property of men and continued to be so after such declarations.

The drafters of the document could not have intended these rights to apply to Black people because enslaved Black people were the property of white men, including those who drafted such declarations. One must be free to seek liberty; Black people in the Americas in that time period were neither free, nor did they own property. Even after the abolishing of slavery, Black people were not allowed to own property and a plurality of instruments and public policy tools were invented and applied to deny Black people the right to own property.

The drafters of these three rights could not have included Native Americans because white men usurped their land. Importantly, the right to property was not intended to benefit Indigenous people of the Americas because many of the Native peoples did not have the same relationship with land as white men. Native peoples were denied their land when these declarations were made and, even after these declarations were amended, Native Americans have continued to be restricted to living on reservations and with no clear path to reclaiming their ancestral land.

These rights are not *human* rights because human rights are about the most basic of rights, not about liberty beyond freedom, property beyond dignity, and happiness beyond want. These are reaffirmation of privilege and entitlement, not a declaration of basic *human* rights.

Talbott acknowledges the limits of these declarations and legal documents, and offers to amend them based on what we now know. However, his package of rights echoes the same conditions and the same intent as the Enlightenment-era statements often seen as the springboard of modern human rights.[4] His package of basic rights is for "normal" people, and he admits that this package of rights does not cover persons with cognitive, emotional, of functional issues because they may have to depend on the paternalism of the State or some other entity to secure some rights appropriate for them. The progress in liberal thought takes us from a package of rights applicable to white men who owned land to citizens who are "normal," leaving behind the most vulnerable social groups. In this paradigm, the function of the State is to guarantee the rights of "normal" people, not those most vulnerable. That is not a package of rights, it is a package of privileges, one that empowers the State to do as it has done throughout history: label anyone who challenges its power as being "abnormal" and ignore them, commit them, drug them against their will, imprison them, kill them, or forcibly sterilize them. Abusers will always use every tool available to them to enable their abuse, including the instruments of the State.

Talbott and Sachedina both believe in liberalism as the most appropriate political framework for developing and universalizing human rights. They differ on how to get there. For Sachedina, liberalism and religious thought are compatible and through reason, a God-given capacity, human beings can construct a moral and metaphysical foundation of human rights norms. Such a foundation would then serve as "a springboard for international conventions about common moral standards for the entire human race, the very secular foundation of the Declaration." He is confident in this approach because he is confident that "even the staunchest opponents of the Universal Declaration of Human Rights, who regard the document as being morally imperialistic and culturally ethnocentric, concede the fact that human beings have rights that accrue to them as humans."[5] For Sachedina, liberal views about human individuality and dignity are compatible with Islamic revelation as developed in Islamic philosophical theology and juridical methodology to understand human personhood.[6] Today, however, Sachedina finds the challenge of human rights in Islamic societies to be concentrated in three areas: Sectarian and religious intolerance, disregard for the rights of women, and absence of a constitutional and conceptual citizenship.[7] Out of more than one thousand years' history, Sachedina concludes that these three areas of rights are the most challenging for Muslims today. The facts cannot support that conclusion. It is a reactionary prognosis of the problem, for there are other, more serious, problems specific to Islamic societies, including disdain and hostility towards dissent in the name of consensus building, genocide in the name of religious purity, racism in the name of divine selection, exploitation of workers in the name of prosperity, and ethnic supremacy in the name of Quraysh-Arab nobility.

The main problem with Sachedina's approach is that he believes that developing a moral foundation for human rights and rooting it in Islamic traditions will universalize human rights and end abuse. That is a recycled argument. It, or some version of it, was preached and even implemented by the founder of Islam, Prophet Muhammad. Yet within days of his death, those moral commitments started to be rolled back. One striking example is in the origins and evolution of slavery in Islamic thought and practices. The text of the Quran is explicit in holding that owning slaves is bad and freeing them is good. Quranic legal injunctions made it possible for people to remedy a violation of some legal or moral ordinance by freeing enslaved people.[8] Yet, despite these moral and legal judgements, wealthy Muslims continued to own slaves and preserved such an abhorrent institution until it was abolished by the world community. Even after it was abolished, some sects within Islamic communities do not recognize the abolition of slavery. For instance, when ISIL took over large territories in Syria and Iraq and established their modern "caliphate," which they described as representative of the practice of the Prophet (`ala minhaj al-nubuwwa), they reinstated slavery, concubinage, servitude, and Qurayshi entitlement. ISIL did not emerge in vacuum. Its school of thought finds its roots in the teachings of Salafism, the dominant, State-sponsored sect in Saudi Arabia. The reason ISIL was able to publicly reinstate slavery but Saudi Arabia was not is the latter's obligation towards international treaties. ISIL did not sign onto these treaties and would not do so if it continued to exist. We know that because Saudi Arabia resisted many injunctions in a number of treaties for the same reason ISIL rejected them. We also know that many of the human rights crimes that took place during the reign of the caliphate were present during the 2011 wars in SWANA. That tells us that Muslim leaders and Muslim thinkers did not resolve those problems.

Talbott wants guarantees from the government that it will honor a package of basic rights and, in return, the government would be recognized as legitimate. The guarantee is legal, constitutional, or both. Based on historical records, governments have often agreed to codify such rights. But governments have also preserved unmatched power that allows the head of the State to invoke emergency laws, sign executive orders, and issue commands that violate the law, constitution, and treaties. Of course, unconstitutional and illegal actions can be overruled by courts. However, courts are often slow to act and are limited by procedural, political, and institutional factors.

There are many examples of government overreach and abuse from the last two decades alone. Therefore, one way to assess the state of human rights in any society is to test for the independence of the three branches of government: Three truly independent branches of government make it more likely that violations of human rights are addressed and remediated.

From the point of view of advocacy for human rights, and given my contention that the State exclusively commits human rights violations—and while it is true that the executive branch is the likely violator or potential violator of human rights, the other two branches are either enablers or complicit in human rights violations—it is not prudent to trust the government or any of its branches with measures intended to protect against violations of human rights or to promote human rights. What other options are there? The answer: Strengthening civil society institutions, including what I would consider the fourth branch of government—news and information media.

The state of human rights in any society is as strong as the civil society institutions therein. Independent and free press and media is crucial. The press and media cannot be all-corporate enterprises. There must be at least one public option in every category: print, radio, visual, and digital. The public media option must be funded through taxes but free of political influence and control. The third layer of ensuring optimum conditions for safeguarding human rights in society is the strength and diversity of non-government civil society institutions. This layer consists of all organizations, clubs, teaching entities, private clubs, religious entities, professional associations, and others of this kind. The best indicator for assessing the strength of human rights norms in a society is the protection of an organization with which members of some other organizations profoundly disagree. Your rights are likely to be safe if the rights of members of an organization that, in your view, represents fringe values, ideas, and interests are safe.

If we were to develop an index for human rights in a specific society, it must include all variables concerning the state and the standing of all the three layers I identified: How separate are the branches of government? How free and independent are the press and media? And how diverse and secure are the NGOs and civil society entities? It is a complex equation, but it provides a reliable, measurable predictor of the strength and weakness of human rights in any given society. To explain this further, I will illustrate it with an example.

If we want to measure the volume (V) of a simple geometric object, we solve this equation: Length x Width x Depth = Volume. But how can we measure the volume of something whose dimensions are hard or impossible to measure? Say a very oddly shaped stone? Society is like an oddly shaped rock. It is made complex by the plurality of interests, backgrounds, experiences, needs, wants, and infinite other factors. Just like an oddly shaped rock, the state of human rights can be measured through *negative displacement*, or exclusion: the number of civil society institutions excluded through law, morality, bias, discrimination, prejudice, racism, supremacy, power, wealth, and other means, as well as the level of independence of the branches of government and the level of public funding to public press and media. Scores from all these subgroups would give us number, a human rights index if you will, that tell us how committed a society is to respecting and honoring human rights norms.

Human rights advocates have argued for universalizing some or all of the rights enshrined in the Universal Declaration of Human Rights or a separate list. Based on what we now know, in the 50-plus years since the UDHR has been signed and used in treaties, human rights have been and continue to be violated. It doesn't matter whether it's a liberal society or an illiberal society, a democratic government or a non-democratic government; they all abuse the human rights of one social group or another. For example, while European governments protect the rights of their native peoples—white citizens—they abuse the rights of immigrant Muslims by placing on them more restrictions like the ban on minarets, headscarf wear, and other rights.[9]

The best strategy, then, is to accept that there is no consensus and that there will never be a consensus about a set of universal rights. Some people may agree to honor them from a moral standpoint. Politicians, empowered by a majority vote, may agree and reach a consensus to honor some basic rights. However, human rights will always be violated. So what is a viable alternative? Instead of trying to argue for a list of absolute, inviolable rights, human rights advocates should think of systems that can minimize the harm governments cause when they violate human rights. Since government abuse of human rights is the only certainty in this equation, the goal should be focused on confronting that certainty, not squandering resources on developing lists. Every government, be it clannish—favoring a specific clan over others, democratic—honoring the popular wish of the majority, a republican kind of democracy or institutional democracy—following the ground rules from a dominant social group, or a king/caliph—ruling as he wishes depending on his temperament and his dispositions, all these governments have a history of violating human rights and we have no evidence that this will change in the future simply due to a strong argument, a moral discovery, or a legal guarantee that some rights should be universal. The effective approach for increasing the probability that governments might respect human rights should be centered on harm reduction, not on full compliance at all times. Because abuse of rights is certain, the best thing to do is to minimize the harm.

Human rights abuses have happened in the past, they occur around us in every country, and they will continue to occur. The root motivations behind these violations vary in context: culture, religion, or politics; they can be security-based, racism-driven, or supremacy-inspired. What is constant, however, is that all these violations occur at the hands of the State, an entity that is enabled by the State, or an organization that stands for the State (as in the case of failed states).

Human rights violations occur either through direct government action or through government proxies. In all cases, the government violates rights or allows others to violate rights and therefore it should be held responsible since the social contract that granted it a monopoly on the use of violence requires it to protect everyone from abuses of power.

The burden of proof should fall to the State, and the benefit of doubt ought to go to the weaker side. A society respecting human rights would become reflexively more inclined to believe the weaker, non-State actor. This position has to do with balancing the dynamic equilibrium socially, whereby when the power shifts to the government side, civil society action gravitates towards supporting non-State actors. And so, what is happening here is not eliminating abuses of human rights and violations of human rights; rather, it is mitigating the abuse and making it difficult for the State to get away with it.

There is nothing unusual about creating a separate category of crime that applies to one class of legal persons and not others. Many actions, when an ordinary person commits them, would lead to criminal charges resulting in criminal punishments. However, the same crimes—when an agent of the State, like the president or a judge, commits them—would lead to criminal charges resulting only in political punishment such as removal from office. These are some of the consequences of inventing the State as a legal person. Human rights crimes should be categorized as State crimes,[10] but the consequences should be more than civil action, which would require addressing the uses and abuses of the doctrine of qualified and sovereign immunity.[11]

Another thing we learn from historical human rights crimes: No one was held responsible for these crimes. No redress and no remediation have taken place related to slavery, colonialism, genocide against Native Americans, the Holocaust, or any other crime governments committed and nothing of consequence has happened to remediate these historical abuses.

Western human rights discourse has occurred in the context of a grand project designed to reinvent governance and society. Such efforts directly produced the modern systems of Society and State. The many shades of liberalism, conservatism, communism, and capitalism, notwithstanding their conceptual and ideological difference, share the same origins and premise: Material wealth and ownership of resources and capital are good. The disagreement has been about who should control the wealth, resources, and capital—the State (or community) or individuals. This singular focus, then, has shaped the value systems and institutional systems not just in Western societies, but around the world. All governments throughout the world, therefore, see their main function as facilitators or creators of *prosperity*, through public policies, culture, and value systems. Consequently, this singular focus docketed poverty as problematic and wealth as virtuous. What is often ignored is the fact that prosperity and wealth are inherently negative. They are not quantities carrying an absolute value, since in the social sense one cannot be prosperous unless the opposite, poverty, is present to provide comparison. Therefore, a human rights discourse cannot be built on one designed to create prosperity. Rather, it must be built on the anticipation that the pursuers of prosperity and extreme wealth will necessarily produce poverty, pollution, need, degradation, exploitation, and abuse. This is what those involved in the liberal side of the project fail to grasp: Human rights abuses cannot be mitigated by amplifying the workings of a system deliberately designed to produce inequity, difference, and exclusion. A genuine human rights project is not one that promotes the rights of people with property rights to protect or autonomy to preserve, such as Talbott's "normal" citizens. A human rights project is one that changes the value systems to emphasize and promote the dignity of the most vulnerable. That societies are biased in favor of prosperity-generating systems and against the poor is evidenced in both Islamic and Western social history, notwithstanding the modern roots of the human rights discourse.

Applying systems thinking to human rights has the benefit of doing two things at the same time: understanding and solving the systemic abuse of human rights. Human rights abuse is not produced by a single ill-designed system functioning parallel to other systems to produce other desired outcomes. Human rights are outcomes of social configurations whereby either the Overall System is designed to have one of its byproducts be human rights abuses, or a numeric minority of State-enabled Determinant Systems result in human rights abuses. To solve the problem of human rights abuse, the former would require the redesign of the majority of systems within the overall social system; the latter would require disabling the Determinant State power. In some societies, both social configurations are present, and the solution would require action on both tracks. The instances of human rights abuses, therefore, come in three categories. In the first instance, human rights abuses are majority-driven. In the second instance, human rights abuses are power-driven. In the third instance, human rights abuses are both majority-driven and power-enabled.

Human rights discourse is the product of modernity for two reasons. First, the emergence of the nation-state replaced old forms of government, replacing submission to the dominant ruler (ruler with *ghalaba*[12]) with individual citizenship and society as an expression of empowered individuals and social groups. The second reason, related to the first, is the function of the State in relation to social tension. All communities have economic and social tensions and those tensions often result in stratification, creating a social hierarchy based on power. This social order allows social groups to dictate national agendas and to determine the distribution of resources. The modern nation-State, when it chooses a side in this social conflict, opens the door for human rights claims. Therefore, we can speak of human rights in a way that is new and unique to the modern era. Rights before then were individual claims against rulers in their individual capacities. That was true at least in the context of Islamic civilization. Now, rights claims are groups' claims against the State. This difference is significant, and it can be informative in the process of developing human rights mitigation capacities through systems thinking.

172 Globalism, history, and human rights today

Unlike human rights norms, which are the subject of may attempts to universalize them, human rights abuses are already universal. That in and of itself points to the dark origins of human rights discourse: Bad things have been happening, and these bad things are unlikely to stop happening, after the publication of countless works of scholarship and the ratification of countless treaties.

The evidence presented in this work leads to one conclusion: The State, in all of its iterations in every culture and throughout history, stands charged of human rights crimes. Any project focused on human rights should empower civil society institutions, nationally and globally, to create new instruments and systems that reduce the harm the State causes when it violates rights of vulnerable social groups, and to find systems that force States and social groups profiting from human rights abuses to provide appropriate reparations to the communities whose rights they have violated. This charge should stand without prejudice, and free of the effects of any statute of limitation that will cause the expiry of future claims, to ensure that historical wrongs are remedied.

Notes

1. The institution is generally referred to as *Ijara* or *Istijara*.
2. Quran 9:6; al-Tawbah, 6.
3. To understand property rights in proper context, and the reason why property was referenced in Western bills of rights documents, it should be noted that even today, the Queen of England is the legal owner of more than 17% of the total land surface on the planet Earth—6.6 billion acres.
4. Riane Eisler, "Human Rights: Toward an Integrated Theory for Action," *Feminist Issues* (1987): 26.
5. Sachedina, *Human Rights*, 6.
6. Ibid, 16.
7. Ibid, 101.
8. See Quranic passages on expiatory emancipation and manumission including, 4:92, 5:89, and 58:3.
9. One factor seems to be present in Western countries with a record of low instances of human rights abuses: least diverse societies. For instance, in some Nordic countries, governments not only provide strong social programs to its citizens and raise the living standard for larger segments of their populations, but also extend those benefits and services to immigrants of different backgrounds. However, these countries do not have large diverse communities with a history of marginalization, disempowerment, and systemic exclusion. Quite the contrary; many of the immigrant communities in these countries are highly skilled and educated professional and/or well-financed entrepreneurs. Moreover, in many of these countries, governments adopted aggressive "integration" policies and practices that are designed to forcefully assimilate social groups into the dominant culture and worldview.
10. For more detailed discussion of the evidence and reasoning, see dynamic equilibrium and definition of rights in the previous section.
11. Sovereign immunity and qualified immunity shield agents from the state from liability when they commit violation while carrying out their duties. These doctrines have direct consequences on human rights abuses, and perhaps by

categorizing human rights offenses as State crimes, these doctrines will be dissolved. There is growing support already for action against the doctrine of qualified immunity, and recent abuses by administration officials could focus attention of sovereign immunity as well. For an example of how qualified immunity is perceived by those working in the justice system, see the opinion of Judge Carlton Reeves in in his order granting qualified immunity in Jamison v McClendon, where he asserted that "Immunity is not exoneration… And the harm in this case to one man sheds light on the harm done to the nation by this manufactured doctrine."

12. For background on the political theory explaining the doctrine of dominance in Islamic societies, see 'Abd al-Rahman Ibn Muhammad Ibn Khaldun, *al-Muqaddima* (Beirut: Dar Ihya' at-Turat al-Arabi, 1970).

Appendix
Notes for an Islamic reader of which rights should be universal?

By William J. Talbott
University of Washington, Seattle

I am grateful to Professor Souaiaia for the invitation to include in his book an essay on addressing some questions raised by him and others about my book *Which Rights Should Be Universal?* (2005). He and I have been discussing human rights for over 20 years. This essay gives me the opportunity to share some of our discussions with the readers of his book.

Before I address specific questions, let me provide a brief overview of some of the important themes of my book. The main project of my book is to understand how it could even make sense to believe in universal human rights and then to use that understanding to attempt to articulate a list of nine basic human rights. At the time I wrote the book, and still today, it was and is generally thought that there were only two possible routes to reasonable belief in universal human rights: Either (1) some kind of infallible insight into moral truth (e.g., "We hold these truths to be self-evident ...") or (2) some kind of consensus (e.g., a universally agreed upon human rights law).

In my book, I rejected both of these alternatives. The first alternative, infallible insight into moral truth could not be the way that human rights were discovered. Human rights have never been self-evident, or rationally unquestionable. Even today there is no shortage of philosophers and other commentators who argue against universal human rights. In my book, to emphasize my rejection of this first alternative, I acknowledged that my view is epistemically modest—that is, that it is fallible, and subject to correction. I believe that all of our beliefs, including all of our moral beliefs, are fallible.

I realize that many people have moral authorities that they regard as infallible. In my book I do discuss a religion that claims infallibility for its moral deliverances, Roman Catholicism, because I have much more knowledge of the Roman Catholic doctrine of the infallibility of the Pope when speaking *ex cathedra* than I do of Islam. In the book, I point out that even though Pope Paul VI declared *ex cathedra* that contraception is a sin, polls show that overwhelming majorities of Catholics in the United States (and elsewhere) do not agree (5).

When we look at traditions that claim to have infallible authorities, we find that the general understanding of those authorities evolves over time. I believe that this is because individual human moral judgment plays a role in textual interpretation. The development of a widespread agreement on the wrongness of human slavery—and, indeed, on a human right not to be enslaved—is one of many examples of this evolutionary process. There may never be a complete consensus on any human right, but, in spite of many setbacks, I think there has been a clear evolution in that direction.

The evolution of human rights is not driven by infallible insight into exceptionless moral principles. Indeed, it is difficult to find any exceptionless moral principles. Judaism, Christianity, and Islam all regard the Book of Exodus as the word of an infallible deity. It includes the admonition "Thou shalt not kill." None of these three religious traditions is a pacifist tradition, though some branches are pacifist. The dominant branches of all of these traditions make exceptions to the admonition, and even today, there are disagreements about how to interpret it. If, as I believe, someday there will be general agreement that the death penalty is wrong and that even criminals have a right not to be put to death, that change will take place in the same way that the consensus against slavery developed, even though slavery is clearly endorsed in the Book of Leviticus. I would make the same prediction about rights of gays and lesbians, even though homosexuality is declared an abomination in the Book of Leviticus.

The most widely accepted understanding of the universality of human rights is based on the idea of consensus. The thought is that it only makes sense to think of human rights being universal if the belief in universality is based on a consensus or general agreement of some kind. I reject this alternative, also. I believe that the idea of a human right is a moral idea that has played the role of providing a standpoint from which to criticize all historical traditions, all cultural traditions, including religious traditions, and any other kind of consensus that you might appeal to. This is because there is no human rights tradition. All historical traditions have been based on a consensus *against* human rights. Even today, there is not a single right in the U.N. Universal Declaration of Human Rights on which there is world-wide consensus, not even the right against torture. The idea of universal human rights is an idea that had developed only in the past few centuries and, it seems to me, it is still at a relatively early stage of development. Although, historically, all traditions are anti-human rights traditions, I believe that all traditions have the potential to become traditions with a commitment to human rights.

The development of human rights begins with individual moral judgments that certain practices are morally wrong or unjust, even though the groups that engage in those practices have a consensus that they are morally justified. These judgments of wrongness can be made by insiders (i.e., members of the group that engages in and endorses the relevant practice) or by outsiders, but the judgments have more power when they are made by insiders. In my book, I discussed at length the example of Bartolomé de las Casas, an insider who opposed the treatment of Native Americans by Spanish colonists, because I focus my book primarily on examples of the moral blind spots of Western cultures. However, I also discussed the example of Tecumseh, an insider who opposed the Shawnee practice of burning prisoners alive, to emphasize that this kind of moral development takes place in all cultures.

It is fashionable to claim that there are no universal concepts of morality and justice—for example, because they are just culturally relative constructs. My account of the development of universal human rights builds on a different kind of universality—the universality of concepts of injustice, exploitation, and oppression. If these concepts were culturally relative, there would be no standpoint from which to criticize practices such as slavery, the Hindu caste system, or the near universal norms of discrimination against women, because they have all been regarded as just or moral or legitimate by the groups that engaged in those practices. When we are struck by the injustice, the immorality, or the illegitimacy of such practices, we have taken the first step toward the discovery of universal human rights, because the universal human rights are those rights that are necessary to protect vulnerable populations and individuals from unjust, exploitative, and oppressive practices.

Here is another way of putting much the same point. Everyone learns to make moral judgments as part of their training in a social practice in some historical tradition. My test for whether the moral training is successful is this: If the individual acquires a genuine capacity for moral judgment—as opposed to mere blind rule-following—then the individual will be able to morally critique some of the parts of the historical tradition in which they acquired the ability to make moral judgments. I do not claim infallibility for any of my moral judgments. But the mere fact that someone disagrees with it does not invalidate an individual's moral judgment. When Bartolomé de las Casas told his fellow Spaniards that enslaving the Indians was wrong, they not only disagreed, they also threatened his life. But they did not give him a moral reason for thinking that he was mistaken about the wrongness of slavery.

In my reconstruction of the history of the development of human rights, there are towering figures such as Bartolomé de las Casas and Tecumseh. But there are many millions of unknown heroes. They are ordinary people who recognized injustice and acted in some way, large or small, to try to correct it or eliminate it. There are lots of historical examples, but there are also many recent examples: The "Arab Spring" protests in 2011; the pro-democracy protests in Hong Kong in 2019; and the worldwide anti-racism protests in 2020.I could mention many others. If my crystal ball is correct, even though now is a dark time for human rights, someday all three of those protests will be textbook cases of the people-driven, bottom-up process by which human rights come to be recognized and established in law.

With this background, let me now briefly address some challenges to what I say (and don't say) in *Which Rights Should Be Universal?*

1. As a white male who grew up in a middleclass family in the United States you are a member of multiple oppressor classes. On your own account, your moral judgments are fallible, and you are quite confident that you have moral blind spots. Why should we think that you have anything useful to say to people who are exploited and oppressed?

I do not set myself up as someone with exceptional moral insight. I believe that everyone, myself included, has moral blind spots. In the book, I look at the historical development of human rights to try to articulate an explanatory theory of what that development is. It is because there have been millions of ordinary people who have exercised their moral judgment and worked to change their societies to eliminate injustices that there is something for me to write about. Anyone from any background can potentially contribute to our understanding of this process.

2. Your book is hostile to Islam for many reasons. First, it denies that there are any infallible moral texts, but Islam is founded on moral texts regarded to be infallible. Second, in your book you do not discuss any Islamic advocates of human rights. Third, you give only negative examples of Islamic practices, such as the Taliban's treatment of women.

Let me begin by saying that I regret that some readers of my book have gotten the impression that I am hostile to Islam. If I were rewriting the book today, I would be even more explicit that I did not mean to single out Islam for its negative practices. However, I must add that I said very little about Islamic practices in my book. Because I am sensitive to Westerners writing books critical of other traditions, in my book, almost all of my examples of human rights violations are example involving practices of Western European traditions. For example, I quote with approval Zagorin's claim that Christianity has been by far the most intolerant of the world's major religions (40).

In Chapter 5 of my book, I discuss women's rights. One reason that I focus on this topic is that *all* major traditions have norms of discrimination against women. Focusing on rights for women enabled me to discuss "how it is possible to criticize a culture's internal norms without inviting invidious distinctions between cultures" (89). As I stated above, I don't believe that there is any human rights tradition, but all traditions have the potential to become traditions with a commitment to human rights.

With that introduction, let me address the three parts of this challenge. I replied to the first with my discussion of infallible authorities above. My response to the second is that my failure to discuss Islamic advocates of human rights was due to ignorance, not hostility. At the time that I wrote the book, the students in my class on human rights read selections from an essay by Abdullahi Ahmed An-Na'im. I did not think I was knowledgeable enough about An-Na'im and other Islamic advocates of human rights to discuss them intelligently in my book. I thought it would be much more valuable to have someone who is part of an Islamic tradition discuss the relation between Islam and human rights. That is one of the reasons that I am so pleased that Professor Souaiaia has written this book.

After I finished my book, a friend of mine encouraged me to read the work of Fatima Mernissi. Reading her book *The Veil and the Male Elite* was eye-opening for me. Mernissi convinced me that the Prophet Mohammed was a feminist. I now have selections from Mernissi's book as required reading in my human rights course. If I were to rewrite my book today, I would include a section on Mernissi's interpretation of Mohammed in my discussion of women's rights.

The third part of this challenge is that I give only negative examples of Islamic practices. As I said, this charge is potentially misleading, because I have so little discussion of Islamic practices. Even though almost all of my negative examples are from Western traditions, I do give some examples from other traditions, including Islam, in order to emphasize that no historical tradition is a human rights tradition.

3 In your book, you limit human rights to human beings with "normal" cognitive, emotional, and behavioural capacities. How can you claim to be an advocate of human rights when you exclude some human beings from their protection?

This is a challenge that I felt very keenly when I was writing the book. It is the reason that I was reluctant to use the word "normal" at all. It is also the reason that, in the book, I took pains to emphasize that I was not denying that human beings without "normal" cognitive, emotional, and behavioural capacities have no rights. Indeed, they have some of the rights that I classify as human rights—for example, the right not to be tortured. As I say in the book, I do not regard the right not to be tortured to be a distinctively human right, because I believe that all sentient beings have a right not to be tortured (7).

I still have qualms about using the word "normal." So often in the past, "abnormal" has been used stigmatize groups so as to deny them their human rights. Here is how, in my book, I explained my use of "normal" as applied to adults: "*Adult human beings who surpass a minimum level of cognitive, emotional, and behavioural functioning.*" (7; emphasis in original).The idea is that there is some minimal threshold. It is difficult to say what the minimal threshold is, but here is one kind of test: If a human being can be held morally responsible for their actions, they are above the threshold.

Some of the most important rights on my list of nine basic human rights simply do not apply to human beings who lack "normal" cognitive, emotional, and behavioural capacities. These include the full right to an education; democratic rights, including the right to vote; and rights against paternalism. Even human beings below this threshold have moral rights, just not all the rights on my list of basic human rights. Let me emphasize again that I think that all sentient beings have some moral rights, just not all the rights on my list of basic human rights.

4 In your book, human rights guarantees are used as a test of the moral legitimacy of governments. But laws and other government actions are neither necessary nor sufficient for human rights to be recognized and respected. Why do you focus so much on governments?

I think that this challenge is based on a misunderstanding. Although I think it is important that governments enact human rights laws and I think that, from a moral point of view, government legitimacy should depend on the extent to which they adopt and enforce such laws, I do not believe that the development of human rights is typically a process that is top-down, in which those in power take the lead. In the book, I emphasize that the social process of the development of human rights is primarily the result of bottom-up social movements of ordinary people. Often, those in authority are the last to get the message. Even when it seems that human rights are being implemented top-down, as in the U.S. Supreme Court's recognition of a right to same-sex marriage in *Obergefell v. Hodges*, the court's decision is inconceivable without the grass-roots movements for equality that preceded it. And no laws protecting human rights will be effective unless they are supported by large numbers of ordinary people.

Let me conclude by saying that I am grateful to Professor Souaiaia for this opportunity to clarify the views that I express in my book *Which Rights Should Be Universal?* Even though my book focuses mostly on examples from Western traditions, it addresses themes that can be understood, appreciated, and improved upon by members of any tradition. My book is only one fallible contribution to the continuing conversation about human rights. I am pleased that Professor Souaiaia has written this book to make his own contribution to that conversation.

Select Bibliography

Primary works (Islamic):

References

`Abbās, Iḥsān. *Dīwān shi`r al-khawārij*. Cairo: Dar al-Kitab, 1982.
Abū al-`Arab, Muḥammad Ibn Aḥmad Ibn Tamīm al-Tamīmī. *Kitāb al-miḥan*. Beirut: Dar al-Gharb al-Islamī, 1983.
Abū Na`īm, Aḥmad Ibn `Abdullāh al-Aṣfahānī. *Hilyat al-awliyā` wa-ṭabaqāt al-aṣfiyā'*. Beirut: Dar al-Kutub al-Ilmiyyah, 1988.
Abū `Ubaydah, al-Qāsī Ibn Sallām al-Harwī. *al-Amwāl*. Beirut: Mu`assasat Nasir, 1981.
Abū Zakkariyā, Yaḥyā Ibn Abī Bakr. *Kitāb al-siyar wa-akhbar al-ayimmah*. Tunis: al-Dar al-Tunusiyyah li-'l-Nashr, 1985.
Albānī (al-), Muḥammad Nāṣir al-Dīn. *Irwā' al-ghalīl fī takhrīj aḥādith manār al-sabīl*. Beirut: al-Maktab al-Islami, 1985.
Asbahani (al-), Ahmad Ibn Abdullah. *Hilyat al-awliya*. Cairo: Dar Umm al-Qura, 1932.
Aṣfahānī (al-), Abū Na`īm. *Ḥilyat al-awliyā' wa-ṭabaqāt al-aṣfiyā'*. Beirut: Dar al-Kitab al-Arabi, 1985.
Ash`arī (al-), Abū al-Ḥassan `Alī Ibn Ismā`īl. *Maqālāt al-islāmiyyīn*. Beirut: al-Maktabah al-`Asriyyah, 1990.
Baghdādī (al-), `Abd al-Qāhir Ibn Ṭāhir Ibn Muḥammad. *al-Farq bayna al-firaq*. Beirut: al-Maktabah al-`Asriyyah, 1990.
Balādhirī (al-), Aḥmad Ibn Yaḥyā` Ibn Jābir. *Ansāb al-ashrāf*. Beirut: Dar al-Fikr, 1996.
Barrādī (al-), Abū al-Qāsim Ibn Ibrāhīm. *al-Jawāhir al-muntaqāt fī itmām mā akhalla min kitāb al-ṭabaqāt*. Cairo: Tab`ah al-Ḥajriyyah, 1884.
Bayyāsī (al), Yūsuf Ibn Muḥammad Ibn Muḥammad Ibn Ibrāhīm al-Anṣārī. *al-I`lām bi-'l-ḥurūb al-wāqi`ah fī ṣadr al-islām*. Amman: Dar al-Kitab, 1987.
Dhahbī (al-), Shams al-Dīn. *al-`Ibar fī khabar man ghabar*. Beirut: Dar al-kutub al-`Ilmiyyah, 1985.
Dhahbī (al-), Shams al-Dīn. *Tārīkh al-islām*. Beirut: Dar al-Kitab, 1999.
Dhahbi, *Siyar a`lam al-nubala*. Beirut: Bayt al-Afkar al-Duwaliyya, 2004.
Fayyash (al-), Muḥammad Ibn Yūsuf. *Haymān al-zād ilā dār al-mi`ād*. Oman: Wizarat al-Turath, `1980.
Ghazzāli, *Ihya' Ulum Ad-Din*. Beirut, Lebanon: Dar Al-Kotob Al-ilmiyah, 2011.

Ghurābī (al-), `Alī Muṣṭafā. *Tārīkh al-firaq al-islāmiyyah wa-nash'at `ilm al-kalām `inda al-muslimīn*. Cairo: Matba'at al-Anglu al-Masriyyah, 1985.
Ḥarīrī (al-), Muḥammad `Īsā. *al-Dawlah al-rustumiyyah bi-'l-maghrib*. Dar al-Qalam, 1987.
Ibn `Abd al-Barr, Yūsuf. *al-Istī`āb fī ma`rifat al-aṣḥāb*. Beirut: Dar al-Jil, 1992.
Ibn `Abd Rabbuh, Aḥmad Ibn Muḥammad. *al-`Iqd al-farīd*. Beirut: Dar al-Hilal, 1990.
Ibn `Adiyy, `Abdullāh al-Jarjānī. *al-Kāmil fī du`afā' al-rijāl*. Beirut: Dar al-Fikr, 1988.
Ibn al-Athīr, `Alī. *al-Kāmil*. Beirut: Dar Sadir, 1989.
Ibn al-Athīr, `Ali. *Asad al-ghābah fī ma`rifat al-ṣaḥābah*. Beirut: Dar al-Fikr, 1989.
Ibn al-Jawzī, `Abd al-Raḥmān Ibn `Alī Ibn Muḥammad. *Kitāb al-ḍu`afā' wa-'l-matrūkīn*. Beirut: Dar al-Kutub al-`Ilmiyyah, 1986.
Ibn al-Jawzī, `Abd al-Raḥmān. *al-Muntaẓam fī tārīkh al-umam wa-'l-mulūk*. Beirut: Dar al-Kutub al-`Ilmiyyah, 1992.
Ibn al-Mundhir, Muḥammad Ibn Ibrāhīm. *al-Iqnā`*. Cairo: Dar al-Ḥadīth, 1994.
Ibn Ḥajr, Aḥmad Ibn `Alī al-`Asqalānī. *Taqrīb al-tahdhīb*. Cairo: Dar al-Salam, 1992.
Ibn Ḥajr, al-`Asqalānī al-Ḥāfiẓ Aḥmad Ibn `Alī. *Fatḥ al-bāri'*. Beirut: Dar al-Fikr, 1993.
Ibn Ḥazm, Abū Muḥammad `Alī Ibn Aḥmad al-Ẓāhirī. *al-Faṣl fī al-milal wa-'l-ahwā' wa-'l-niḥal*. Beirut: Dar al-Jil, 1992.
Ibn Ḥazm, Abū Muḥammad `Alī Ibn Aḥmad al-Ẓāhirī. *Jamharat ansāb al-`arab*. Beirut: Dar al-Kutub al-`Ilmiyyah, 1983.
Ibn Ḥazm, Abū Muḥammad `Alī Ibn Aḥmad al-Ẓāhirī. *al-Muḥallā*. Beirut: Dar al-Jil, 1980.
Ibn Ḥibbān, Muḥammad. *Mashāhīr `ulamā' al-amṣār*. Beirut: Dar al-Kutub al-`Ilmiyyah, 1959.
Ibn Hishām, Abū Muḥammad `Abd al-Mālik. *al-Sīrah al-nabawiyyah*. Beirut: Dar al-Jil, 1991.
Ibn Kathīr, Ismā`īl. *al-Bidāyah wa-'l-nihāyah*. Beirut: Maktabat al-Ma`arif, 1990.
Ibn Khaldūn, `Abd al-Raḥmān. *al-Muqaddimah*. Beirut: Mu'assat al-A`lami, 1974.
Ibn Qutaybah, `Abdullāh Ibn Muslim. *al-Imāmah wa-'l-siyāsah*. Beirut: Dar al-Ma`rifah, 1992.
Ibn Sa`d, Muḥammad. *al-Ṭabaqāt al-kubrā*. Beirut: Dar Sadir, 1986.
Jāḥiẓ (al-), `Amr Ibn Baḥr. *al-bayān wa`-'l-tabyīn*. Beirut: Dar al-Jil, 1991.
Khaṭīb (al-), Aḥmad Ibn `Alī Ibn Thābit. *Tārīkh baghdād*. Beirut: Dar al-Fikr, 1987.
Kindī (al-), Abū Bakr Aḥmad Ibn `Abdullāh Ibn Mūsā. *al-Muṣannaf*. Oman: Wizarat al-Turath, 1984.
Mas`ūdī (al-), `Alī Ibn al-Ḥussayn Ibn `Alī. *Murūj al-dhahab*. Beirut: al-Maktabah al-`Asriyyah, 1988.
Munqirī (al-), Naṣr Ibn Muzāḥim. *Waq`at ṣiffīn*. Beirut: Dar al-Jil, 1990.
Qarnī (al-), `Abdullāh Ibn Muḥammad. *Ḍawābit al-takfīr `inda ahl al-sunah wa-'l-jamā`ah*. Beirut: Mu'assasat al-Risālah, 1992.
Shahrastānī (al-), Abū al-Fatḥ Muḥammad Ibn `Abd al-Karīm. *al-Milal wa-'l-niḥal*. Beirut: Dar Sa`b, 1986.
Shantiri (al-) al-Andalusi, Ali Ibn Bassam. *al-Dhakhira fī mahasin ahl al-jazira*. Beirut: Dar al-Gharb al-Islami, 2000.
Ṭabarānī (al-), Sulaymān Ibn Aḥmad. *Musnad al-shāmiyyīn*. Beirut: Mu'assasat al-Risālah, 1989.
Ṭabarī (al-), Abū Ja`far Muḥammad Ibn Jarīr. *Tafsīr jāmi` al-bayān*. Beirut: Dar al-Kutub, 1992.

182 Select Bibliography

Ṭabarī (al-), Abū Ja`far Muḥammad Ibn Jarīr. *Tārīkh al-umam wa-'l-mulūk*. Beirut: Dar al-Kutub, 1988.
Ṭūsī (al-), Muḥammad Ibn al-Ḥassan. *Tahdhīb al-aḥkām*. Beirut: Dar Sa`b, 1981.
Ya`qūbī (al-), Aḥmad Ibn Abī Ya`qūb Ibn Ja`far Ibn Wahb Ibn Wāḍih. *al-Tārīkh*. Beirut: Dar sadir, 1992.

Secondary Sources

Key Sources Examined in this Work:

References

Sachedina, Abdulaziz. *Islam and the Challenge of Human Rights*. New York: Oxford University Press, 2009.
Talbott, William J. *Which Human Rights Should Be Universal?*. New York: Oxford University Press, 2007.

General Bibliography:

Berkeley, George. *A Treatise Concerning the Principles of Knowledge*, 1710; edited with an introduction by Jonathan Dancy. Oxford & New York: Oxford University Press, 1998.
Browne, Peter. *Things Divine and Supernatural Conceived by Analogy with Things Natural and Human*. London: 1733.
Butler, Joseph. "The Analogy of Religion." In *The Works of Joseph Butler*, edited by S. Halifax, Vol. I. Oxford: Oxford University Press, 1849.
Cohen, Marshall, Thomas Nagel, and Thomas Scanlon, eds. *Marx, Justice, and History*. Princeton, NJ: Princeton University Press, 1980.
Crenshaw, Kimberlé, Neil Gotanda, Gary Peller, and Kendall Thomas, eds. *Critical Race Theory: The Key Writings That Formed the Movement*. New York: New Press, 1995.
Darby, Derrick. *Rights, Race, and Recognition*. New York: Cambridge University Press, 2009.
Dawson, Michael C. *Black Visions: The Roots of Contemporary African-American Political Ideologies*. Chicago: University of Chicago Press, 2001.
Descartes, Rene, "Meditations on First Philosophy." In *The Philosophical Writings of Descartes*, translated by J. Cottingham, R. Stoothoff, D. Murdoch, Vol. II. Cambridge: Cambridge University Press, 1984.
Ellison, Ralph. *Invisible Man*. New York: Vintage, 1995.
Fanon, Frantz. *Black Skin, White Masks*. New York: Grove Press, 1991.
Feagin, Joe R. *The White Racial Frame: Centuries of Racial Framing and Counter Framing*. New York: Routledge, 2013.
Fredrickson, George M. *Racism: A Short History*. Princeton, NJ: Princeton Classics, 2015.
Fredrickson, George M. *White Supremacy: A Comparative Study in American and South African History*. New York: Oxford University Press, 1981.
Fricker, Miranda. *Epistemic Injustice: Power and the Ethics of Knowing*. New York: Oxford University Press, 2007.

Select Bibliography   183

Gaines, Kevin K. *Uplifting the Race: Black Leadership, Politics, and Culture in the Twentieth Century*. Chapel Hill, NC: University of North Carolina Press, 1996.

Garvey, Marcus. *The Philosophy and Opinions of Marcus Garvey*. Edited by Amy Jacques-Garvey. Vols 1–2. New York: Atheneum, 1992.

Goldenberg, David M. *The Curse of Ham: Race and Slavery in Early Judaism, Christianity, and Islam*. Princeton, NJ: Princeton University Press, 2003.

Hay, Carol. *Kantianism, Liberalism, and Feminism: Resisting Oppression*. New York: Palgrave Macmillan, 2013.

Haynes, Stephen R. *Noah's Curse: The Biblical Justification of American Slavery*. New York: Oxford University Press, 2002.

Hobbes, Thomas, *The Citizen [Philosophical Rudiments Concerning Govrnment and Society]*, 1642; edited and introduced by B. Gert, *Man and Citizen*, Indianapolis: Hackett, 1991.

Hobbes, Thomas. *Human Nature and De Corpore Politico [The Elements of Law]*, 1640; edited with an introduction by J.C.A. Gaskin, Oxford & New York: Oxford University Press, 1994.

Hobbes, Thomas, *Leviathan*, London, 1651; edited with an introduction by E. Curley, Indianapolis: Hackett, 1994.

Isaac, Benjamin. *The Invention of Racism in Classical Antiquity*. Princeton, NJ: Princeton University Press, 2004.

Jung, Moon-Kie, João H. Costa Vargas, and Eduardo Bonilla-Silva, eds. *State of White Supremacy: Racism, Governance, and the United States*. Stanford: Stanford University Press, 2011.

Kant, Immanuel. *Groundwork of the Metaphysic of Morals*. New York: Harper Torchbooks, 1964.

Kant, Immanuel. *The Metaphysics of Morals*. New York: Cambridge University Press, 1991.

Kant, Immanuel. *Political Writings*. Edited by Hans Reiss. Translated by H. B. Nisbet. New York: Cambridge University Press, 1991.

King, Desmond. *Separate and Unequal: African Americans and the U.S. Federal Government*. Revised edition. New York: Oxford University Press, 2007.

Kleingeld, Pauline. "Kant's Second Thoughts on Colonialism." In *Kant and Colonialism: Historical and Critical Perspectives*, edited by Katrin Flikschuh and Lea Ypi, 43–67. New York: Oxford University Press, 2014.

Lebron, Christopher J. *The Making of Black Lives Matter: A Brief History of an Idea*. New York: Oxford University Press, 2017.

Leibniz, G.W. *Theodicy*, 1710; translated. E.M. Huggard, edited with an introduction by A. Farrer, London: Routledge & Kegan Paul, 1951.

Locke, John. *An Essay Concerning Human Understanding*, London, 1690; edited with a foreword by P.H. Nidditch, Oxford: Clarendon Press, 1975.

López, Ian F. Haney. *White by Law: The Legal Construction of Race*. New York: New York University Press, 2006.

Louden, Robert B. *Kant's Impure Ethics: From Rational Beings to Human Beings*. New York: Oxford University Press, 2000.

Marx, Anthony. *Making Race and Nation: A Comparison of the United States, South Africa, and Brazil*. New York: Cambridge University Press, 1998.

Mikkelsen, Jon M., ed. *Kant and the Concept of Race: Late Eighteenth-Century Writings*. Albany, NY: SUNY Press, 2013.

Mills, Charles W. *The Racial Contract*. Ithaca, NY: Cornell University Press, 1997.

Muthu, Sankar. *Enlightenment against Empire*. Princeton, NJ: Princeton University Press, 2003.

Rawls, John. *A Theory of Justice*. Cambridge, MA: Harvard University Press, 1999.

Rothstein, Richard. *The Color of Law: A Forgotten History of How Our Government Segregated America*. New York: Liveright Publishing/W. W. Norton, 2017.

Schott, Robin May, ed. *Feminist Interpretations of Immanuel Kant*. University Park, PA: Pennsylvania State University Press, 1997.

Shelby, Tommie. *Dark Ghettos: Injustice, Dissent, and Reform*. Cambridge, MA: Harvard University Press, 2016.

Index

'aqa'id, 104
'asabiyya, 110
'Ilmani, 134
'ulamā', 102, 103, 114, 181
'ulum, 104, 112
'Uthman, 92, 94, 95, 98, 120

Abbas, 96
Abbasid, 93, 96, 97, 111, 112, 139
abstract, 2, 6, 7, 9, 10, 24, 38, 39, 49, 56, 82, 109, 156
Abu Abbas, 96
Abu Bakr, 91, 92, 111, 125
Abu Bakr al-Baghdadi, 125
Abu Muhammad al-Julani, 125
Africa, 3, 13, 16, 21, 29, 40, 58, 65, 66, 72, 76, 79, 86, 93, 96, 113, 117–119, 121, 122, 142, 143, 148, 149, 157, 158, 161, 183
Afrin, 144
Ahl al-Bayt, 96
Alcoran, 67
Aleppo, 123, 144
allocation of resources, 14
ambiguous, 101
amendments, 122
Ansar, 92
apartheid, 2, 161
Arab, 13, 63, 70, 87–89, 93, 95, 111, 120–125, 128–133, 135, 139, 143, 144, 148, 149, 152, 153, 155, 159–161, 167, 176, 180
assessment systems, 38
assumptions, 25, 29, 51
atrocities, 2, 3, 42, 48, 78, 81, 85, 117, 118, 158, 161
Authority, 36
autonomous, 11, 50, 93, 96, 98
autonomy, 5, 11, 21, 71, 74, 81, 171

Azhar, 103, 106, 114, 131

basic human rights, 23, 24, 31, 174, 179
Bay'a 'amma, 93
Bay'a khassa, 93
bias, 2, 8, 12, 15, 47, 50, 51, 74, 128, 168
Black Hand, 142
Black Lives Matter, 161, 183
Blacks of Africa, 68
Blood Spiller, 96
bottom-up, 24, 28, 31, 32, 34, 36, 44, 164, 177, 179
bureaucracy, 13, 76, 94, 96
business, 12, 13, 36, 88, 90

caliph, 54, 92–99, 102, 103, 108, 111, 112, 119, 169
caliphate, 93, 94, 96–99, 102, 108, 110, 115, 140, 167
caliphs, 93, 94, 97–100, 102, 108, 110–112, 120, 139, 158
Canadian savage, 71
capitalism, 170
Christian. *See* Christianity
Christianity, 49–51, 57, 67, 70, 72, 78, 79, 84, 175, 177, 183
citizenry, 36
civilization, 2, 15, 16, 21, 24, 37, 40, 43, 59, 61, 63, 82, 93, 97, 100, 113, 135, 171
clan, 13, 14, 27, 30, 86, 87, 90, 93–97, 110, 124, 131, 162, 163, 169
coalitions, 125, 127, 143
Coercion, 97
cognitive, 4, 33, 166, 178, 179
collaboration, 97
colonial powers, 79, 97, 139

186 Index

colonialism, 1, 2, 13, 39, 43, 51, 66, 72–78, 80, 83, 121, 139, 158, 170
commandments, 101
communism, 170
conservatism, 170
consumers, 36
Crusaders, 70, 134
cultural cost, 36
cultural practices, 14

Daesh, 127, 134, 136, 157
dalīl, 105–107
dalīl al-shar'ī, 105
Darfur, 49
Dawa Party, 160
Declaration. *See* UDHR
dehumanize, 24
Deir Ezzor, 127, 144
deliberate systems, 15, 16
democracy, 14, 27, 47, 143, 150, 169, 176
democratic. *See* democracy
Determinant Systems, 171
Dey, 97
dignity, 4, 6, 8, 22, 47, 50, 55, 73, 80, 109, 143–146, 150, 155, 156, 162, 166, 171
din, 106
discourse, 2, 3, 8, 16, 19, 22, 24, 26, 28, 30, 32, 34, 36–38, 40, 42–46, 48–50, 52, 54, 56–60, 62, 63, 68, 76, 80–82, 85, 110, 119, 121, 122, 128, 133, 138, 141, 143, 144, 153, 156, 170–172
discovery, 10, 19, 24, 25, 31, 32, 34, 37, 45, 48, 59, 149, 169, 176
discriminate, 33, 152
discursive, 36
dissent, 1, 34, 36, 37, 92, 95, 98, 100, 111, 139, 152, 164, 166
dominance, 11, 14, 109, 110, 115, 173
dominant, 8, 11, 13–15, 22, 23, 27, 43, 47, 52, 59, 63, 75, 100, 118, 131, 148, 158, 167, 169, 171, 172, 175
dominant social groups, 8, 11, 13–15
dynamic equilibrium, 145
dynasties, 98, 115

economic sanctions, 35, 41, 80, 144
elite, 22, 25, 26, 91, 93, 111, 162
elitism, 12, 89, 92
emotional, 4, 32, 33, 41, 71, 83, 121, 143, 166, 178

empathy, 96, 142
Empire, 84, 97, 98, 159, 184
empirical evidence, 25
enhanced interrogation, 138
Enlightenment, 1, 3, 5, 15–17, 21, 25, 40, 41, 43, 49, 50, 51, 61, 63, 65–69, 71, 73–75, 77–85, 89, 119, 142, 149, 162, 164–166, 184
entitlements, 45, 71, 108
environment, 10, 14, 36, 69, 71, 81, 88, 110, 146, 152
epistemic grounding of rights, 51
epistemic modesty, 25, 28, 31, 32, 66
epistemology, 21, 44
equality, 5, 17, 38
equilibrium, 14, 36, 110, 145–147, 149, 153, 170, 172
ethical value systems, 15
exclusion, 13, 15, 81, 92, 168, 171, 172
exploitation, 21, 23, 39, 56, 60, 66, 77, 89, 97, 121, 148, 167, 171, 176

fallibility, 25
fallible, 25, 28, 174, 177, 179
Fallujah, 144
fanaticism, 37
fiqh, 41, 44, 52, 101, 103–109, 114
firqah, 101
fitra, 46, 53
Fitra, 5, 46
forced conversions, 59
Fostat, 93
France, 17, 76, 77, 120, 124–126, 129, 136, 143, 148, 154
Freedom, 17, 73
furū', 106

genocide, 2, 15, 19, 36, 39, 42, 73, 77, 80, 96, 97, 117, 121, 133, 139, 151, 158, 160, 166, 170
ghalaba, 110, 115
ghana'im, 87
Globalism, 36, 74, 117, 120, 122, 124, 126, 128, 130, 132, 134, 136, 140, 142, 144, 146, 148, 150, 152, 154, 156, 158, 160, 164, 166, 168, 170, 172
globalization, 36
government, 4, 5, 11–13, 21–23, 25–28, 30, 32–35, 37, 43, 49, 50, 54, 55, 57–59, 71, 74, 75, 77, 83, 95–99, 102, 109, 110, 114, 120, 122–125, 127, 129–134, 136, 138, 140–144,

146–148, 151, 153, 154–160, 164, 165, 167–171, 179
greed, 15, 74, 138

habashi, 87
Hadith, 7, 92, 103, 113, 115
Hanafism, 98, 101
Hanbalism, 101
harm, 7, 16, 22, 35, 75, 82, 110, 140, 145, 146, 155, 169, 172, 173
Hashemite, 131
Hayat Tahrir al-Sham. *See* Nusra
headscarf, 169
Henri Dunant, 141, 144, 159
Hezbollah, 127, 130, 132–134, 143
hierarchy, 107, 171
hikma, 104
Hindus, 79
hoarding, 15, 81, 82, 117, 162
hoarding resources, 15, 117
holocaust, 142
homeland, 72, 73, 76, 81, 133
human rights, 1–16, 19, 21–31, 33–61, 63, 65–67, 69, 71, 73–77, 79–83, 85, 87–89, 91, 93, 95–101, 103, 105, 107, 109–111, 113, 115, 117–122, 124, 126, 128, 130, 132–134, 136, 138–161, 164–179
human rights abuses, 1–3, 5, 7–9, 14–16, 21–24, 29, 39, 50, 59–61, 63, 65, 66, 76, 77, 81, 82, 85, 95, 100, 109, 110, 117, 118, 121, 122, 138–140, 144, 146–148, 151–154, 157, 158, 171, 172
Hussain, 95, 98, 111, 112, 120, 130
hybrid wars, 138, 139

Ibadism, 92, 101, 111
Ibn Taymiyya, 104
identity, 43, 60, 87, 127, 135, 137, 158
ideology, 10, 15, 127, 136, 150
Ijara, 162, 163, 172
ijmāʿ, 105
ijmaʾ, 104
ijtihād, 105, 106
illegal combatant, 138
illiberal, 23, 24, 26, 27, 34, 36, 117, 169
Imami Shia, 54, 120
immigrants, 172
imperialism, 19, 21, 23, 25, 31, 32, 35, 109, 154
imperialistic. *See* imperialism

indigenous, 11, 21, 29, 36, 65, 66, 70, 71, 74, 75, 77, 79, 80, 81, 88, 97, 143, 148, 150, 154, 158
Indigenous communities, 97
infallible, 45, 98, 102, 174, 175, 177
inheritance rights, 38, 108
injustice, 25, 60, 72, 73, 122, 176
institutions, 31
instrumentalized, 66, 138, 139, 141, 143, 145, 147, 148, 149, 151, 153, 155, 157, 159, 161
International Criminal Court, 1, 16
intersubjective, 36
intolerance, 13, 15, 21, 139, 166
intrasubjective, 36
Iran, 17, 57, 91, 120, 126, 130, 131, 134, 135, 137, 143, 161
Iraq, 35, 61, 91, 94, 95, 120, 121, 123–127, 130–132, 135, 136, 138, 143, 148, 149, 153–155, 157, 159–161, 167
irhab al-takfiri, 130
ISIL. *See* ISIS
ISIS, 134
Islam, 13, 19, 21, 41, 43–47, 50–58, 60, 61, 63, 66–68, 70, 79, 84–89, 91, 93, 95–101, 103–109, 111–115, 120, 127, 131, 134, 135, 137, 159, 167, 174, 175, 177, 178, 182, 183
Islamic. *See* Islam
Islamic State. *See* ISIS
Islamic thought, 16, 40, 43–45, 48, 53, 57, 61, 83, 85, 108, 113, 164, 167
Ismaʿilism, 101
isolation of the system, 14
istajarak, 163
istushhida, 129

Jaʿfarism, 101
Jabhat nusrat ahl al-sham, 125
Jahiliyya, 3, 63, 85, 88, 162
Judaism, 57, 79, 175, 183
juridical methodology, 50, 166
jurisprudence, 21, 44, 51, 52, 56, 98, 101, 104, 108, 111
justice, 29, 39, 42, 53, 55, 66, 67, 71, 73, 78, 92, 97, 99, 102, 104, 109, 140, 173, 176
justification, 22, 23, 39, 53, 119, 126, 155

Karbala, 96
khawarijism, 139

188 Index

Koran, 70, 79
Kufa, 96

legal guarantees, 5, 33, 51, 52, 71, 110, 164
legal judgments, 37, 104
legitimacy, 25, 28, 32, 55, 71, 110, 113, 124, 130, 131, 137, 179
legitimate, 25, 28, 32, 54, 59, 71, 74, 98, 132, 133, 143, 167, 176. See legitimacy
legitimize, 71, 97, 102, 103, 131
liberal, 5, 7, 19, 23, 24, 26, 27, 32–34, 42, 49, 50, 58–60, 73–75, 77, 79, 80, 110, 117, 166, 169, 171
liberal societies, 5, 23, 26, 27, 33, 34, 42, 59, 74, 80
liberalism, 46, 166, 170
liberty, 15, 66, 71, 75, 81, 85, 165
life, 4, 8, 11, 17, 31, 36, 40, 45, 46, 56, 57, 63, 67, 81, 85, 88, 90, 91, 97, 105, 124, 133, 138, 141, 146, 152, 165, 176
linear, 25, 29, 32, 77

Ma'lula, 127
Madina, 86, 87, 90–94, 114, 119, 131, 162
Mahometans, 67, 68
majlis, 106
makruh, 56, 104
Malikism, 98, 101
mamluks, 110
Marja', 45
market of ideas, 35
Marwan II, 96
maslaha, 105
massacre, 96
Mauritania, 97, 123
mazlumiyya, 110
Mecca, 86, 88, 90, 91, 94, 111, 119, 131, 137, 162, 163
metaphysical foundation, 166
Mihna, 54, 139
military, 14, 34, 35, 41, 51, 58, 88, 95, 97, 110, 113, 124, 125, 132, 136, 140, 141, 144, 149, 151, 153, 154, 159
military intervention, 34, 35, 41, 140, 144
mitigate, 7, 8, 10, 22
modern intellectuals, 40
modernity, 44, 50, 109, 171

Mohametanism, 66
Mohammedans, 66, 79
Mohomet, 67
Mongolia, 97
moral authority, 25, 37, 45, 158
moral cognition, 46
moral development theory, 45
moral imperialist. *See* imperialism
moral judgment, 21, 25, 27, 45, 175–177
moral principles, 36, 68, 175
moral progress, 24
Mosul, 144
mu'āmalāt, 107
Mu'awiyya, 94, 111, 120
mubah, 104
Muhammad, 7, 55, 66, 67, 87–92, 94, 95, 102, 106, 111–113, 120, 125, 131, 162, 163, 167, 173
muharram, 104
murtaddin, 130
Muslim Brotherhood, 130, 131, 132, 137, 149
Muslims, 5, 21, 30, 33–37, 40, 41, 43–48, 50–63, 66, 67, 82, 85, 87, 88, 90–103, 105–109, 112–115, 120, 130–133, 135–137, 139, 148, 152, 158–161, 166, 167, 169, 181
myth, 23

Najaf, 131, 132
narrative, 45, 59, 70, 102, 119, 121, 126, 127, 129, 132–135, 143, 150, 152
nass, 103
Native Americans, 70, 81, 165, 170, 176
Natural condition, 72
Negroes, 66, 70, 79
normal, 4, 7, 33, 34, 109, 166, 171, 178, 179
Nusayri, 134
Nusra, 125, 127, 134, 136

occupation, 6, 76, 90, 97, 112, 120, 136, 138, 141, 153
Occupy movement, 118, 161
oppressor, 15, 177
orthodoxy, 37, 50, 54, 59
Ottoman, 93, 97, 98, 100, 114, 115, 120, 131
outcomes. *See* systems outcomes

Palestine, 123, 130, 161
paternalism, 23, 24, 39, 166, 179

paternalistically, 22, 23, 26, 27, 40.
  See paternalism
patriot, 75
patriotism, 75
Persian, 52, 87, 88, 93, 130, 133, 134, 135, 161
personhood, 48, 50, 166
philosophers, 21, 25, 26, 27, 35, 37–40, 42, 45, 65, 66, 68, 73, 77, 80, 81, 83, 110, 119, 163, 174
philosophy, 19, 27, 28, 31, 32, 38, 39, 48–50, 52, 62, 66, 68, 81, 83
pluralism, 50, 158
political theology, 50, 52
Pope, 45, 51, 61, 102, 174
positivizes riches, 15
poverty, 14, 15, 17, 81, 89, 96, 112, 117, 170, 171
power, 14, 15, 21, 22, 24, 33, 38, 39, 48, 53, 56–59, 74, 78–80, 89, 95, 97, 98, 102, 108, 110, 113, 121–124, 128, 137, 140, 144–149, 152–159, 163, 164, 166–168, 170, 171, 176, 179
predetermine outcomes, 16
predetermined, 105, 107
prejudice, 168, 172
pride, 74
privilege, 8, 12, 30, 82, 166
process, 5, 9, 10, 24–28, 32, 34, 37, 38, 93, 107, 140, 171, 175, 177, 179
progress, 25, 28, 32, 56, 65, 77, 78, 82, 96, 165, 166
property, 4, 21, 23, 76, 81, 85–89, 105, 108, 117, 137, 165, 171, 172
prosperity, 15, 48, 96, 148, 167, 170, 171
public policy, 14, 22, 24, 57, 163, 165
public reason, 46, 49, 51, 59
punishments, 100, 101, 103, 109, 170

Qaeda, 123, 125, 127, 131, 134, 136, 143
Qatar, 13, 122, 124–126, 128–132, 143, 154, 160, 161
Quran, 55, 56, 66, 70, 86, 88, 90–92, 94, 98, 101–108, 115, 163, 167, 172
Quraysh, 86, 87, 89, 91–94, 99, 111, 167
qutila, 129
quwwat al-nidham, 129

R2P, 34, 35, 42, 58, 154
racial biology, 68
racialized, 15, 80, 81, 83, 150
raciological thought, 68
racism, 3, 13–15, 24, 29, 39, 42, 65, 67, 69, 71, 73–75, 77, 79–83, 85, 120, 121, 134, 137–139, 142, 145, 148, 167–169, 176
rafida, 130
rafidi, 127, 135
Raqqa, 144
Rawls, 34, 36, 41, 42, 45, 46, 66, 184
reason, 5, 11, 22, 23, 26, 28, 30, 32, 33, 36–39, 43, 45, 46, 48–54, 56–61, 63, 66, 67, 69, 71, 75, 81, 89, 99, 124, 146, 150, 151, 164, 166, 167, 171, 172, 176, 177, 178
reasoned arguments, 25
rebellion, 92, 97, 98, 100, 111–113, 119, 121, 140, 152, 164
Rechtsstaat, 80
Red Crescent, 142
Red Cross, 142, 159
redundancy, 9, 13
refugees, 123
regress, 25, 56
religion, 4, 12, 19, 21, 27, 44–47, 50, 51, 54, 57–60, 67, 68, 70, 72, 78, 79, 87, 106, 119, 133, 150, 169, 174
remediate, 22, 60, 156, 170
remediation, 2, 5, 170
remedied, 147, 172
revolution, 76, 89, 144, 149, 150, 152, 153, 155, 164
righteous, 98, 99, 150

Sachedina, 2, 5, 19, 43–63, 85, 110, 164, 166, 167, 172, 182
Safawis, 130
Saffah, 96, 111
salaf, 104
Salafism, 59, 98, 104, 131, 167
sanctions, 13, 34, 35, 91, 109, 127, 136, 139, 149, 160
Saudi Arabia, 13, 57, 98, 106, 114, 120, 122, 123, 125, 127, 129–132, 135–137, 152, 154, 160, 161, 167
sectarian purity, 15
sectarianism, 13, 60, 85, 121, 139, 142
secular. *See* secularism
secularism, 46, 49, 58
security, 4, 11, 34, 85, 86, 94, 95, 96, 124, 126, 130, 155, 160, 169

Index

serfdom, 72
Shafi'ism, 101
Sham, 90, 125, 127, 134
Sharia, 55, 99, 100–110, 113–115
Shia, 44, 45, 53, 54, 61, 90, 95, 112, 120, 127, 130–133, 135, 150
Shi'ism, 101
similarity, 30, 43, 58, 119
slavery, 2, 12, 13, 16, 23, 39, 42, 56, 72, 73, 77, 78, 83, 111, 158, 165, 167, 170, 175, 176
Social Contract, 74
social equilibrium, 36
society, 7–12, 14–16, 19, 22, 25–27, 33, 34, 36–39, 45, 47, 50, 52, 54, 56, 57–60, 65, 67, 71, 73–77, 79, 82, 86, 88, 89, 94, 95, 100, 103, 105, 109–111, 117, 141, 142, 145–148, 150, 153, 154, 156–158, 162–165, 167–173
soft intervention, 34–36, 42
Somalia, 13
sovereign immunity, 140, 170, 173
status, 7, 8, 12, 39, 87, 98, 102
stigmatizes the poor, 15
storytelling, 102
subjugation of women, 22
Sultanate, 97, 100, 114, 115, 120
Sunna, 92, 94, 102–104, 106, 107, 108, 112, 115
Sunni, 30, 45, 53, 54, 99, 106–108, 110, 111, 120, 123, 130–133, 135, 150, 151
Sunnism, 15, 45, 53, 54, 98, 101
supremacist. *See* supremacy
supremacy, 3, 13–15, 24, 25, 29, 30, 37, 60, 65, 79, 80, 82, 83, 85, 87, 89, 91, 93, 95, 97, 99, 101, 103, 105, 107, 109, 111, 113, 115, 121, 135, 137, 138, 139, 167–169
SWANA, 3, 117–119, 121–123, 125–127, 129, 131, 133–141, 144, 149, 157–159, 161, 167
Syria, 9, 61, 118–136, 140, 141, 143–145, 149, 151, 152, 154, 159, 161, 167
systemic. *See* systems thinking
systems, 1, 6–17, 21, 24, 25, 27, 30, 38–40, 43, 47–49, 52, 54, 59, 61, 67, 68, 73, 76, 78–82, 88, 98–101, 108–110, 114, 117, 118, 120, 122, 128, 131, 132, 140, 145, 148, 150, 152, 157–159, 169–173, 176

systems thinking, 1, 7–11, 13–16, 24, 40, 82, 117, 128, 171

ta'ifah, 101
Talbott, 2, 4, 5, 16, 19, 21–45, 48, 49, 51–55, 58–61, 63, 65, 66, 71, 77, 80, 85, 110, 162–167, 171, 174, 182
Tang Dynasty, 96
ta'zīr, 109
Thawrat al-zanj, 97
the State, 2, 3, 5, 14, 15, 17, 23, 33, 34, 39, 40, 57–59, 71, 75–77, 110, 138–141, 146, 147, 151, 152, 156, 158, 161, 164, 166–172
theocracy, 98
theological, 48, 50, 51, 53, 91, 103, 105, 106, 107
theories, 2, 3, 26, 44, 57, 66, 68, 74, 77, 82, 99, 108, 156
torture, 14, 73, 81, 109, 117, 121, 133, 138, 142, 148, 150, 153, 160, 175
treaties, 1–3, 31, 46, 62, 86, 138, 144, 164, 167, 169, 172
Tunisia, 35, 38, 121–123, 149, 152, 155, 157, 159
Turkey, 120, 124–126, 129–131, 154, 157, 160
Turkic, 97

UDHR. *See* Universal Declaration of Human Rights
Umar II, 103
Umayyad, 57, 93–96, 99, 111
unequal. See equality
universal, 1, 4–6, 10, 16, 19, 21–26, 28, 29, 31, 33–35, 37, 39, 40, 46, 49–52, 55, 58–60, 73–76, 79, 85, 101, 106, 110, 119, 126, 133, 144, 151, 152, 156, 158, 159, 162, 163–165, 169, 172, 174–176
Universal Declaration of Human Rights, 1, 3, 6, 21, 31, 47, 48, 55, 85, 110, 142, 164, 166, 169, 175
universalism, 49
universalized human rights abuses, 16
universalizing human rights, 19, 26, 37, 110, 119
UNSC, 35, 143, 144
usul al-din, 101
usul al-fiqh, 52, 101

value systems, 15, 117, 118, 159, 170
veil of ignorance, 2
vulnerable, 5, 8, 33, 35, 39, 47, 54, 75, 110, 148, 150, 154, 156–158, 161, 163, 166, 171, 172, 176
vulnerable social groups, 5, 33, 39, 54, 75, 148, 156, 158, 166, 172

Wahhabists, 98, 131
wajib, 56, 104

wealth, 14, 15, 22, 23, 81, 82, 86, 89, 97, 112, 122, 137, 148, 162, 168, 170, 171

Yazid, 95, 98, 103, 112, 120
Yazid Ibn Mu'awiyyah, 103

Zahirism, 98
Zaydism, 101
Zine El Abidine Ben Ali, 122
zulm, 104